Ecotourism Book Series

General Editor: David B. Weaver, Professor of Tourism Management, George Mason University, Virginia, USA.

Ecotourism, or nature-based tourism that is managed to be learning-oriented as well as environmentally and socioculturally sustainable, has emerged in the past 20 years as one of the most important sectors within the global tourism industry. The purpose of this series is to provide diverse stakeholders (e.g. academics, graduate and senior undergraduate students, practitioners, protected area managers, government and non-governmental organizations) with state-of-the-art and scientifically sound strategic knowledge about all facets of ecotourism, including external environments that influence its development. Contributions adopt a holistic, critical and interdisciplinary approach that combines relevant theory and practice while placing case studies from specific destinations into an international context. The series supports the development and diffusion of financially viable ecotourism that fulfils the objective of environmental, sociocultural and economic sustainability at both the local and global scale.

Titles available:

1. *Nature-based Tourism, Environment and Land Management*
   Edited by R. Buckley, C. Pickering and D. Weaver
2. *Environmental Impacts of Ecotourism*
   Edited by R. Buckley
3. *Indigenous Ecotourism: Sustainable Development and Management*
   H. Zeppel
4. *Ecotourism in Scandinavia: Lessons in Theory and Practice*
   Edited by S. Gossling and J. Hultman
5. *Quality Assurance and Certification in Ecotourism*
   Edited by R. Black and A. Crabtree
6. *Marine Ecotourism: Between the Devil and the Deep Blue Sea*
   C. Cater and E. Cater
7. *Ecotourism and Conservation in the Americas*
   Edited by A. Stronza and W.H. Durham
8. *Island Tourism*
   Edited by J. Carlsen and R. Butler

Now in paperback

1. Nature-based Tourism, Environment and Land Management
   Edited by R. Buckley, C. Pickering and D. Weaver
2. Environmental Impacts of Ecotourism
   Edited by R. Buckley

ISLAND TOURISM
Sustainable Perspectives

Edited by

Jack Carlsen

Curtin University
Western Australia

and

Richard Butler

University of Strathclyde
Scotland

www.cabi.org

CABI is a trading name of CAB International

CABI Head Office
Nosworthy Way
Wallingford
Oxfordshire OX10 8DE
UK

Tel: +44 (0)1491 832111
Fax: +44 (0)1491 833508
E-mail: cabi@cabi.org
Website: www.cabi.org

CABI North American Office
875 Massachusetts Avenue
7th Floor
Cambridge, MA 02139
USA

Tel: +1 617 395 4056
Fax: +1 617 354 6875
E-mail: cabi-nao@cabi.org

A catalogue record for this book is available from the British Library, London, UK.

Library of Congress Cataloging-in-Publication Data
Island tourism : towards a sustainable perspective / edited by Jack Carlsen and Richard Butler.
    p. cm.
  Includes bibliographical references and index.
  ISBN 978-1-84593-679-2 (alk. paper)
  1. Sustainable tourism. 2. Islands--Economic conditions. 3. Islands--Environmental aspects. 4. Sustainable development. I. Carlsen, Jack. II. Butler, Richard, 1943–.

  G156.5.S87I85 2010
  910.68′4--dc22

                                        2010030664

ISBN-13: 978 1 84593 679 2

Commissioning editor: Sarah Hulbert
Production editor: Kate Hill

Typeset by Columns Design Ltd, Reading, UK.
Printed and bound in the UK by MPG Books Group.

Contents

Contributors

Professor Tom Baum is Professor of International Tourism and Hospitality Management in the Strathclyde Business School, University of Strathclyde, Glasgow, Scotland. He holds first and masters degrees from the University of Wales, Aberystwyth and a PhD in tourism labour market studies from the University of Strathclyde. Tom has published extensively on tourism-related topics and is author and/or editor of seven books and over 150 scientific papers. He has researched and written extensively on the theme of small island development and the role of tourism.

Dr Susanne Becken is an Associate Professor at Lincoln University, New Zealand, where she is currently leading two government-funded programmes, namely 'Tourism and Oil' and 'Preparing the Tourism Sector for Climate Change'. Susanne is on the editorial boards of the *Journal of Sustainable Tourism*, *International Tourism Review*, and *Journal of Policy Research in Tourism, Leisure and Events*, and she is a Resource Editor for *Annals of Tourism Research*. She co-authored (with Professor Hay) a book on tourism and climate change, and acted as a contributing author to the Fourth IPCC (Intergovernmental Panel on Climate Change) Assessment Report.

Professor Richard Butler is Emeritus Professor in the Business School of the University of Strathclyde, Glasgow, Scotland. He has published widely in tourism journals, and produced 15 books on tourism and many chapters in other books. His main fields of interest are the development processes of tourist destinations and the subsequent impacts of tourism, issues of carrying capacity and sustainability and tourism in remote areas and islands. He is a founding member and past president of the International Academy for the Study of Tourism.

Professor Jack Carlsen is Professor of Sustainable Tourism at Curtin University, Western Australia and Founder and Codirector of the Curtin Sustainable Tourism Centre, Western Australia. He has an extensive research track record, having produced more than 200 scholarly publications on various topics related to tourism planning, markets, development and evaluation. He was leader of the

Sustainable Enterprises Research Program for the Sustainable Tourism Cooperative Research Centre and leader of the Technical Team that developed the Maldives Third Tourism Master Plan 2007–2011. His other books include *The Family Business in Tourism and Hospitality* (CAB International, 2004), *Global Wine Tourism: Research, Management and Marketing* (CAB International, 2006) and *Innovation for Sustainable Tourism* (Goodfellow Publishers, in press).

Dr Johnny Coomansingh was born and raised in the town of Sangre Grande, Trinidad and Tobago, and received his education from Kansas State University, Fort Hays State University, Kansas and Andrews University, Michigan. He read for his masters and doctoral degrees in geography at Kansas State University, after which he accepted a position at Minot State University, North Dakota, where he serves as an Assistant Professor of Geography. Before his appointment at Minot State, he served as a tourism/geography lecturer at Missouri State University. His research interests include sacred and contested landscapes, Caribbean culture, festivals and tourism, and global Afro–Indo conflicts.

Dr Malcolm Cooper is Pro-Vice President Research and Professor of Tourism Management at Ritsumeikan Asia Pacific University, Beppu, Japan. He is a specialist in tourism management and development, environmental planning, water resource management and environmental law, and has published widely in these fields. He has held appointments at the Universities of New England, Adelaide and Southern Queensland, Australia, at Waiariki Institute of Technology, New Zealand and in the environmental planning and tourism policy areas for federal, state and local governments in Australia. He has also been a private consultant and a consultant to the governments of China and Vietnam.

Dr Glen Croy is a Senior Lecturer and a member of the Tourism Research Unit at Monash University, Victoria, Australia. Glen's teaching and research interests are in tourism. His special areas of research interest are in the role of media in tourism and in tourism education. He also has an active research interest in tourism in natural and protected areas. Glen has a PhD in tourism from the University of Otago, New Zealand, which investigated the role of film in destination decision making and he is a co-convener of the International Tourism and Media (ITAM) Conference.

Dr Patricia Erfurt-Cooper is a lecturer in Tourism at Ritsumeikan Asia Pacific University, Beppu, Japan and has authored or co-authored a number of books and articles in the field of tourism and environmental planning. Her research interests are risk management in volcanic environments and geothermal resources for human use.

Dr Stephen Espiner is a Senior Lecturer in Parks, Recreation and Tourism at Lincoln University, New Zealand. His research interests are largely in the field of human dimensions of protected natural area management, with particular reference to natural resource recreation and tourism, and to visitor management issues, including recreational value conflicts, social impacts, risk perception, communication and influencing visitor behaviour.

Professor John E. Hay has over 35 years experience in academia, the private sector and governmental organizations. His work has focused on bringing an interdisciplinary approach to the environmental sciences and to technical and policy-relevant assessments, especially in relation to climate variability and change. As a lead author for the Intergovernmental Panel on Climate Change (IPCC),

John was a recipient of the 2007 Nobel Peace Prize, awarded jointly to the IPCC and Al Gore. John is Visiting Professor at Ibaraki University, Japan, and an Adjunct Professor at both Lincoln University in New Zealand and the University of the South Pacific, a regional university.

Dr Ranjith Ihalanayake is a Lecturer at the School of Economics and Finance, Victoria University, Australia. His research interests include applied econometrics, tourism taxation and CGE (computable general equilibrium) modelling in tourism, tourism impact studies and tourism in developing countries, with specific reference to Sri Lanka. He was the recipient of the Best Paper Award (Economics) at the 9th International Business Research Conference 2008 in Melbourne, Victoria, Australia, was a national finalist of the Lecturer of the Year Competition 2008 conducted by UniJobs and was nominated as one of the top ten lecturers from Victoria University.

Dr Fathilah Ismail obtained her PhD from Victoria University, Melbourne, Australia in 2009. She is now lecturing at Universiti Malaysia Terengganu, Malaysia. Her research interests include island tourism, tourism impacts, cross-cultural study in tourism and tourism sustainability, as well as carrying capacity. Her present research works and publications are focused on various issues related to island tourism, particularly in Malaysia. These include tourism impact perceptions, tourist expectations, tourist satisfaction and destination attributes.

Dr Julia Jabour has been researching, writing and lecturing on matters to do with Antarctic law and policy at the University of Tasmania, Australia for nearly 20 years. She has visited Antarctica five times and has twice been a member of the Australian delegation to Antarctic Treaty Consultative Meetings. Julia has a Bachelor of Arts degree majoring in politics, philosophy and sociology, and a Graduate Diploma (Honours) in Antarctic and Southern Ocean Studies. For her PhD she researched the changing nature of sovereignty in the Arctic and Antarctic in response to global environmental interdependence. Julia's research interests are eclectic and cover Antarctic tourism, international law, environmental law, threatened species conservation, international marine management and scientific ethics.

Dr Hiroshi Kakazu, currently Chairman, Board of Directors at Meio University in Okinawa, Japan, was born on the island of Okinawa. He received his PhD in Economics from the University of Nebraska in 1971. Since then, Hiroshi has served as Visiting Research Fellow at the London School of Economics, UK, at the East-West Center, Honolulu, Hawaii, where he was a Fulbright Senior Research Fellow, and as Visiting Professor to the University of Hawaii, and the University of the Philippines (Japan Foundation). He is also the co-founder of the International Small Islands Studies Association (ISISA), Vice President of the International Scientific Council for Island Development (UNESCO-INSULA) and Emeritus President of the Japan Society of Island Studies. He has served on various governmental panels, including the Okinawa Development Promotion Council (currently Vice Chairman). Nissology (island study) is his life's work.

Professor Brian King is Professor of Tourism Management and Acting Pro-Vice-Chancellor (Industry and Community) at Victoria University, Australia. His research interests include tourism planning in developing countries and island microstates, resort operations and marketing, tourism education and human resource development, tourism in emerging Asian markets and tourism/migration linkages. He has authored several books on island resorts, tourism marketing and tourism in the Asia-Pacific region. He is founding and current Joint Editor-in-Chief of *Tourism, Culture and Communication* and chairs the Tourism and Hospitality Education International Centre of Excellence (THE-ICE), an international accreditation agency. He is a Visiting Professor at AILUN University in Sardinia, Italy.

Dr Jithendran Kokkranikal is a Senior Lecturer in the Department of Marketing, Events and Tourism at the Business School, University of Greenwich, London, UK. His research interests concentrate on tourism and development, with particular focus on entrepreneurship, community networks and human resource issues in tourism. Jithendran is currently researching issues in decentralized tourism planning and the role of community networks in tourism in developing countries, with a geographical focus on South Asia. He is also interested in studying quality and social issues in wellness tourism.

Dr Janne J. Liburd is an Associate Professor and Director of the Centre for Tourism, Innovation and Culture at the University of Southern Denmark. She is a cultural anthropologist and her research interests are in the field of sustainable tourism development. She has published on national park development, heritage tourism, open innovation and Web 2.0, tourism education, tourism crisis communication, NGOs (non-governmental organizations) and accountability. Janne has conducted a number of research projects relating to competence development for tourism practitioners and tourism educators. She is the chair of the BEST Education Network and steering committee member of the Tourism Education Futures Initiative.

Dr Gui Lohmann is a lecturer in transport and tourism at the School of Tourism and Hospitality Management of Southern Cross University (SCU) in Sydney, Australia. Previously he has worked for the School of Travel Industry Management (TIM) at the University of Hawaii at Manoa. Dr Lohmann has taught and conducted research on many different aspects of the tourism transport relationship. Apart from Australia and the USA, he has undertaken research in places such as Brazil, the United Arab Emirates, New Zealand and Singapore.

Dr Brent Moyle completed his PhD research, which focused on host–guest interactions and their implications for sustainable tourism to islands, at Monash University, Victoria, Australia. He also holds a Bachelor of Business and Commerce (Hons), majoring in Management and Tourism. His Honours research focused on visitor satisfaction in natural and protected areas. His research interests include host–guest interaction, sustainable island development, natural and protected areas, strategic planning and destination management. Brent is currently a researcher at the Tourism Research Unit, Monash University and at the School of Tourism, University of Queensland, Australia.

David Ngoc Nguyen is a graduate student at the Department of Geography at the University of Hawaii at Manoa. Nguyen is an alumnus of the East-West Center, Honolulu, Hawaii and specializes on research related to transportation and economic geography in the Asia-Pacific. He has conducted research on transportation in the Japanese islands, Hawaiian islands and islands in the South Pacific.

Dr Girish Prayag is an Assistant Professor of Marketing at SKEMA Business School in France. Before this appointment, he was a lecturer at the University of Mauritius and a doctoral student at the Waikato Management School in New

Zealand. His research interests are related to destination management, airline marketing, consumer behaviour and sustainable tourism. His work has been published in journals such as *International Journal of Quality & Reliability Management*, *Tourism Analysis*, *Current Issues in Tourism* and *Journal of Travel & Tourism Marketing*. He is specifically interested in marketing issues associated with island destinations.

President Giovanni Ruggieri is a lecturer on Tourism Economy at Palermo University, Italy and is the President of The Observatory on Tourism in the European Islands (OTIE). His research interests are innovation and tourism, tourism economy and impacts, island tourism development and sustainability, and tourism and poverty. His major publications are on the topics of the effects of cruise tourism on the economies of the Mediterranean islands (*World Journal of Tourism*, 2009), the economic impact of tourism in private homes in the Lipari Archipelago (*Real Estate and Development in Tourism: Successful Strategies and Instruments*, Erich Schmidt Verlag, 2008) and expenditure behaviour in official and hidden tourism in small Italian islands (*Actas de las Jornadas de Economia del Turismo*, 2006).

Professor Betty Weiler leads a team of researchers at Monash University, Victoria, Australia, specializing in visitor services and tourist experience management. Her qualifications include a PhD from the University of Victoria, British Columbia, Canada and a Masters degree in planning from the University of Waterloo, Saskatchewan, Canada. A widely published author, particularly in the fields of visitor communication and ecotourism, Betty is known for her collaborative approach to research, particularly with park agencies, tourism attractions and industry associations. She has managed or co-managed projects on nature and heritage tourism and tour guiding, interpretation, persuasive communication, tourism–protected area partnerships and wellness tourism.

Dr Heather Zeppel is a Senior Lecturer in Tourism at James Cook University, Cairns, Queensland, Australia. She lectures on tourism and the environment, Australian ecotourism, tourism analysis and tourism issues in developing countries. Her research interests include indigenous tourism, ecotourism, wildlife tourism, environmental interpretation and sustainability. She completed her doctoral research on Iban longhouse tourism in Borneo. Heather is the author of *Indigenous Ecotourism: Sustainable Development and Management* (CAB International, 2006). In 2010, Heather graduated with a Master in Education for Sustainability degree from James Cook University. She is now also an Associate Professor at the Australian Centre for Sustainable Business and Development, University of Southern Queensland, Brisbane, Australia.

Dr Mariyam Zulfa graduated with a PhD from Curtin University of Technology, Perth, Western Australia in 2010; her thesis investigated the competitiveness of small-island tourism destinations. Mariyam is also a graduate in law from the University of Western Australia. Before that she completed the degree of Bachelor of Arts in Urban and Regional Planning at the University of South Australia and the degree of Master of Business Administration at Waikato University, New Zealand. She has worked as a town planner in the government for many years and is now a practising lawyer in the Maldives. Mariyam was appointed Minister for Tourism in the Maldives in November 2010.

Preface

There is already a significant body of knowledge of sustainable island tourism development presented in previous books by authors including Apostolopoulos and Gayle, 2002 (*Island Tourism and Sustainable Development: Caribbean, Pacific and Mediterranean Experiences*), Briguglio *et al.*, 1996 (*Sustainable Tourism in Islands and Small States: Issues and Policies*) and Briguglio *et al.*, 1996 (*Sustainable Tourism in Islands and Small States: Case Studies*), among others. These previous volumes, along with this present book, would not have materialized without the contributions of the numerous island tourism researchers dedicated to developing an understanding of the important and complex topic of sustainable island tourism development. The chapters in this book are all based on original research and were subject to peer review before publication.

This growing interest in studying island tourism development from a sustainable perspective is probably attributable to the fact that islands form perfect 'living laboratories' that enable researchers to isolate the causal and immediate effects of tourism development on the community, environment and economy of islands, and to study them at a level of detail that is not possible in other tourism destinations. Islands attract not only tourists, but also those who seek to study the effects of tourism, and the chapters in this book add to that substantial body of research from the perspective of sustainable tourism researchers. Additionally, research questions and implications arising from each of the chapters are included in the final chapter, which will stimulate interest in specific topical or geographical areas of future research.

Acknowledgements

We wish first to acknowledge the contributors to this volume, without whose efforts the book would not have appeared. We thank them not only for their chapters, but also for their support, cooperation and patience during the completion of the project. We hope that they are happy with the result, and we, as editors, accept responsibility for any errors or misinterpretations.

We are also grateful to the staff at CABI, particularly Sarah Hulbert and Katherine Dalton, for their support and encouragement as the book has progressed. We really appreciate their patience and understanding in the process of production.

We would also like to thank Shirley Bickford from Curtin Sustainable Tourism Centre for her excellent editorial support during the 2 years that it took to produce this publication.

Dedications

Jack Carlsen

This book is dedicated to my sons Lawrence, Vincent and Dominic, who have inspired me to work towards an understanding of the world of islands that they will inherit.

Richard Butler

This book is dedicated to my grandchildren, Elspeth, Thomas, Graeme and Evelyn, in the hope that they can still find some unspoilt islands to enjoy as much as I have.

1

Introducing Sustainable Perspectives of Island Tourism

JACK CARLSEN[1] AND RICHARD BUTLER[2]

[1]Curtin University, Western Australia; [2]Strathclyde University, Scotland

Islands have been considered idyllic tourism destinations for centuries. They offer authentic cultural and natural experiences in unique settings far from the urbanized and banal locales that provide the source of island tourists. Islands often present the antithesis of urbanized life, offering the perceived distance and difference from the normal routine necessary to provide the basic ingredients for a holiday.

Islands have long held a place in the traveller's psyche, representing a combined journey over water and exploration of a bounded area that holds fascination, mystique and the unknown (Baum, 1997). They are also often used to represent paradise. Islands in the Mediterranean, Caribbean and South Pacific are major tourist destinations (Butler, 2008), and increasing air and sea access has enabled the growth of tourism to islands in the Atlantic and the Indian Ocean.

In spite of this, the consensus in the tourism literature is that island tourism, however defined and studied, is confronted with multiple challenges and problems, and is the source of social, environmental and economic distortion on a large scale (Lockhart and Drakakis-Smith, 1997). Lockhart (1997), in his overview of islands and tourism notes that 'As a result of tourist development, many islands have experienced dramatic landscape changes that reflect growing demand for accommodation, amenities and transportation systems, which in most places have been built to serve the needs of foreign visitors'. This quote reflects the economic, physical and social impacts that growing demand for island tourism was found to be responsible for in the 1990s.

For example, an economic perspective on island tourism development presents multiple challenges with common characteristics, including isolation, small scale, weak economies (Lockhart and Drakakis-Smith, 1993; Robinson, 2004), and commensurate costs of development, access to markets and expertise. These 'structural' weaknesses also include a limited resource base, small domestic market, diseconomies of scale, poor accessibility, limited infrastructure and institutional mechanisms, and dependency on external forces (Ioannides *et al.*, 2001), which impose a 'handicap of insularity' (Robinson, 2004). Limited transport access to and between island groups, and increasing costs of movement, mean that residents often require subsidization and compensation, so creating another cycle of dependency (Britton, 1991; Milne, 1997). Tourism has been described as a new form of 'monocrop' (Robinson, 2004), which in many islands has displaced the traditional agricultural activities of the past, without alleviating the risk, vulnerability and seasonal uncertainty that has characterized many island economies for decades (Britton and Clarke, 1987).

Their general relative isolation gives rise to the notion of peripherality of islands, not only in a geographical but also in a political–economic sense, whereby the 'core' centres of governance and the economy (usually the mainland capital cities) receive most of the economic benefits in return for generating investment funds. Economic and financial challenges of operating island tourism abound as well, including domestic inflation, resource-use competition, economic 'leakage', and low-paid, low-skilled and seasonal employment (Baldacchino, 2008). Even when island tourism generates economic benefits, the distribution of those benefits remains an issue. Most importantly, islands remain vulnerable to market vagaries and dependent on the economic conditions in tourist-generating countries (Robinson, 2004).

From a social perspective, island tourism developers have been cast in the mould of neocolonialists, responsible for the exploitation and destruction of fragile living cultures and of traditional ways of life. Tourism has a pervasive impact on small island communities owing to higher levels of social interaction (Robinson, 2004). Anthropologists, ethnographers and human geographers have identified a raft of social and cultural impacts, including cultural commodification and 'demonstration' effects (Kokkranikal *et al.*, 2003). Mass tourism to small islands such as Bermuda and Malta has resulted in the swamping of local culture and has contributed to domestic inflation and damage to fragile ecosystems (Baldacchino, 2008). Many bemoan the predominance of '3S' tourism in association with mass tourism (Ryan, 1995; Wing, 1995; Kokkranikal *et al.*, 2003) and the pervasive image of islands offering these attributes. The irony is that sun, sand and sea (plus the fourth 'S', sex) are probably the main experiences on islands that are sustainable, if properly managed. Furthermore, the markets, especially those originating from Europe in winter, are seeking exactly these experiences. The experience is compromised when beaches are overcrowded, polluted or eroded, usually as a result of mass tourism and the overdevelopment of coastal areas along with weak or non-existent resource and environmental management (Conlin and Baum, 1995).

From an ecological perspective, tourism development is often found to be responsible for more wanton destruction of more fragile island ecosystems, both marine and terrestrial, than any other human activity in history. That is, of course, excluding residential development, infrastructure projects and other primary production activities such as mining and fishing, all of which are depressingly commonplace on many islands. The litany of the ecological impacts of island tourism development is immense, including terrestrial and marine pollution, habitat destruction and species extinction. More recently, long-haul travel to islands via aircraft has been identified as a source of greenhouse gases (GHGs) contributing to climate change; hence island tourism is not only contributing to its own demise, but also to the impacts of global warming, including rise in average sea level and extreme weather events. Many authors have subscribed to the view that island nations in the Pacific and Indian Oceans are destined to be inundated as a result of the combined effects of global warming and rise in sea level (Mimura *et al.*, 2007). Even if islands manage to survive periodic inundation, and may in fact be expanding in size in response and adaptation to rise in sea level (Webb and Kench, 2010), numerous ecological threats remain.

Finally, there are those that believe that peak oil supply has been reached and that once the remaining oil runs out, island tourism development will end (Zubair *et al.*, 2010). The almost exclusive reliance on air services to most island tourism destinations renders them vulnerable to the fortunes of the global air transport sector, which itself is undergoing rapid change and cost pressures. It can be argued that the concept of sustainable development of islands is redundant in the face of this vulnerability to mounting ecological and economic pressures that will first and foremost have an impact on islands, no matter how committed they may be to sustainability.

None the less, island tourism continues to develop because demand is increasing, and tourism is a market-driven industry. Zubair *et al.* (2010) claim that the rate of growth in arrivals to island tourism destinations over the last two decades exceeded the rates of growth in tourism arrivals worldwide, with some islands e.g. the Maldives, experiencing a doubling of arrivals over that period. However, limited capacity and resources mean that island tourism development may not be able to keep pace with increasing arrivals and the increasing pressure on the social, economic and environmental fabric that ensues.

On reading the literature on island tourism, a scholar new to the field would surely wonder why and how this form of tourism development would and should ever continue, given the magnitude of barriers, problems and impacts that have been identified over the past two decades. Furthermore, a new scholar would be confused by the proposition that island tourism development could in any way be viewed from the perspective of sustainability.

Nevertheless, that is indeed what this book is about: moving away from the generalizations concerning island tourism impacts and identifying specific cases where islands are not only confronting the challenges of tourism development, but also responding in ways that place them on a path towards sustainability. It may indeed be the first of many books on island tourism that highlights this process of change, rather than the problems of island tourism and, as such, provides an optimistic view of the topic, more in line with the perceptions that many island tourism communities, developers and tourists themselves have of these places.

Structure of This Book

The book is presented in three parts which exemplify the ecological, social and economic perspectives of sustainable island tourism development, each with five chapters. This partial approach could be perceived as a false trichotomy, given that all three perspectives should be considered in every case when documenting true sustainability; but we live in a world where all important sustainability issues can be viewed from multiple perspectives, and in such a world greater insights can be provided by those with specific perspectives in these issues. In order to gain more detailed insights into the specific ecological, social and economic perspectives of island tourism development, expert researchers from around the world were invited to contribute to this book. The contributions introduce a range of highly qualified researchers in disciplines including anthropology, geography, law, economics, planning, marketing and business. Cases in this book include cold water islands in the Atlantic and Southern Oceans, as well as islands in the more popular warmer climes of the Mediterranean, Caribbean, and the Pacific and Indian Oceans. The following section provides an introduction to the chapters on island tourism development from each of the three perspectives chosen: ecological, social and economic sustainability.

Towards Ecologically Sustainable Perspectives of Island Tourism Development

Macquarie Island's journey towards sustainability is the subject of Chapter 2. Tourism to subantarctic Macquarie Island in Tasmania, Australia, is largely focused on ecological matters, but the purpose of this chapter is to investigate the nature of limits to tourism to the subantarctic islands in the Peninsula region, including the Antarctic Peninsula itself, and how such limits might have an impact on Macquarie as an alternative destination.

The difficult journey of Fraser Island towards sustainability is reviewed in Chapter 3. This chapter describes the setting and historical context of tourism development, covering the previous sand mining and logging economy and describing the process of attaining world heritage listing in the 1990s, and the impetus that this has given to tourism development. As this book goes to press, another sand island off the Queensland coast in Australia, North Stradbroke island, is undertaking a similar transition from sand mining to ecotourism.

Environmental management of Green Island has been the key driver of sustainability according to the account in Chapter 4. This chapter reviews the environmental management of tourism on and around Green Island, a coral cay located 45 minutes from Cairns in tropical North Queensland, Australia.

Tourism to the ecologically fragile Lakshadweep Islands of the Indian Ocean is described in Chapter 5, which considers the development of tourism in the islands within the context of sustainability. Through an examination of the structural and developmental features of Lakshadweep tourism, the chapter seeks to identify specific development and management patterns, if any, and to explore potential strategies for promoting sustainability-oriented tourism in the Lakshadweep Islands.

Climate change has been recognized as both a threat and an opportunity for low-lying islands such as the Maldives. This important threat to sustainability, and the opportunities for response and adaptation, are explored in Chapter 6.

Towards Socially Sustainable Perspectives of Island Tourism Development

Cross-cultural exchanges in Malaysian island tourism development are discussed in Chapter 7. This chapter investigates the exchanges between hosts and guests, and the potential impacts of cultural differences on perceptions of sustainable tourism development in the small island settings of Malaysia.

Particular forms of island tourism development may represent the antithesis of social sustainability, as is found to be the case in Chapter 8 for casino development in St Croix, USA Virgin Islands, and in Christmas Island. These reviews of island casino development facilitate an understanding of how policy processes can work against social sustainability if they fail to be informed by values and context.

Adverse social conditions and sexual tensions arising from the 'carnival mentality' of Trinidad and Tobago represent a major threat to social sustainability, as is described in Chapter 9. The objective of this chapter is to portray the true nature of the present social condition of Trinidad and Tobago as it relates to the fledgling tourism industry. The pre-Lenten Trinidad Carnival will be used as a springboard to facilitate study of the dynamics of a society locked into a 'carnival mentality'.

An understanding of the social interactions on two Australian islands – the Bruny and Magnetic Islands – is developed in Chapter 10. This chapter uses social exchange theory as a framework to explore the process of tourism interaction on islands from the perspectives of both visitors and the local inhabitants.

The nature of sustainable tourism planning on the Shetland Islands of Scotland is reviewed in Chapter 11. This chapter discusses the nature of tourism planning, control and development on the Shetland Islands, which were recently selected as one of the most sustainable tourism destinations in the world in a global survey. The importance is emphasized of local control of planning and development if a more sustainable approach is to be taken.

Towards Economically Sustainable Perspectives of Island Tourism Development

The Tourism Area Life Cycle (TALC) model is used in Chapter 12 to describe the economics and markets for sustainable tourism in Mauritius. The chapter aims to explain the rejuvenation of the island of Mauritius in terms of its changing products, visitor profile and generating markets.

The transformation of the Ryukyu Islands of Okinawa, Japan towards a more sustainable economic footing is the subject of Chapter 13. This chapter will describe how islands such as those in Okinawa can be transformed rapidly into tourism-dependent economies because they have maintained internal political stability and offer warm hospitality to visitors.

A comparison of 24 Mediterranean islands highlights some of the economic barriers to sustainability in Chapter 14, which analyses the main dimensions of tourism in islands representing seven European countries. Islands are classified by area into large, medium, small and micro, and also by population density – from high to low. The Mediterranean islands represent a wide variety of situations and common problems, and every economic decision has had an immediate impact on the sustainability of the economies of each island.

Sustainable transport policies and practices in Hawaii are detailed in Chapter 15. This chapter aims to elaborate further on the issue of sustainable tourism transportation, not only reviewing the major indicators to measure sustainable transportation practices but also discussing them from the perspective of tourism transportation in Hawaii.

Finally, the planning processes for tourism development in the Maldives are reviewed in Chapter 16. This chapter reviews the history and development of tourism in the Maldives, and analyses the legal, planning and political structures and processes that should enable the ongoing economically sustainable development of tourism.

Summary

Sustainability provides the lens through which island tourism can be considered as positively contributing to the economic, social and ecological conditions of islands. It is hoped that this book, by bringing a sustainable perspective to the study of island tourism, will increase our understanding of how best to manage these ecologically fragile, socially sensitive and economically vulnerable places as tourism is developed further.

References

Baldacchino, G. (2008) Island tourism. In: Lück, M. (ed.) *Encyclopedia of Tourism and Recreation in Marine Environments.* CAB International, Wallingford, UK, pp. 254–255.

Baum, T.G. (1997) The fascination of islands: a tourist perspective. In: Lockhart, D.G. and Drakakis-Smith, D. (eds) *Island Tourism: Trends and Prospects.* Cassell, London, pp. 21–35.

Britton, S.G. (1991) Tourism, capital and place: towards a critical geography of tourism. *Environment and Planning D: Society and Place* 9, 451–478.

Britton, S.G. and Clarke, W. (1987) *Ambiguous Alternative: Tourism in Small Developing Countries.* Institute of Pacific Studies, University of the South Pacific, Suva, Fiji.

Butler R. (2008) Islands. In: Lück, M. (ed.) *Encyclopedia of Tourism and Recreation in Marine Environments.* CAB International, Wallingford, UK, p. 254.

Conlin, M.V. and Baum, T. (1995) *Island Tourism: Management Principles and Practices.* John Wiley, Chichester, UK.

Ioannides, D., Apostolopoulos, Y. and Sonmez, S.F. (2001) *Mediterranean Islands and Sustainable Tourism Development: Practices, Management and Policies.* Pinter, London.

Kokkranikal, J., MacLellan, R.L. and Baum, T. (2003) Island tourism and sustainability: a case study of the Lakshadweep Islands. *Journal of Sustainable Tourism* 11, 426–447.

Lockhart, D.G. (1997) Islands and tourism: an overview. In: Lockhart, D.G. and Drakakis-Smith, D. (eds) (1997) *Island Tourism: Trends and Prospects.* Cassell, London, pp. 3–20.

Lockhart, D.G. and Drakakis-Smith, D. (1993) *The Development Process in Small Island States.* Routledge, London.

Lockhart, D.G. and Drakakis-Smith, D. (1997) *Island Tourism: Trends and Prospects.* Cassell, London.

Milne, S. (1997) Tourism, dependency and South Pacific micro-states: beyond the vicious cycle? In: Lockhart, D.G. and Drakakis-Smith, D. (eds) *Island Tourism: Trends and Prospects.* Cassell, London, pp. 281–301.

Mimura, N., Nurse, L., McLean, R.F., Agard, J., Briguglio, L., Lefale, P., Payet, R. and Sem, G. (2007) Small islands. In: Parry, M.L., Canziani, O.F., Palutikof, J.P., Linden, P.J. van der and Hanson, C.E. (eds) *Climate Change 2007: Impacts, Adaptation and Vulnerability. Contribution of Working Group II to the Fourth Assessment Report of the Intergovernmental Panel on Climate Change.* Cambridge University Press, Cambridge, pp. 687–716.

Robinson, M. (2004) *Tourism, Globalisation and Cultural Change: An Island Community Perspective.* Channel View Publications, Clevedon, UK.

Ryan, C. (1995) Islands, beaches and life-stage marketing. In: Conlin, M.V. and Baum, T. (eds) *Island Tourism: Management Principles and Practices.* John Wiley, Chichester, UK, pp. 79–94.

Webb, A.P. and Kench, P.S. (2010) The dynamic response of reef islands to sea level rise: evidence from multi-decadal analysis of island change in the central Pacific. *Global and Planetary Change* 72, 234–246.

Wing, P. (1995) Tourism development in the South Indian Ocean: the case of Mauritius. In: Conlin, M.V. and Baum, T. (eds) *Island Tourism: Management Principles and Practices.* John Wiley, Chichester, UK, pp. 229–236.

Zubair, S., Bowen, D. and Elwin, J. (2010) Not quite paradise: inadequacies of environmental impact assessment in the Maldives. *Tourism Management*, doi:10.1016/j.tourman.2009.12.007.

Ecologically Sustainable Perspectives of Island Tourism

2 Aliens in an Ancient Landscape: Rabbits, Rats and Tourists on Macquarie Island

JULIA JABOUR

Institute for Marine and Antarctic Studies, University of Tasmania, Australia

Introduction

Macquarie Island, in the subantarctic south of Tasmania, Australia, is one of the few refuges in the vast Southern Ocean for seabirds, seals and penguins. Their presence contributes nutrients to the substrate upon which cold temperature flora, grasses and mega-herbs (but not trees), rely. Exotic animals such as elephant seals and king penguins, plants and, more generally, the physical vista of the island, are integral to the island tourism experience. The sustainability of Macquarie Island tourism relies in large part on the continued existence of an experience of this calibre and therefore its fortunes are tied to the fortunes dictated by the physical processes that continue to shape the island. Tourism is not a major contributing factor to island disturbance, but it may be a hapless victim of these physical changes. The sustainability of future tourism to Macquarie Island is discussed here in the context of contemporary physical changes to climate and the resulting ecological effects.

Hundreds of thousands of years ago, oceanic crust that was about 9 million years old was thrust out of the Southern Ocean and Macquarie Island was born. It is the only one of the subantarctic islands (Fig. 2.1) to be formed in this way, and earned it World Heritage Area status in 1997. Its modern history began with its discovery by sealers only 200 years ago; there followed a grizzly history of mass slaughter of its wildlife, particularly of seals and penguins, which were clubbed to death or driven alive into trypots and boiled for their oil (Parks Tasmania, 2009a). The legacies from the island's first visitors are a double-edged sword. Macquarie Island's unusual genesis and the abuse of its wildlife have earned it a host of prestigious designations as a place of outstanding universal value, giving significant protection to its biodiversity. The downside has been the intentional and accidental introduction of non-native species. Today there is evidence of the significant effect of these aliens (especially rabbits and rats) on the endemic flora and fauna. This, in turn, threatens to

Fig. 2.1. The Subantarctic islands (Antarctic Tasmania, 2006. Map by Peter Boyer, South Wind.)

compromise the island's appeal as a tourist destination in its own right and as a stepping-stone for tourism to East Antarctica.

The early 21st century is a time of transitional climate warming, with the effects being noted first on the subantarctic islands. Early indications, although still somewhat ambiguous, point to the possibility of more extreme local weather conditions, which are already extreme in the subantarctic; conditions that are more conducive to the survival and colonization of introduced species, including microorganisms, with the resultant biosecurity issues; and changing climatic conditions, making Macquarie Island, for example, even wetter and possibly less appealing to all but the hardy few (Pendlebury and Barnes-Keoghan, 2007).

Fragile is not an adjective that is usefully applied to this or the other subantarctic islands that have stood in the path of keening winds, driving rain and chilling temperatures for millennia. Their plants and animals are relatively robust, otherwise they would not have survived in what humans would call an *extreme* environment. However, these remote subpolar ecosystems are most certainly *vulnerable* and, in contemporary times, it is the introduction of alien species in a warming climate that will continue to have the greatest effect. It will be impossible for the administrators of any of the subantarctic islands, including Macquarie Island, to ameliorate extrinsic factors, such as the effects of climate warming, but it is possible to manage and regulate intrinsic factors such as the introduction of alien vertebrates and human activity. If the ecological integrity of Macquarie Island can be maintained relatively free from anthropocentric stressors, then there will be a better chance of withstanding the pressure from sources that cannot be controlled.

The Process of Development of Tourism to Macquarie Island

There has been no planned development of tourism to Macquarie Island. The first visitors to this remote, uninhabited place were sealers ranging across the southern oceans in search of fur seals in the early 1800s. Whalers and explorers followed, and then scientists who have operated a research base on the island since the early 1950s. In fact, it was the Australian Antarctic scientist and explorer, Sir Douglas Mawson, who first proposed protection for Macquarie Island after his 1911 Antarctic expedition (which established wireless communication facilities on the island in support of their polar exploits) exposed the cruelty and indefensibility of the animal oil industry. Mawson was influential in having the first protection bestowed on Macquarie Island in 1933, when it was declared a wildlife sanctuary under the Tasmanian *Animals and Birds Protection Act 1928*. Protection was further strengthened in 1979 when the island became a restricted area. Admission for any reason required a permit from Parks and Wildlife Service Tasmania (hereinafter Parks Tasmania), the government department with responsibility for the island (Parks Tasmania, 2009a).

Commercial tourism has developed in an ad hoc manner, linked to increasing interest in the eastern part of Antarctica. Located at 54° South, Macquarie Island is only as far south of the equator as the mid-English counties are north, yet nobody lives there. At about 1500 km south-south-east of Tasmania, travel to this speck in the ocean entails a 3-day voyage from the port of Hobart. Once a ship arrives, there is no guarantee that passengers will be able to land owing to the strong and gusty winds (an annual average of 268 days of strong wind). Because there is no wharf to berth at, ships must anchor offshore and transport tourists by landing craft (a Zodiac, for example) to the shore. This latitude is known as the Furious Fifties and, because passenger safety is paramount, landings are not always possible. Sometimes it is only possible to view the island's scenery and wildlife through a stormy veil as the vessel cruises along its 34 km coastline. This expedition-style of tourism has ensured that numbers have remained low (Fig. 2.2). One operator forewarns its high-end passengers:

> Although our itinerary to the extreme sub-Antarctic and Antarctic regions is based on many years of collective experience, prevailing weather and ice conditions in this area of the world are unpredictable, mother nature dictates our course. These are not cruises they are true expeditions to what can be the most inhospitable region on earth. Bring with you a spirit of adventure and flexibility
>
> (Orion Expedition Cruises, 2009).

Notwithstanding this, the upward trend in numbers is steady. Carmichael (2007), for example, notes that increasing educational tourism interest is one of the most important and pressing management issues facing Macquarie Island because of the potential for increased environmental risk, 'particularly from a quarantine perspective'.

There is only a handful of regular Australian and New Zealand operators using Macquarie Island as a stopping-off point on route to and from the

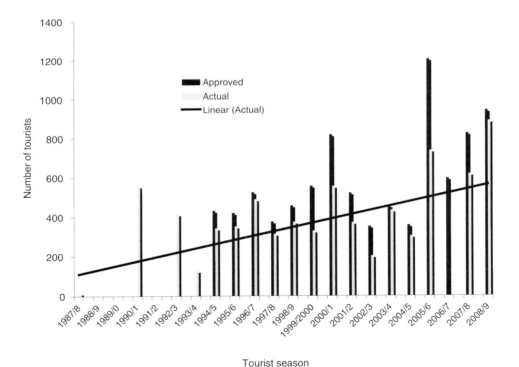

Tourist season

Fig. 2.2. Macquarie Island tourist numbers. Note that no actual data were collected for the 2006/07 season. Variation between approved and actual numbers occurs because operators have failed to make landings, for reasons usually related to weather. (After Noel Carmichael, Hobart, personal communication, 2009.)

Antarctic continent. There are three Australian operators and one from New Zealand who are full members of the voluntary industry body, the International Association of Antarctica Tour Operators (IAATO). The IAATO is the principal source of information about Antarctic and subantarctic tourism. It reports that the East Antarctic component, which has Macquarie Island and the other subantarctic islands in the region (Auckland, Campbell and Enderby) on its itinerary, is only a very small percentage of the annual total of all Antarctic tourism (which itself is very modest in global terms). For example, in the 2008/9 season, out of 563,497 landings, only 6213 (just over 1%) were made at East Antarctic destinations and, of those, only around 880 were on Macquarie Island (IAATO, 2009).

Planning for Sustainability

Originally there were no management plans for Macquarie Island. As it is so far away from the state of Tasmania (formerly Van Diemen's Land), to which it has belonged since 1825, it is virtually out of sight and out of mind. Comprehensive planning became obligatory, however, with its World Heritage Area designation in 1997.

There was only very limited human activity initially, after the early animal oil industry ceased in 1919. Since 1948 though, there has been a continuous presence of research scientists and personnel, including those attached to the Australian National Antarctic Research Expeditions (ANARE), the Australian Bureau of Meteorology and, since 1972 when it became a Tasmanian Reserve, Parks Tasmania rangers and researchers. Small numbers of tourists visit the island each year to view the historical artefacts, the wildlife, the spectacular wild landscape and the current research facilities. The nature and level of all human activities are prescribed within the Macquarie Island Nature Reserve and World Heritage Area Management Plan (hereinafter, the Management Plan) (Parks Tasmania, 2009b).

The Macquarie Island Management Plan

The Management Plan is a blueprint for strategies to protect the island's physical and ecological integrity. It employs, among other techniques, spatial differentiation (management zoning) to prescribe and regulate human activities. It aims to allow the continuation of scientific research, management and long-term monitoring programmes providing that they do not cause any long-term adverse effects on the island. This includes any compromise to the values that make Macquarie Island a place of outstanding universal interest (e.g. World Heritage status, Biosphere Reserve status, Tasmanian National Park status and listing on the Australian Register of the National Estate) (Parks Tasmania, 2009b).

The objectives of the Management Plan are to implement and enforce the Plan's provisions efficiently and effectively; these include protecting and conserving the island's values; coordinating and integrating scientific research, monitoring and management activities; and ensuring safety and prompt response to emergencies (Parks Tasmania, 2009b). A Parks Tasmania Ranger in Charge is stationed on the island, together with other personnel who are deputized to help carry out administration functions, including observation aboard tourist vessels.

Management approaches for the island are site specific and involve three different layers of differentiation (Fig. 2.3). First, there are three broad management zones: Zone A, a services zone (at the Isthmus where the research station and facilities are located); Zone B, a limited access zone (the whole of the remainder of the island); and Zone C, a marine zone (Tasmanian waters out to 3 nautical miles). Secondly, within the large zones there are smaller special management areas (SMAs), including tourism management areas (TMAs, discussed later). Thirdly, the SMAs are themselves further differentiated into categories with opened and closed seasons. The SMAs are revised annually, as regards both areas included and dates of opening/closing. In 2006, for example, there were three categories: Category 1, described as very sensitive to human disturbance because of difficulty of entry; Category 2, a high-density breeding area described as difficult to enter without disturbance; and Category 3, a more sporadic breeding area, but still vulnerable (Parks Tasmania, 2009b).

Strict rules apply to the zones and areas, with scientific permits and/or access authorizations only available for research or management purposes during specific times. With the broad objectives of protecting the physical and ecological integrity of the island, the special reserve status of Macquarie Island effectively prohibits the public from general access (Parks Tasmania, 2009b).

The greatest risk posed by even the low numbers of visitors is, as was mentioned earlier, one of biosecurity. The administrators of Macquarie Island have had a long and not so glorious history of attempts to restore and maintain its ecological integrity following breaches of biosecurity best practice.

Ecological Integrity: Barriers and Indicators

It is logical to assume that the extreme isolation of Macquarie Island should, at least, have buffered it against human impact. Sadly, this was not the case (Bergstrom and Selkirk, 2007). Its vulnerability is exemplified in this banner, which is on the public domain website of the administrator, Parks Tasmania (Parks Tasmania, 2009c):

> Rabbits and rats are posing a severe threat to World Heritage values on Macquarie Island, as research reveals widespread damage to terrestrial eco-systems. These impacts include devastating effects upon native fauna, flora, geomorphology, natural landscape values and nutrient recycling systems.

Unfortunately, rabbits were naively introduced as a food source in case of emergencies, such as a shipwreck for sealers and whalers. Because there were minimal quarantine controls in place at the time, shipboard rats (and mice)

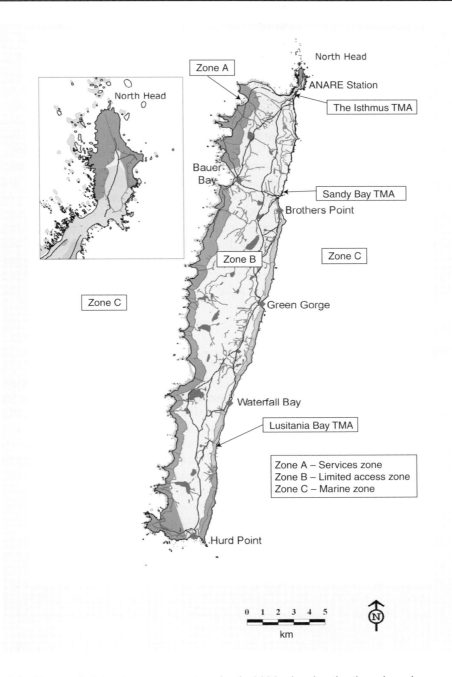

Fig. 2.3. Macquarie Island management zoning in 2006, showing the three broad management zones (A, B and C), the three special management areas (SMAs), which are included in the darker shaded areas on the western and eastern coasts of the island and at its northern tip, and the three tourism management areas (TMAs). ANARE, Australian National Antarctic Research Expeditions. (With permission from Tasmania Parks and Wildlife Service.)

came ashore even though rat guards are traditionally used on ships to prevent disease-ridden rodents from coming on board in the first place. Once established in the ecosystem of Macquarie Island, these aliens were much more tenacious and difficult to eradicate than first thought. The problem was made momentarily worse when cats were introduced to control the rabbits and rats. They too colonized and became feral, but were eventually eradicated in 2000 (Carmichael, 2007). The rabbit and rat numbers increased as a result of diminished predation by cats and today the damage they have caused is visible and devastating.

Macquarie Island may be only a small speck in the middle of the ocean, but it is a large area when trying to eradicate every single mouse, rabbit and rat (and a plant or two as well). It is not necessary to rake over the history of attempts at pest eradication on Macquarie Island here, except to note that commentators acknowledge how difficult the job was given the size of the island and the lack of suitable technology, calm weather or experience (Scott and Kirkpatrick, 2008; Turbett, 2008). Today, major Management Plan actions now include, under the general rubric of *Values*, three broad items relating to threatened species, rare plants and pest eradication (Appendix 9 of the Management Plan).

Key indicators of sustainability

Appendix 10 of the Management Plan lists a range of key indicators that will provide a guide to evaluating the success of its strategies, particularly those related to the three items noted above. Success relies heavily on the effective implementation of and compliance with the Management Plan. For example, as an indicator of species health, any national recovery, threat abatement or action plans for at-risk species should be seen to be working. This could mean that monitoring would show a slowdown in decline of these species, or even a recovery to the point where a more favourable conservation status is evident. In addition, the pest eradication programme (proposed to commence in winter 2010) should be shown to have eradicated all alien species. A crucial part of this strategy is to introduce concomitant quarantine and environmental protection measures, which will be assessed as being successful if no further alien species have been introduced and no new species have been found (Parks Tasmania, 2009b). As the Management Plan is to be reviewed 7 years after entry into force (July 2006–July 2013), it is assumed that key indicators will have at least a 7-year time frame during which some improvement should become evident (Parks Tasmania, 2009b).

There is no evidence to suggest that tourists have been responsible for introducing alien species to Macquarie Island or for compromising its ecological vitality. Yet tourism is sometimes used as a convenient environmental scapegoat, unjustly, it would seem. It could be argued, rather, that Macquarie Island's ecological integrity is partly maintained by the fact that tourism is tightly controlled, both naturally by the tyranny of distance and the weather, and through highly prescriptive regulation. Environmental integrity is crucial to the island tourism experience, and in the past it has been reports from tourists, tourism operators and non-governmental organizations (NGOs) that have helped to gain a higher media profile for Macquarie Island's pest problem.

Sustainable Tourism: Barriers and Indicators

There is no purpose-built tourism infrastructure on Macquarie Island except for boardwalks and viewing platforms and limited interpretation signs, all of which have been constructed partly using funds generated by access fees. Operators must pre-purchase permits from Parks Tasmania to land a specified number of visitors on the island each season. Quotas are in place, and in the 2008/9 season the limit was 940 tourists. Operators who have missed a landing as a result of extreme weather are not permitted to trade unused permits with other operators who missed the ballot. This explains the disparity between the 'Approved' and 'Actual' figures in Fig. 2.2, and why the long-term average of 'Approved/Actual' is only 76% (Noel Carmichael, Hobart, personal communication, 2009).

Selection criteria for visiting operators are categorical and include: demonstrated capacity to minimize environmental impacts (best verified by an independent environmental impact assessment); safety and self-reliance; tangible benefits to the management and protection of Macquarie Island and to the state of Tasmania; education of clients, crew and staff; operator accreditation and relevant qualifications and experience; and timetable flexibility (Parks Tasmania, 2009d).

The Management Plan is unequivocal in relation to tourism: 'controlled tourism for educational purposes is the only form of tourism permitted in this reserve' (Parks Tasmania, 2009b). It delineates tourism management areas (the aforementioned TMAs) and, perhaps more importantly, areas where tourism is prohibited. In conjunction with an annually reviewed document titled 'Guidelines for Tourist Operations and Visits to Macquarie Island Nature Reserve and World Heritage Area' (Parks Tasmania, 2009e), these approaches effectively limit tourist numbers and therefore tourism impact. This, in turn, goes some way towards making the activity sustainable in the longer term.

Tourism management areas

Parks Tasmania recognizes the value of tourists to Macquarie Island and makes provision for 'limited access for educational tourism purposes' (Parks Tasmania, 2009b). Visitation is confined to the three TMAs, one in each of the three zones A, B and C (Fig. 2.3). These areas have been carefully designed to allow tourists safe and low-impact access to wildlife, flora and the landscape. It is not possible to sleep ashore; tourism can only be ship based (and vessels carrying more than 200 passengers are prohibited from entering Reserve waters). Visits into restricted areas are also not possible, primarily for safety reasons, but also with the aim of minimizing impact on the flora and fauna.

The TMAs are best placed to promote public understanding and appreciation of the values that the island holds. The irony is that without such public scrutiny, the significance of the pest problem may not have been uncovered as convincingly as it has been, and may have become far worse before it was verified and a plan of action adopted. In that sense, island tourism is helping to restore the environmental integrity of the island itself.

Guidelines for tourist operations and visits

The documented Guidelines issued by Parks Tasmania are used to assist operators in seeking access to Macquarie Island (Parks Tasmania, 2009e). Prior approval to visit must be obtained from the Director. Unlike some Antarctic continental destinations where the presence of a yacht or ship may easily go unnoticed, seasonal staff on Macquarie Island will more readily notice unauthorized visits, possibly putting operators in breach of Tasmanian law as a result.

Although only a guideline, this document is prescriptive and contains important information for operators. In the context of this chapter, two topics within the Guidelines are noteworthy: quarantine and wildlife. Biosecurity has already been flagged as a management headache, and no soil, plants, animals, animal products, other organic material or food may be taken ashore (emergency provisions notwithstanding) in order to minimize the potential for alien species to be translocated. For the same reason, clothing and equipment taken ashore must be decontaminated before each landing. No rubbish is to be left ashore and no shipborne rubbish or ballast water can be disposed of in the Reserve waters. To prevent the accidental introduction of shipborne invertebrates, no mooring lines are connected to shore and no vessel is to approach closer than 200 m. Vessels must be certified 'clean' (Parks Tasmania, 2009e).

In relation to wildlife, there are provisions about safe small boat operation, including avoiding collisions with marine life. Safe viewing distances are mandatory. A cruising speed limit of 5 knots is in place, and propeller guards must be fitted. Small vessels cannot refuel anywhere other than on board ship (Parks Tasmania, 2009e).

Key indicators of sustainability

As with the key indicators for success of the Management Plan generally, Appendix 10 to the Plan notes that, in relation to tourism, success will be measured by monitoring the compliance of tour operators. Indicators might include signs that threatened species are recovering, that already-disturbed sites have recovered naturally and that rehabilitated sites also show recovery. These signs will indicate that the spatial containment of tourist impact will have been generally effective (Parks Tasmania, 2009b).

In relation to the specific TMAs, monitoring might show high compliance with the strategy: that the boardwalks and viewing areas are not degrading the environment and that the flora and fauna are showing only minor or transitory impact from tourist visitation (Parks Tasmania, 2009b). Overall, and in spite of the presence of alien species (rabbits, rats and some plants) tourism to Macquarie Island can hardly be anything other than sustainable given the strict regulation and enforcement.

Discussion

There is no empirical evidence to suggest that tourism has contributed to either the degradation of the Macquarie Island environment, or threatened its endemic species. The tourism industry does have the potential, though, to be the loser in the event that restrictions on human activity become too onerous. Under the current circumstances, the Management Plan is being used to both protect the island's values (including its terrestrial vista and biodiversity) and at the same time to promote limited self-sufficient, environmentally responsible, educational tourism. It is not clear under what circumstances this scenario might change in the short term.

Macquarie Island tourism generates a small amount of revenue for the Tasmanian government each year through access fees. The money is used to help pay the salaries of Parks Tasmania rangers stationed there; to provide, maintain and upgrade visitor infrastructure (safety boardwalks, viewing platforms and interpretation signs, for example); and to plan and initiate management measures such as the pest eradication programme (Noel Carmichael, Hobart, personal communication, 2009). The fee per person (tourist and volunteer crew) for the 2009/10 season is set at AUS$165, plus an AUS$2000 non-refundable bond for each vessel visit. The fees have remained at this level for some years. Given the figures of 940 tourist access approvals and 14 ship visits in the 2008/9 season, this would have generated around AUS$183,000 in revenue. The Tasmanian government is not going to profit financially from Macquarie Island tourism; in fact, maintaining a presence there to carry out the research and management functions associated with the national park costs in excess of the small return from the low numbers of tourists. The Australian federal government, which underwrites shipping and infrastructure costs for the research carried out there, is supporting the Tasmanian government, and while this arrangement remains in place, tourism management is unlikely to change.

It is also probable that Macquarie Island will remain low on the agenda of Antarctic tour operators while the tourist numbers are still relatively modest for the Antarctic as a whole. The vast majority of tourists visit the Antarctic Peninsula from departure ports in South America because of the advantage of proximity (Fig. 2.1). The principal operators are from the USA and the main market is in the USA, thus the costs are relatively low by comparison with costs accruing to operators from say, Europe, or Australia. However, like the subantarctic, the Antarctic Peninsular environment is also in transition: for example, the greatest warming is being recorded on the western side of the Peninsula where both scientific and tourism effort is focused (ACE CRC, 2009). This area corresponds with the largest concentration of readily accessible wildlife, which empirical data suggests is the number-one motivation for tourists travelling to the Antarctic (Bauer, 2001). Unfortunately, changes in climate have the potential to impose added stress on wildlife: more or less sea ice may interfere with foraging behaviour and success; bigger icebergs might block the path of penguins to the sea; the populations of some species, such as Antarctic fur seals, are growing rapidly in some areas and may cause added competition for food; and perhaps worst of all, a warming climate may provide a more conducive habitat for the introduction and colonization of alien species (particularly microorganisms). Increasingly, difficult or risky operating conditions in the Peninsula may see the imposition of added regulation on tourism, which may in turn have a flow-on effect to the East Antarctic destination. There are changes that are happening now.

Antarctic Peninsula tourism is almost exclusively ship based. Between October 2008 and April 2009, official port records indicate that 36 vessels departed Ushuaia (Argentina) on 233 voyages to the Antarctic Peninsula (Government of Argentina, 2009). Shipping is an inherently dangerous activity, and the risk is heightened in the polar context by – among other things – inadequate charts, extreme weather and the presence of icebergs and sea ice. There have been a number of groundings and a recent sinking on the Peninsula tourist route which, understandably, have operators and managers nervous about possible future trends given the exigencies of operating there. These include remoteness from search and rescue capacity and the changing climate and its effect on the formation, composition, extent and duration of sea ice (ACE CRC, 2009).

The world's shipping regulator, the International Maritime Organization (IMO), has adopted an Arctic shipping code (IMO, 2002) which might prove useful as the basis for an Antarctic code. This task has been an Antarctic Treaty Consultative Meeting chestnut for some years now and progress towards its completion was best described as glacial. However, at their 2009 meeting, the Antarctic Treaty Consultative Parties adopted a Resolution (8/2009) giving their imprimatur to the IMO for a mandatory polar code to be struck as soon as practicable (Antarctic Treaty Secretariat, 2009). The tightening of shipping regulations (including a recent ban on heavy fuel oil) is likely to have a significant impact on Peninsula tourism but it is not speculated here whether this will affect the volume of seaborne tourism to East Antarctica (including Macquarie Island).

Finally, the Antarctic Peninsula receives the lion's share of tourism but there is no barometer for measuring how close the destination is to saturation. Quite possibly, this is something of a subjective assessment, based on the fact that the unique wilderness experience offered by the tourism operators will become increasingly difficult to sustain while there are many ships, many operators and many tourists all vying for the same thing. The recent financial downturn has seen Antarctic tourism numbers drop; one long-term operator anticipated a 20% decrease in numbers across the board in the 2009/10 season because of global financial constraints (Greg Mortimer, Hobart, personal communication, 2009). If the downturn continues, it should ease the congestion for the time being. A combination of more difficult operating conditions, higher costs (especially for environmentally benign fuel) and tighter shipping regulations might slow the growth of Antarctic tourism generally. If this does flow on to Macquarie Island, then the administrators need only sit back and relax for the moment, confident that they have all possible controls in place.

Conclusion

The sustainability of Macquarie Island tourism is dependent on a number of key factors, including the conditions under which the governments with conjoint jurisdiction proceed; for example, will the federal government continue to underwrite state presence on the island, how will a warming climate affect the island's ecological values and thus the island tourism experience, and in the current global financial crisis, what will happen to the cost of doing business and other idiosyncrasies of the Antarctic tourism market? It will be important in the future for administrators to do all they can to maintain the ecological integrity of Macquarie Island by ensuring that it remains as free as possible from human-induced stress, which might give it better odds of withstanding the pressure from sources that cannot be controlled.

Tourism has not contributed to the degradation of the Macquarie Island environment because boardwalks and viewing platforms control tourist movements, or to its vulnerability as official observers monitor all activities. The industry does have the potential, however, to be the loser in the event that restrictions on human activity become onerous, either on Macquarie Island or in the Antarctic context more broadly.

Tourism to Macquarie Island is a commercial venture and government access charges are used to help pay salaries, maintain infrastructure and commission research. As numbers are low and capped on an annual basis, the industry is very well controlled through the Management Plan and Guidelines. Under these conditions it is unlikely that tourism will have more than a minor or transitory impact on the island environment.

The presence of tourists helped alert the media and then the public to the gross degradation of the environment resulting from alien species and forced the hands of the joint administrations into a co-funded agreement for an eradication programme. The programme was only possible once they acknowledged that technology and experience from elsewhere were necessary to try to manage such large-scale invasions. Once the programme is complete, and after several seasons of monitoring, it might be possible to conclude that these aliens have been removed from Macquarie Island. The other aliens, the tourists, will continue to have a positive effect while their presence is so tightly controlled.

References

ACE CRC (2009) Changes to Antarctic sea ice: impacts. *Position Analysis*, 11 June 2009. Antarctic Climate & Ecosystems Cooperative Research Centre, Hobart, Tasmania. Available at: http://www. acecrc.org.au/drawpage.cgi?pid= publications&aid=797037 (accessed 18 June 2009).

Antarctic Tasmania (2006) Sub-Antarctic Map, 2006. In: *International Forum on the Sub-Antarctic*. Available at: http:// www.sub-antarctic.org/ifsa.html (accessed 3 September 2009).

Antarctic Treaty Secretariat (2009) Antarctic Shipping Code. In: ATCM XXXII (Thirty-second Antarctic Treaty Consultative Meeting – Twelfth Committee on Environmental Protection Meeting, Baltimore, USA, 6 April–17 April 2009). Available at: http://www.ats.aq/devAS/ ats_meetings_meeting.aspx?lang= e&id=72 (accessed 4 September 2009).

Bauer, T.G. (2001) *Tourism in the Antarctic: Opportunities, Constraints, and Future Prospects*. Haworth Hospitality Press, New York.

Bergstrom, D.M. and Selkirk, P.M. (2007) Human impacts on sub-Antarctic terrestrial environments. *Papers and Proceedings of the Royal Society of Tasmania* 141, 159–167.

Carmichael, N. (2007) Macquarie Island, its conservation and management. *Papers and Proceedings of the Royal Society of Tasmania* 141, 11–17.

Government of Argentina (2009) Report of activities of Antarctic tourism cruise ships operating from Ushuaia during austral summer season 2008/2009. *Information Paper* (IP) No. 119. Submitted to ATCM XXXII (Thirty-second Antarctic Treaty Consultative Meeting – Twelfth Committee on Environmental Protection Meeting, Baltimore, USA, 6 April–17 April 2009) – CEP XII – Meeting Documents. Available at: http://www.ats. aq/devAS/ats_meetings_documents. aspx?lang=e (accessed 23 April 2009).

IAATO (2009) Tourism Statistics, 2008/2009 Statistics. International Association of Antarctica Tour Operators, Providence, Rhode Island. Available at: http://www. iaato.org/tourism_stats.html (accessed 3 September 2009).

IMO (2002) Guidelines for ships operating in Arctic ice-covered waters. MSC/Circ. 1056–MEPC/Circ.399, 23 December 2002. International Maritime Organization, London.

Orion Expedition Cruises (2009) Voyage Summary: Antarctica. Orion Expedition Cruises, Sydney. Available at: http:// www.orionexpeditions.com/expeditions/ antarctica/voyage_summary (accessed 3 September 2009).

Parks Tasmania (2009a) History of sealing at Macquarie Island. Parks and Wildlife Service, Hobart, Tasmania. Available at: http://www.parks.tas.gov.au/index. aspx?base=1819 (accessed 3 September 2009).

Parks Tasmania (2009b) Management Plans, Site Plans and Other Publications: Macquarie Island Nature Reserve and World Heritage Area Management Plan 2006. Parks and Wildlife Service, Hobart, Tasmania. Available at: http://www. parks.tas.gov.au/index.aspx?base=5957 (accessed 30 August 2009).

Parks Tasmania (2009c) Macquarie Island World Heritage Area. Parks and Wildlife Service, Hobart, Tasmania. Available at: http://www.parks.tas.gov.au/index. aspx?base=394 (accessed 30 August 2009).

Parks Tasmania (2009d) Guidelines for Tourist Operations and Visits: Criteria for Selection of Macquarie Island Tourist Vessels. Parks and Wildlife Service, Hobart, Tasmania. Available at: http:// www.parks.tas.gov.au/index.aspx?base= 2999 (accessed 30 August 2009).

Parks Tasmania (2009e) Guidelines for Tourist Operations and Visits: Guidelines for Tourist Operations and Visits to Macquarie Island Nature Reserve World

Heritage Area. Parks and Wildlife Service, Hobart, Tasmania. Available at: http://www.parks.tas.gov.au/index.aspx?base=2999 (accessed 30 August 2009).

Pendlebury, S.F. and Barnes-Keoghan, I.P. (2007) Climate and climate change in the sub-Antarctic. *Papers and Proceedings of the Royal Society of Tasmania* 141, 67–79.

Scott, J.J. and Kirkpatrick, J.B. (2008) Rabbits, landslips and vegetation change on the coastal slopes of subantarctic Macquarie Island, 1980–2007: implications for management. *Polar Biology* 31, 409–419.

Turbett, A. (2008) Macquarie Island: progress in managing an island of outstanding universal value. Bachelor of Antarctic Studies (Honours) Thesis, University of Tasmania.

3 From Sand Mining to Sand Bashing in About 30 Years: a Difficult Journey Towards Sustainable Tourism for Fraser Island

MALCOLM COOPER AND PATRICIA ERFURT-COOPER

Ritsumeikan Asia Pacific University, Beppu, Japan

Introduction

It is September 2009, the heart of the whale-watching season in Australia (July–November) when this chapter is being finalized. Tourists are everywhere in Hervey Bay and on the large sand island some 15 km offshore (Fig. 3.1).

Hervey Bay is both the name of the city that has grown up on mainland Australia opposite Fraser Island and the name for the extensive but relatively quiet stretch of water that separates Fraser Island from Queensland. Within the bay, female whales, their babies and the occasional male humpback rest for up to 2 weeks on their long journey back to the Antarctic from their summer breeding grounds in the north (Corkeron, 1995). Without the bulk of Fraser Island lying just offshore, this Mecca for whale watchers would be nothing more than just another place on the east coast of Australia from which tourists can observe humpback whales as they move past on their way north or south. The island is what makes this area unique for tourism, both in respect of its own environment and its influence on the surrounding marine environment.

Located just below the southern end of Australia's Great Barrier Reef, Fraser Island is the world's largest sand island, with just over half its land surface in national park managed under the State *Recreational Areas Management Act 1988* by the Queensland Parks and Wildlife Service. It is also one of the 16 World Heritage listed areas in Australia (it was listed in 1992), and is iconic for its perched lakes (see below) and its reducing but still important 'pure' dingo (native dog) population. More will be said about these two factors affecting Fraser Island's quest for sustainability later.

Island tourism contributes a significant proportion of Australia's share of the world tourism market, mainly as a result of the attraction of the islands in

Fig. 3.1. Fraser Island, Queensland, Australia. (Adapted from Wikipedia, 2009, and State of Queensland Environmental Protection Agency Map MAQ250.)

and adjacent to the Great Barrier Reef, one of the seven natural wonders of the world. Sustainable tourism development in an island context has thus become a significant goal for Australian tourism operators, regulators and tourists, as it is concerned with visitors experiencing natural environments without threatening their viability. In this respect, Fraser Island, 300 km north of Brisbane and just south of the Barrier Reef, has important advantages due to its location, but also important problems in terms of the protection of its natural values. In the late 1990s, the *Final Report of the Review of Tourism Activities in the Great Sandy Region* noted that the region that includes Fraser Island ranked higher than other comparable areas in Queensland in terms of 'naturalness' (Cooper, 2001). However, while that review clearly identified the value of nature-based ecotourism activities based on these values, it also flagged potential problems – both for the environment and visitors – of uncontrolled access to the island. The report supported the view held among many visitors and locals that Fraser Island was already 'overused'. At the time, for the Queensland Department of Environment and Heritage (DOEH – now the Department of Environment & Resource Management, or DERM), this evidence led to the question: how to find ways of meeting visitor expectations of a sustainable environment while allowing as many people as possible to experience Fraser Island?

The journey to sustainability

The journey to sustainability based on tourism for Fraser Island is not yet complete, and along the way several major problems have emerged. This chapter describes the setting and historical context of its development; it covers the previous sand-mining and logging economy – as this has had significant impacts on the government policies and community attitudes that constrain current use of the island and its resources (a very important source of fresh water is locked up as a result), the process of attaining World Heritage listing in the 1990s and, more recently, the listing of the surrounding Great Sandy Straits area as a UNESCO Biosphere Reserve (26 May 2009). We also cover the vulnerability of sustainable island tourism in the face of management policies that have an impact on some of the iconic attractions, such as the treatment of the dingo by the National Parks and Wildlife Service, the prevention of water pollution (the unique perched lakes on the island are affected by this), the heavy reliance on revenues from tourism to fund the protection of the national park on the island (possibly a self-defeating conundrum), and the attitudes of the tourists themselves to sustainable development of this industry in an island context. The latter includes sand bashing in four-wheel drive (4WD) vehicles, large-scale fishing competitions that strain limited accommodation and waste management systems, illegal feeding of the dingo population and the problems that stem from inadequate information and training for visitors.

Fraser Island is a significant but quite recent major tourist attraction in the Australian and world tourism contexts; its 30-year journey towards sustainable tourism development has been a complicated one since extensive sand mining (which ceased in 1976) and logging of significant tree resources (which ceased in 1991) were discontinued. The discussion here provides important insights into the practical problems of replacing one set of intensive resource-using industries with another – tourism – in an island context that includes World Heritage listing on the basis of environmental values and the need for revenue generation in order to protect these values.

The History, Environment and Exploitation of the Island

Geology and environment

Fraser Island is some 123 km in length and is 22 km at its widest. It comprises almost entirely drift sand that has consolidated around rocky outcrops at Indian Head, Middle Rocks and Waddy Point, and has an area of 184,000 ha, making it the largest sand island in the world. The island is the only place in the world where tall canopy rainforests have been found growing on sand dunes at elevations of over 200 m. The low 'wallum' heaths on the island are also of particular evolutionary and ecological significance, and provide attractive wildflower displays in spring and summer.

The island forms a protective barrier to the Hervey Bay and Great Sandy Straits Marine Park and Biosphere Reserves. The Great Sandy Strait is also listed under the Ramsar Convention, and provides shelter for rare patterned ferns, mangrove colonies, seagrass beds and up to 40,000 migratory shorebirds. Rare, vulnerable or endangered species include dugongs, turtles, Illidge's ant-blue butterflies and eastern curlews (Williams, 2002; Cooper and Erfurt, 2003).

The lakes

Fraser Island's 100 plus dune lakes are unique, with typically small catchment areas, no inflow or outflow streams and no connection to the regional aquifer. As basins of rainwater with low nutrient concentrations and unique biodiversity, these ecosystems have biological and ecological characteristics that attract the attention of researchers, environmentalists and tourists alike (Hadwen, 2009). Maintaining the ideally low nutrient concentrations in the lakes poses a severe problem for the sustainability of tourism in the face of increasing visitor pressure; rubbish on the shoreline, trampling of fringing vegetation and the resultant accelerated delivery of nutrients into the lakes represent just a few of the consequences of visitor use and activities. Nutrients entering the lake environments can drastically increase algal production and, in turn, have considerable potential to alter the way the food webs in these systems function, and thus, eventually, to reduce the attractiveness of the lakes for tourism.

The sand

Fraser Island formed over hundreds of thousands of years as winds, waves and ocean currents carried sands from the far south-east of Australia, and from as far away as Antarctica, to form a string of sand islands along the Queensland coast. These sand islands reach from South Stradbroke Island, off the Gold Coast, to Fraser Island. As the largest of these islands, Fraser Island was formed as the sand was deposited over what was once a low but hilly terrain formed over a million years ago by volcanic activity. This dynamic landscape has formed a series of overlapping sand dune systems dating back at least 700,000 years. The immense sand blows and cliffs of coloured sands characteristic of Fraser Island are part of the longest and most complete age sequence of coastal dune systems in the world, and they are still evolving. The highest dunes on the island reach up to 240 m above sea level (Williams, 2002).

The rainforest

Two of Fraser Island's unique features are its diversity of vegetation and its ability to sustain this vegetation in sand, a soil that is notoriously low in nutrients essential to plant growth. Plants growing on the dunes can obtain their nutrients (other than nitrogen) from only two sources – rain and sand. Sand is coated with mineral compounds such as iron and aluminium oxides. Near the shore, the air contains nutrients from sea spray which are deposited on to this matrix. In a symbiotic relationship, fungi in the sand make these nutrients available to plants and, in turn, the plants supply various organic compounds to the fungi which, having no chlorophyll cannot synthesize these for themselves.

The apex of this system is the rainforest that grows on the sand dunes. Subtropical rainforests can be found in the centre of the island in the moist gullies. These communities have a thick canopy of leaves which allows minimal light to reach the forest floor. This causes the trees to grow tall and straight to reach the sunlight, making the trees suitable for logging. Kauri pine, satinay and the piccabeen palm are common species found in the rainforests (Williams, 2002).

The fauna

Fraser Island is home to a diverse array of native terrestrial and water fauna, many of which are at the northern or southern limit of their distribution or are considered to be rare or vulnerable. The dingo or native dog is the largest predator (their major food source in recent times being the brumbies or wild horses introduced to the island in 1879, but since removed), and there are 47 other species of mammals on the island, including the swamp wallaby, small eared mountain possum and the sugar glider. More than 354 species of birds have been sighted, in a wide range of habitats providing different food sources, and nesting and breeding areas. The island is also home to 79 species of reptiles, including 19 kinds of snakes. Finally, dolphins, dugongs, turtles, rays, and – from July to November – migrating humpback whales frequent the waters around the island (Williams, 2002).

Aboriginal settlement

The Butchulla people were the indigenous inhabitants of Fraser Island. There were six clans in the Butchulla Nation and their traditional name for Fraser Island was *K'gari*, which means paradise (Williams, 2002). It is uncertain how long Fraser Island has been occupied by the Butchulla people, but local evidence suggests that it is more than 5500 years and may be up to 20,000 years. Early population numbers are unknown although it has been said that during times of plentiful resources up to 2000 people lived on the island, with the stable number around 300 to 400.

The English explorer Captain Cook first sighted the Fraser Island and Butchulla people during 1770, and named Indian Head on the eastern beach after them. Subsequently, Captain Matthew Flinders was one of the first white men to have contact with the islanders, and had peaceful meetings with them in 1799 and 1802. However, colonization by Europeans caused great conflicts with the Aboriginal people as the European settlers did not understand or respect their tribal boundaries, their social structure or the importance to them of their environment. Land was cleared and agricultural practices established which, in turn, disturbed the natural supply of food cycles of the native people, who were eventually removed from the island as a consequence of one of the many injustices perpetrated by colonizers anxious to get their hands on the natural wealth of Australia. The Fraser Island Aboriginal story is particularly poignant as it involved how the island came to have that name – a classic case of misrepresentation and the resulting maltreatment of the 'natives' (Williams, 2002).

European exploitation

Logging was started on Fraser Island in 1863 by 'Yankee Jack' Piggott (Williams, 2002) and continued until December 1991, when the state government's Fitzgerald Inquiry Recommendations of May 1991 to cease logging resulted in the withdrawal of the last contractor (Williams, 2002). The major timber on the island (satinay and kauri) was progressively extracted under controlled conditions, especially from 1925 when the satinay was found to be resistant to marine borers and became popular for use in marine conditions around the world. This timber was used in the construction of the Suez Canal and to rebuild the UK's London Docks after World War II. The logging railways and sawmills have since been removed and Central Station, a former logging camp, is now a Queensland Parks and Wildlife Service ranger information station and interpretive centre.

The real economic attractiveness of the island though was found in its deposits of rutile, ilmenite, zircon and monazite sands. Sand-mining leases were first granted in 1950 and were in force until 1977, when environmental concerns caused the suspension of mining by the federal and state governments under the terms of Cabinet Decision 1794 (Australian Federal Government, 1976). Direct employment in the industry was some 300, with

200–300 additional jobs in support. Forestry and tourism were suggested as the replacement industries for sand mining, tourism having begun in a small way in the 1970s and the timber resources of the island being well known (although requiring a subsidy of AUS$9000 per job per year to maintain, according to Cabinet Decision 1794). The federal government offered the Queensland government a grant to cease sand-mining operations without a phase-out period owing to the environmental degradation that was feared if the normal period of up to 5 years was allowed (Australian Federal Government, 1976).

Tourism

Tourism generates in excess of AUS$9 billion a year in revenue for Queensland and AUS$3.9 billion in exports in the early 21st century, making it the state's second largest export industry, and it employs approximately 119,000 people. In the year ended December 2008, there were 19 million visitor trips recorded in Queensland. Of those, 60% were made by intra-state visitors, 29% were interstate visitors and 11% were international visitors. An additional 28 million day trips were recorded. The Fraser Coast/South Burnett Region (within which Hervey Bay/Fraser Island contribute the major destination and the fastest growing city) attracts some 2.5 million visitors each year, of which approximately 67% are from intra-state Australia, 17% are from interstate Australia and 16% are international. The majority of the visitor expenditure in the Wide Bay/ Burnett area (69%) is generated by domestic overnight tourism but there is a significant and growing international visitor market. Overall, tourism's contribution to gross regional product totals 5.9% and the industry supports approximately 7% of total regional employment (15,000), highlighting the significance of the tourism industry to the regional economy (Tourism Queensland, 2009).

   The Fraser Coast/South Burnett region of Queensland has the advantage of iconic tourism attractions in Fraser Island and the migratory humpback whales. Such attractions represent a significant area of competitive advantage for the region, especially given the worldwide interest in wildlife and geotourism. With these natural assets undoubtedly being a major drawcard for both international and domestic visitors, effective conservation of the associated marine park and world-heritage listed sand island is critical in sustaining current levels of visitation, particularly that of international visitors. The international visitors are largely made up of backpackers, who almost invariably include a visit to Fraser Island in their itinerary when following a coastal route from Cairns (tropical North Queensland) to Sydney, or vice versa, and domestic visitors are largely families on camping tours who include Fraser Island as a day trip or camping location (Cooper *et al.*, 2004). There are also major resorts on the island that attract senior international and Australian tour groups, conventions, meetings and major sporting events.

The Journey to Sustainable Management

In recent years, an increasing demand for island-based environmental tourism has been noted (Morgans, 2000; Harrison, 2003). As Hall (1994) commented, however, the selling of 'sun, sand and surf experiences', the development of beach resorts and the increasing popularity of marine tourism have all placed pressure on coastal environments and adjacent islands throughout the world. In this respect, Fraser Island continues to have important problems in terms of the protection of its natural values. Access for tourists to the island is controlled by the Department of Environment and the large resort owners, such as the Kingfisher Bay Resort. The Department regulates its use by backpackers and other tourists wishing to take vehicles to and/or camp on the island, while the resorts bring in tour groups and individuals to accommodation in fixed locations. Management of the Fraser Island National Park resource is again the responsibility of the Department, while private land owners and tour operators control the use of those parts that are not in the National Park.

Regulation of behaviour

This picture is complicated by the system that has developed to regulate the visitors to the National Park itself. A variable set of 4WD and tour-bus operators actually handle the demand for travel to and on Fraser Island. All the island operators are licensed by the Queensland Department of Environment and Heritage, and are subject to rules and regulations regarding the environment of Fraser Island, and in the interest of their own businesses they do appear to abide by these (Cooper *et al.*, 2001). A permit system controls both the number of visitors that can be landed by each company and the locations that they may visit. Obviously, those who conduct tours using their own vehicles/ facilities or who contract to the island resorts potentially have a much greater level of control over what actually happens on the island than those who simply hire out vehicles to groups of visitors, but even the latter do insist upon organized information sessions before travel. However, if tourists come with their own vehicles there are no compulsory information sessions and a lot of people therefore go to the island without any prior instructions on how to act within that environment. Such independent travellers receive only a set of pre-printed brochures from the Park Management as they buy their visiting and/or camping permits on the barge to the island (Cooper, 2001).

Within this pattern, the information sessions for escorted tour groups and those hiring 4WD vehicles are very similar; comprising observations on required behaviour and illustrative videos on the environment being delivered, usually on the night before travel. These can in no way be classified as comprehensive training sessions though, as they are essentially only related to driving skills and behaviour in emergencies while driving, and to basic environmental behaviour, while the time available for digesting the information doesn't allow for much real understanding or for the development of an ability to apply it when on the island. From the 4WD-hire people, the main emphasis is to keep the vehicles away from saltwater, because any damage from this source will cost the driver, who is solely responsible for the vehicle. Night driving, except in real emergencies, is also prohibited for several reasons: too dangerous, more animals are moving about, track conditions can't be observed properly and distance to water can be deceiving (Cooper and Erfurt, 2003).

This evidence points to a dichotomy between consistently held definitions of sustainable behaviour and the seeming inability of island tour operators to impart these to their clients, or of the clients in conforming to them (Conlin and Baum, 1995). All operators hold that sustainability is visitors in harmony with the environment, is sustainable use of the environment without degradation, and is concerned with visitation conducted in a responsible and sustainable manner in order to increase awareness of the value of natural attractions. All operators also want to educate tourists and locals to preserve Fraser Island's natural beauty, and all want to train their staff in protection of the environment while they are introducing tourists to it. In addition, all tour operators also want profitable businesses and the respect of government environmental regulators for their efforts, but within a framework of greater facility development and considerably higher investment in roads on the island.

As might perhaps be expected therefore, if tour and resort operators are surveyed in situations like that on Fraser Island they will generally be adamant that they follow all rules and regulations, and attempt to educate visitors to respect the island's environment by briefing them before travel. However, the reality is that most visitors are not given enough training or interpretation for environmental protection to be anything other than very low on their priority list when visiting the island (Morgans, 2000). When this is coupled with very poor roads, signage and level of usable information (in English only – Cooper and Erfurt, 2003), it can be seen that the desire on the part of operators to have their clients act responsibly, and even the existence of the permit system with its associated regulations, need not necessarily lead to responsible behaviour, as noted by Shelby and Shindler (1992).

Impact on management

There seems no doubt that the managers of the important Fraser Island environment will face increasing pressure from visitors, and that many of these visitors will be backpackers and/or family and other free independent travellers or tourists (FITs) for the foreseeable future. While in management for sustainability terms, there seems no doubt that visitors are interested in the protection of the environment that they have come to see, just at the point where they might become a useful resource for the authorities on Fraser Island with respect to environmental conservation, they are let loose in off-road vehicles, without adequate education, to make their own ways to attractions.

Small wonder then that in this situation the visitors seem content with only sketchy outlines of both appropriate routes to take and how to treat the environment, and take full advantage of the 'freedom and flexibility' to indulge their other passions in the absence of more structured experiences. These passions range from sand 'bashing', to an almost complete disregard of environmental protection instructions (signage). In fact, it has been noted by park rangers that various groups have appeared to disregard signs just because they were in English and not in their native language, despite understanding the message (Cooper and Erfurt, 2003)!

Political factors – the dingoes

Further complicating their management task the government, through the Queensland Parks and Wildlife Service, appears to have effectively 'declared war' on the remnant population of native dogs on Fraser Island (Chapman, 2009). Citing their unpredictability, and therefore danger, the government regularly culls individuals and groups suspected of threatening humans. This policy has angered locals and tourists alike, as previous policies of denying food to and enforcing segregation from these dogs has materially contributed to the present situation, even though this is not acknowledged by the government. A AUS$1 million exclusion fence has recently been erected, which local Aboriginal groups and other residents deplore, citing harmonious relations with the dogs if they are not harassed by rangers and tourists.

Sustainability Through Tourism

To be able to deliver on the promise of environmental management through sustainable tourism in the island context it is important that managers, locals and tour operators do not assume fair play on the part of visitors, especially when these visitors are not given a strong practical message on the requirements of environmental protection, or they observe counter-policies being practised by the protectors themselves (as in the case of the dingoes, which are a part of the ecosystem of Fraser Island and have a role in its maintenance), in a World Heritage setting such as Fraser Island. In assuming that sustainable tourism means little environmental impact and that the dingoes are introduced pests, government policy itself has contributed to the environmental problems generated by tourism to the island. Greater control over visitor numbers (and greater investment in infrastructure, regardless of the numbers of visitors required to pay for it), tag-along tours to reduce environmental degradation through irresponsible driving, and far more stringent training in 4WD driving and environmental protection before visiting the island would seem to be prerequisites for true sustainability on Fraser Island.

The Australian Conservation Foundation (ACF), in its Tourism Policy (ACF, 1994), specified six characteristics that it considered essential to sustainable tourism:

- visitation to enjoy nature, wildlife, culture and archaeology;
- a high degree of interpretation;
- high-quality, low-impact design in all infrastructure;
- promotion of conservation knowledge and ethics;

- the provision of net benefits to environmental protection; and
- the provision of net benefits to indigenous communities and other affected communities.

These defining characteristics broadly follow the minimalist impact definition of ecotourism (Whelan, 1991), and have been adopted in the main by responsible Australian state and national government agencies in specifying appropriate ecotourism strategies.

According to Buckley (1994) however, in practice, the tourism industry and responsible government agencies have been inclined to focus on the product supply side and to treat ecotourism as identical to observing nature, while taking fees to pay for management. By doing this, it is possible to promote more intensive visitation in parks to raise more revenue by giving the nature observation experience a veneer of respectability as ecotourism. This attitude is derived in part from an appeal to the desire in many tourists to protect the environment they have come to appreciate. This changes the way people view these environments, and enables them to suspend disbelief at increasing numbers and lack of real engagement with the ecosystem. However, as Pearce and Moscardo (1985) point out, using the attraction of nature-based tourism as a justification for increasing visitor numbers without appropriate planning, and without the matching of particular types of visitors with particular environments, can put at risk the very attractions that are supposed to benefit from this 'low-impact' form of tourism.

As a result, the 'reality' of the sustainable tourism experience on Fraser Island is largely of the presentation and use of natural attractions as a means of selling a destination which has the fortunate appellation of being on the World Heritage List, rather than of ensuring sustainable impact on the environment through tourism. In our view, this is little different from the 'mining and logging (extractive)' economy approach seen before the 1970s on Fraser Island. In this situation, the tourist actually consumes the environment rather than protecting it, and this is a result which, in turn, has meant that the island managers are faced with considerable environmental pressure from the very people who might have been expected to be predisposed towards assisting them in environmental protection.

Conclusions: Island Destinations and Sustainability

This case study has shown that labelling a part of tourist behaviour ecotourism doesn't necessarily mean that sustainable tourism or environmental management practices will result in a small island environment. The situation on Fraser Island is not sustainable because of this, and as a result the Fraser Island Defenders Organisation (FIDO) has filed a submission with UNESCO to have the island's World Heritage status placed on the 'endangered' list (FIDO, 2009). It is hoped that the close scrutiny that should ensue will spur the Queensland government to modify its management ethos and policies towards sustainable environmental management for tourists and for the fauna and flora. Placing the dingo on the endangered species list would add weight to this change.

References

ACF (1994) *Tourism Policy*. Australian Conservation Foundation, Sydney.

Australian Federal Government (1976) *Decision 1794*. Cabinet Records – Selected Documents, Australian Government Printer, Canberra, Australia.

Buckley, R. (1994) A framework for ecotourism. *Annals of Tourism Research* 21, 661–669.

Chapman, J. (2009) Warnings to parents as dingoes threaten. *Fraser Chronicle* (Hervey Bay, Queensland), Saturday 9 May 2009, p. 8.

Conlin, V.M. and Baum, T. (1995) *Island Tourism, Management Principles and Practice*. John Wiley, London.

Cooper, M. (2001) Backpackers to Fraser Island: why is ecotourism a neglected aspect of their experience? *Journal of Quality Assurance in Hospitality and Tourism* 1, 45–59.

Cooper, M. and Erfurt, P. (2003) Lake management under conditions of heavy tourist pressure: the case of Fraser Island. *Ritsumeikan Journal of Asia Pacific Studies* 12 (October), 61–74.

Cooper, M., Abubakar, B. and Rauchhaupt, P. (2001) Eco-tourism development into the new millennium on Fraser Island: tour operators perspectives. *Tourism* 49, 359–367.

Cooper, M., O'Mahony, K. and Erfurt, P.J. (2004) Harvest trails: nomads join the mainstream? In: Richards, G. and Wilson, J. (eds) *The Global Nomad: Backpacker Travel in Theory and Practice*. Channel View Publications, Clevedon, UK, pp. 180–195.

Corkeron, P. (1995) Humpback whales in Hervey Bay, Queensland: behavior and responses to whalewatching vessels. *Canadian Journal of Zoology* 73, 1290–1299.

FIDO (2009) Fraser Island for World Heritage in Danger List. *Moonbi* 119 (1 June 2009), p. 8. Fraser Island Defenders Organisation, Towong, Queensland. Available at: http://www.fido.org.au/ (accessed 10 September 2010).

Figgis, P.J. (1993) Eco-tourism: special interest or major direction? *Habitat* 21, 8–11.

Hadwen, W. (2009) Perched lakes as focal tourism and recreation destinations on Fraser Island: impacts and management implications. In: *Third Biennial Fraser Island Conference*, 24 July 2009, Brisbane (Shifting Sands: the dynamics of the Great Sandy Region). Fraser Island Defenders Organisation, Toowong, Queensland.

Hall, C.M. (1994). Ecotourism in Australia, New Zealand and the South Pacific: appropriate tourism or a new form of ecological imperialism? In: Cater, E. and Lowman, G. (eds) *Ecotourism: A Sustainable Option?* John Wiley, Chichester, UK, pp. 137–157.

Harrison, D. (2003) *Pacific Island Tourism*. Cognizant, New York.

Morgans, D. (2000) The role of interpretation in protected area management – where does ecotourism fit in? In: Charters, T. and Law, K. (eds) *Best Practice Ecotourism in Queensland*. Tourism Queensland, Brisbane.

Pearce, P. and Moscardo, G. (1985) Conservation and the tourism justification. *Habitat* 13, 34–35.

Shelby, B. and Shindler, B. (1992) Interest group standards for ecological impacts at wilderness campsites. *Leisure Sciences* 14, 17–27.

Tourism Queensland (2009) Tourism Facts and Figures. Available at: http://www.tq.com.au (accessed 20 September 2009).

Whelan, T. (1991) Ecotourism and its role in sustainable development. In: Whelan, T. (ed.) *Nature Tourism: Managing for the Environment*. Island Press, Washington, DC, pp. 3–22.

Wikipedia (2009) Fraser Island Locator Map. Available at: http://en.wikipedia.org/wiki/File:Fraser_island_locator_map.svg (accessed 10 September 2010).

Williams, F. (2002) *Princess K'Gari's Fraser Island*. Merino Harding, Brisbane.

4 Managing Tourism on Green Island, Great Barrier Reef Marine Park: Conservation, Commerce and Compromises

HEATHER ZEPPEL

University of Southern Queensland, Queensland, Australia

Introduction

This chapter reviews the environmental management of tourism on Green Island, a coral cay located 45 minutes from Cairns in Tropical North Queensland, Australia. This 12-ha coral cay is the single most visited destination on the Great Barrier Reef, attracting over 350,000 visitors a year. Green Island is a designated National Park, Marine Park and Recreation Area located within the Great Barrier Reef Marine Park (GBRMP) and Great Barrier Reef World Heritage Area. Since 1990, a Green Island and Reef Advisory Committee (GIRAC) oversees tourism on the cay, with the protected areas managed by a marine park ranger of the Queensland Parks and Wildlife Service (QPWS). Private leaseholders on Green Island are the Green Island Resort and Marineland Melanesia, a captive wildlife attraction with sea turtles and crocodiles on display. Other marine tourism businesses on Green Island include diving, 'sea walking' (helmet diving) and parasailing operators. The history of human use of this coral cay, past and current tourism, the island characteristics and former detrimental impacts are covered first. The chapter then evaluates the regulatory, physical, economic and educational strategies now used to manage tourism sustainably on Green Island. It reviews the collaboration between QPWS, Green Island Resort and other key stakeholders on this coral cay, and describes initiatives undertaken since the mid-1990s to manage tourism sustainably on Green Island, including the park management plans, environmental guidelines, negotiations with traditional Aboriginal owners and the overall impacts of tourism on the island. The cooperative management that is portrayed is necessary for sustainable tourist use of the cay.

Coral Cay Tourism in the Great Barrier Reef

The Great Barrier Reef (GBR) attracts 1.9 million visitors a year and generates AUS$5.1 billion from marine tourism activities including diving, snorkelling, fishing, boating, island resorts and other services (Access Economics, 2009). There are 300 coral cays in the GBRMP, with several sandy cays visited regularly by reef tour operators. These include Michaelmas cay, a major seabird nesting area (Muir, 1993) and Upolu cay, both off Cairns, the Low Isles off Port Douglas and Beaver cay off Mission Beach. Various reef day tours visit these coral cays, which have minimal or no facilities, and no overnight stays are allowed. Only a few coral cays on the GBR in the southern Capricorn section have permanent tourist resorts, such as Heron Island and Lady Elliot Island; there is also a luxury tented camp for 12 guests operating on Wilson Island that is closed from 26 January to 28 February during the bird-nesting season (Delaware North Australia Parks and Resorts, 2010). Camping is allowed on Lady Musgrave, Northwest and Masthead Islands in the southern Capricorn Bunker group. The Green Island Resort near Cairns is the only resort on a coral cay in the northern section of the GBR. All other island resorts in the GBRMP are located on continental islands that are fringed by coral reefs (i.e. Lizard, Fitzroy, Dunk, Bedarra, Hinchinbrook, Orpheus, Magnetic, Lindeman, Brampton, Great Keppel, Keswick and the Whitsunday Islands). This chapter evaluates how tourism is managed for sustainability on Green Island. Information is drawn from published reports, park management plans, conservation and tourism research and news articles about Green Island. Additional site information is drawn from student field trips to Green Island from 2002 to 2009, which were led by the author, with presentations given by QPWS park rangers and environmental managers of Green Island Resort about key management issues.

Green Island

History of human use of Green Island

The Gungandji Aboriginal name for Green Island is *Wunyami*, meaning 'a place of spirits', or *Dabuukji*, 'the place of the hole in the nose', with the island traditionally used as an initiation site for young Aboriginal men (Martyn, 1993). Park visitor brochures mention the Aboriginal significance of Green Island for ceremonies and the traditional use of sea country (the adjacent seas and islands) for hunting and fishing (EPA, 1999, 2007). Captain James Cook named this coral cay as Green Island in 1770. European exploitation of the island in the mid- to late 1800s included bêche-de-mer (sea cucumber) fishermen cutting down the forest to smoke sea cucumbers and also a turtle soup cannery (Baxter, 1990; Martyn, 1993). A turtle cannery also operated on Heron Island (1926–1929) and North West Island (1924–1928) in the southern GBR. In many areas of the reef, early tourists also rode on the backs of nesting turtles

(Lucas, 2008). Green Island has been a popular tourist site for over 100 years, with organized pleasure cruises to the cay made since 1890. Coconut trees were planted in 1899 for shipwreck survivors, while a beachcomber lived on Green Island until his death in 1907 (Martyn, 1993). The island was originally declared as a recreation reserve under Cairns Town Council in 1906, with regulations to prevent the removal of coral and shells around the cay. Passenger ferries have visited the coral cay since 1924, the first hotel was built in 1942, the world's first glass-bottom boat tour occurred in 1948 and the world's first underwater observatory opened in 1954 and is still operating (Green Island Resort, 2009). Coral formations were placed around the observatory to attract reef fish (Martyn, 1993). Two pioneering GBR photographers, Noel and Kitty Monkman, also lived on Green Island from 1956. In 1958, camping was no longer allowed on the coral cay. By 1961, other visitor attractions on Green Island were the Coral Cay Hotel, Great Barrier Reef Theatre and Marineland. Environmental impacts of the hotel included raw sewage seeping on to the reef flat, with cardboard and paper rubbish burnt on the cay (Harris and Leiper, 1995). Up to the 1980s, the hotel and other tourism operators on the cay also relied on collecting rainwater for their needs (EAA, 1983). Seaplane access began in 1978.

Green Island National Park

Green Island National Park comprises 7.93 ha of the island, covering the middle and eastern portions of the coral cay. Green Island was declared a Fauna Sanctuary in 1934; declared as the first island national park in Queensland in 1937 (including the foreshore and reef out to 1 mile below the low-tide mark); declared a marine national park in 1974 (out to 1.6 km beyond the reef platform); and combined into the Cairns Marine Park in 1989 (below the high-tide mark out to 1.6 km). Green Island also became part of the GBRMP in 1975 and part of the Great Barrier Reef World Heritage Area in 1981 (EPA, 2003). The reefs around the island are zoned as a green zone or no-take zone, with no fishing or collecting allowed. In 1990, the surrounding reef, beaches and public areas of Green Island were also declared as a recreation area. The Green Island Recreation Area includes the island national park, a public esplanade and jetty, mooring areas and a navigation channel, and the marine park from the edge of the reef out to 1.6 km. The national park, marine park and recreation area at Green Island are managed by QPWS, with a marine park ranger living on the cay. Since 1990, a recreation area levy of AUS$1.80 per visitor, which is collected by all reef tour operators to Green Island, provides funding to QPWS for the ranger-in-charge, all capital works (i.e. boardwalks, ranger building and bulldozing sand to protect the esplanade), pest control (i.e. rat baiting), interpretive signs and a lifeguard at the designated swimming beach. In 2004, this recreation levy generated AUS$643,915 in funds for QPWS and GIRAC to manage Green Island. A self-guided eco-walk through the rainforest on Green Island has been listed as one of the top ten bushwalks in Queensland (*The Cairns Post*, 2009b). A Queensland Centenary of Parks celebration day was held on Green Island in May 2008, with turtle releases, sea cucumber presentations, a poster display on seagrasses and reef films (Anthony, 2008).

The characteristics of Green Island

Green Island is a sandy coral cay that supports a closed vine-thicket rainforest up to 25 m high with some 134 species of plants. It also has 35 species of seabirds and 28 species of forest birds, with seven species breeding on the cay, including the pied imperial pigeon which nests from October to May (EPA, 2003; DERM, 2010a, b). Flightless buff-banded rails are also commonly seen on Green Island, where they are recovering after a successful rat-baiting programme by QPWS. The island is the only coral cay in the Great Barrier Reef that has a rainforest on it, which is sustained by an aquifer. Green Island has a circumference of 1.6 km and is fringed by coastal plants, sandy beaches and reef flats. It takes about 30–45 minutes to walk around Green Island, with views out over the reef. The coral cay is surrounded by a platform coral reef (710 ha) with giant clams, diverse tropical fish, stingrays, green turtles and hawksbill turtles, dugongs and reef sharks. There are over 190 hard coral species and over 100 soft coral species found at Green Island (Great Adventures, 2010a). The fringing coral reefs around Green Island are still recovering from coral-eating drupella snails and previous outbreaks of crown-of-thorns starfish in 1963–1964, 1969–1972 and 1979–1982 (Baxter, 1990). In 1964, a diver removed over 400,000 crown-of-thorns starfish from the reef around Green Island (Martyn, 1993). Coral bleaching episodes on the GBR in 1998, 2002 and 2006 (far southern section) caused white patches of dead coral on fringing reefs (Siebeck *et al.*, 2006). These bleached patches of coral had been noticeable since 2003 at Green Island, but the reef has since recovered, with no further bleaching recorded at this site on reef surveys in 2006 (GBRMPA, 2007). There are abundant seagrass beds on the reef flats around Green Island grazed by green turtles and dugongs. Mainly juvenile turtles forage around Green Island (Fuentes *et al.*, 2006). A seagrass watch monitoring programme at Green Island since 2000 has found stable coverage of seagrass species at two sites, with the highest abundance recorded in 2008 and no traces of herbicides washed out from sugarcane farms on the mainland (Seagrass-Watch, 2008b). Tourists snorkelling, diving or on boat tours at Green Island can see hard and soft corals, giant clams, colourful reef fish and green turtles. In August 2009, a migrating humpback whale was seen just 100 m offshore inside the reef and observed underwater from a semi-submersible at Green Island (Dickson, 2009). Green turtles are also starting to nest again on Green Island; resort guests watched 100 turtle hatchlings scramble to the ocean in February 2009 (*The Cairns Post*, 2009a). Rangers have recorded up to 640 turtle hatchlings from 12 nests (Wells, 2003); a turtle research and monitoring programme has been operating on Green Island since 1988.

Marine tourism on Green Island

Some 70% of GBR tourism (749,000 visitors) based on coral reef visitation occurs within the Cairns region of the GBRMP (Oxford Economics, 2009). From 1999 to 2004, the number of visitors to Green Island increased from 235,080 to 385,211 a year. The average visitation over the 10 years up to 2004 was 280,000 a year and 787 visitors a day. The maximum number of visitors is capped at 2240 people in any 1 day, mainly allocated to the five reef tour operators with permits to bring passengers to Green Island (EPA, 2003). However, some of this visitor capacity is allocated to roving reef operators who visit other sites, and also to allow for rough weather when the permitted operators cannot go to the outer reef but can still take visitors to Green Island. Daily visitation has been up to 1900 visitors, but has now declined to a maximum of about 1200–1500. A social carrying capacity study on Green Island recommended a daily maximum of 1200 to 1345 visitors (Beaumont, 1996, in EPA, 2003; Beaumont, 1997). About 95% of visitation to Green Island is day-trip visitors (Baxter, 1990). Tourists on Green Island originate from Japan, China, South Korea, Europe, the USA, Australia and other countries. Most tourists arrive at Green Island on two large catamaran services with two to four return trips a day from Cairns, and on other smaller reef tour boats, private boats and yachts. A helicopter and a seaplane also fly to Green Island, with a maximum of five flights a day allowed on a restricted flight path (EPA, 2003).

Current tourist facilities on Green Island include: a jetty; a day-use area with cafes, bars, shops and a pool; a patrolled beach; boardwalks with interpretive signs; Marineland Melanesia, which has captive turtles, fish and crocodiles; and the Green Island Resort. The Monkman Reef Research Station located on Green Island is not usually open to visitors. All buildings on Green Island are below the rainforest canopy, with only a tall radio tower and the jetty visible from the sea. A public esplanade area at the western end includes a retaining sea wall, brick-paved walkways, signage and a patrolled swimming beach with a lifeguard on duty. Marine activities at Green Island include swimming, diving, snorkelling, sea walking, fish feeding by permitted operators, glass-bottom boats and semi-submersibles, the underwater observatory, and boating, fishing or parasailing offshore. Fishing and motorized water sports are not permitted in the waters surrounding Green Island (EPA, 2003). A self-guided snorkel trail previously operated from 1982 to 1987 at the western end of the cay, but was removed (Baxter, 1990). Green Island Resort operates most of the tourist facilities on the coral cay, including accommodation, a restaurant, cafes and bars, a swimming pool, information centre, boutiques and public toilets. The lease for Green Island Resort and the day-use visitor facilities covers 1.8 ha at the western end of the cay. The Resort operates under stringent environmental conditions, such as no gutters or collection of rainwater (to replenish the aquifer), with buildings and walkways erected on piles (so as not to impede animal movement), a tertiary sewage treatment plant and a water desalination plant. QPWS works with the Green Island Resort, reef tour operators and other government stakeholders to manage tourism on

Green Island; the Service has planted *Casuarina* (coastal she-oak) seedlings, monitored nesting turtles, installed public moorings, surveyed for crown-of-thorns starfish, run rat-baiting programmes and built boardwalks (Wells, 2003).

Recent history of Green Island Resort

In 1991, Daikyo Pty Ltd purchased the earlier resort (which had closed in 1989) and ferry service on Green Island. During 1992–1994, Daikyo demolished this previous resort and constructed the current Green Island Resort at a cost of AUS$43 million to accommodate 90 guests and other day visitors. The five-star resort has 46 luxury suites with a pool, restaurant and meeting room. Daikyo developed an environmental code of practice for the construction company and the contractors building the resort, with environmental bonds for any damage caused. This code covered building materials, the removal of rubbish and liquid waste, and the protection of plants and animals. Scaffolding was erected around trees, and the trimming or removal of branches was not allowed (Harris and Leiper, 1995). Permit conditions for the resort redevelopment set by the Department of Environment and Heritage and the Great Barrier Reef Marine Park Authority (GBRMPA) stated that sewage had to be tertiary treated and rainwater had to fall on to the ground to recharge the aquifer (i.e. no gutters on roofs), and also specified natural colours for construction materials, building slabs suspended on concrete piles, a raised wooden walkway and that few trees be cut down.

Landscaping of the resort and lease area involved 6000 native plants from 60 species. This revegetated a previously degraded resort site, providing bird habitat and amenity for visitors (Harris and Leiper, 1995). The resort is described as 'one of the most eco-sensitive developments in the world'. However, air conditioning is left on in rooms for the comfort of guests and to prevent mould growing on surfaces in the humid tropical climate. Green Island Resort and Great Adventures Cruises were sold in 2005 to a local reef tourism company, Quicksilver Connections. A dedicated environmental management officer for the Resort was not replaced in 2009, with this role included in the duties of the overall environmental manager at Quicksilver Cruises. From 2000 to 2004, Green Island Resort won awards for resource conservation and waste management from the Queensland Environmental Protection Agency (EPA), along with cleanest beach awards.

Strategies to Manage Marine Tourism

There are four main strategies employed by park agencies to control and manage marine tourism; these include regulatory, physical (i.e. infrastructural), educational and economic strategies (Orams, 1999). Regulatory strategies include park rules, regulations and zoning plans to restrict visitor numbers, prohibit various activities, separate conflicting activities (temporal and spatial) and allow for closing areas; skill levels (i.e. certification of divers or tour operators) are also required. Regulations are included in permits, lease and licence requirements and also in voluntary codes of practice for marine activities. Physical strategies include site hardening, intensive use or 'sacrifice' areas, placement and design of facilities, alteration of sites and rehabilitation. Economic strategies include fees for operators or visitors, damage bonds or deposits, fines and rewards. There is an environmental management charge of AUS$5 for every visitor to the GBRMP collected by reef tour operators. Ecotourism-certified reef tour operators also receive 15-year operating permits, instead of the usual 5 years (GBRMPA, 2010). Educational strategies include various types of park interpretation, such as brochures, signs, guided or self-guided walks, visitor centres, ranger contact and other educational activities (such as beach clean-up). Outcome indicators are used to measure the success of management strategies in reducing tourism impacts, and to monitor and assess improvements in the environment and visitor behaviour. Improvements to the marine environment include minimizing disturbance, habitat protection and contributing to the longer-term health and viability of marine and coastal ecosystems (Orams, 1999). A cooperative management approach is used in the GBRMP to manage recreation and tourism and minimize the impacts of marine tourism and other reef activities (Ilet *et al.*, 2000; Harriott, 2002; TRRAC, 2002). This next section of this chapter assesses management strategies for sustainable tourism on Green Island.

Managing Tourism on Green Island

Regulatory strategies

A QPWS marine park ranger is responsible for day-to-day management of the Green Island Recreation Area and the surrounding reef. Regulation of tourism activities in the reefs and waters around Green Island comes under Queensland legislation for the GBR Coast Marine Park (*Marine Parks Act 2004)* and under federal legislation for the GBRMP (*Great Barrier Reef Marine Park Act 1975*). The marine parks permit for Quicksilver Connections (2006–2022) authorizes reef tourist activities, vessel charter, guided kayak tours and mooring at Green Island (GBRMPA, 2006). Other Queensland legislation applies for the national park (*Nature Conservation Act 1992*), jetty and public esplanade (*Local Government Act 1993, Integrated Planning Act 1997*). Cairns Port Authority (CPA) manages the jetty at Green Island with the public esplanade and swimming beach under the control of Cairns City Council (CCC). The *Environmental Protection Act 1994 (Qld)* covers environmental impacts and polluting activities in land or sea areas. Under the *Recreation Areas Management Act 2006*, the main public areas of Green Island and the fringing reef are managed for both conservation and nature-based tourism or recreation. The Green Island and Reef Advisory Committee (GIRAC) includes QPWS, GBRMPA, CCC, CPA, the Department of Natural Resources, native title claimants, Green Island Resort and reef tour operators (EPA, 2003). Reef tourism operators and resort staff advise the QPWS ranger of people illegally fishing, collecting shells or marine life and of sick or injured animals, fauna sightings such as nesting turtles or other activities requiring attention on Green Island.

The overall approach to managing visitors and commercial enterprises on Green Island is guided by the zoning, regulations and guidelines set out in the *Green Island Recreation Area and Green Island National Park Management Plans* (EPA, 2003). The plans recognize the natural, cultural and scenic values of Green Island and support low-impact recreational activities that do not adversely affect these values or ecological sustainability. The plans stipulate codes of practice and guidelines for beach hire equipment, helicopter operations, seaplane operations and reef activities on or around Green Island. This includes limitations on vessel size, visitor numbers and areas and types of activities. Fish-feeding guidelines are stipulated in marine parks permits as to location, type and amount of food fed. Guidelines for restricted, prohibited or limited tourism activities are also included in the management plans. Other marine park zoning provisions for the GBRMP as outlined in the *Cairns Area Plan of Management* prohibit fishing and motorized water sports or vessels over 35 m in length at Green Island. In this plan, Green Island is designated as a sensitive location with high natural values and significant tourism use opportunities. There is a limit of four tourism vessels a day on the reef around Green Island, with a maximum group size of 15 on diving or snorkelling trips in the western section of the fringing reef. Anchoring is not permitted within 50 m of moorings installed north of the jetty (EPA, 2003). Limitations on anchoring, and fishing bans, help to protect the fringing reef around Green Island.

Physical strategies

The infrastructure and physical facilities for managing tourism on Green Island include the resort and associated amenities for day-use visitors (i.e. pool, cafe, bar, restaurant, shops, bins, toilets, showers, lockers). This concentrates visitor use around the main arrivals area where these facilities are located. In 2008, a wire mesh enclosure was built over one main food area to keep out birds, but small silvereyes still slip through. Small metal bins and other small portable plastic containers are provided for smokers to extinguish their cigarette butts. The resort operates an AUS$5 million tertiary treatment sewage plant for all toilets on the cay, with sludge residue barged back to the mainland. In 1993, this sewage plant was the first on any island. The outfall pipeline for treated effluent was built through an area with no coral cover to minimize disturbance (Harris and Leiper, 1995). Some 40% of treated water is used in flushing toilets, taps and showers, and garden irrigation. Water is obtained from a seawater desalination plant that started operating in 2001, with an outlet pipe for discharged brine extending underwater to the north of the cay. The plant produces 55,000 litres of freshwater daily (Great Adventures, 2010b). Previously, all freshwater for the resort and for day-visitor use was barged over from the mainland at a significant cost. Other solid waste and recycled material such as cardboard, plastic and tins are sent back to the mainland (EPA, 2003).

Vegetable waste is composted and used on resort gardens, where no pesticides are applied, while only biodegradable and nitrate-free cleaning products are used. Chemicals would affect the bacteria in the tertiary sewage treatment plant that breaks down human wastes. Four diesel generators provide power for the island in an insulated building with concrete troughs under fuel storage tanks to contain any spillage. The resort's hot water system is preheated by the generating system (Harris and Leiper, 1995). Solar panels have been considered for resort power, but this is limited by the rainforest setting. A hybrid solar–diesel power station installed on Lady Elliot Island Eco Resort in the southern GBR has cut use of diesel fuel by 40–55% (Lady Elliot Island, 2009). Biodiesel fuel is used in ten Quicksilver coaches (*Cairns Sun*, 2009).

In 1993, a 230-m brick sea wall was built on the western end of Green Island to protect the esplanade and lease areas from erosion caused by sand and tidal movements around the coral cay. Erosion has continued at the northern end of the sea wall, with QPWS organizing beach restoration work since 1995 at a cost of AUS$10,000 a year (EPA, 2003), using a bulldozer brought over by barge to move sand back to this area. Any machinery brought over to Green Island has to first be cleaned on the mainland while any soil or materials brought to the island must be sterile and weed free. Only plants native to the cay can be grown, using seed stock sourced from Green Island. There are brick-paved walkways around the high-use area of the esplanade between the swimming beach, jetty and snorkelling area. The boardwalk in the main facility area is built around existing trees with holes cut around tree trunks. Raised wooden boardwalks cross other areas of the cay, with seats provided at viewing or rest areas. The infrastructure for reef tour operators includes the navigation channel and jetty for berthing catamarans, with 32 mooring buoys to the north of the jetty for glass-bottom boats, semi-submersibles, the parasailing powerboat, the seaplane and other permitted operators. To facilitate sea walking, a short concrete path and a handrail were built underwater on one section of the sandy reef flat. A concrete helipad is located on the southern side of the cay, jutting out from the bushes over the fringing reef. A raised wooden boardwalk through the rainforest in the middle of the cay has reduced visitor impacts on vegetation, with short sandy paths diverting to the beach or reef edge. QPWS staff have also planted 1000 *Casuarina* seedlings for revegetation and shade around the coastal edge of the cay (Wells, 2003). Reef tourism operators had earlier permits for reef walking on Green Island but chose not to use these to reduce tourism impacts on the fringing reefs. Instead, visitors are taken on glass-bottom boats and semi-submersibles or can snorkel on the fringing reef.

Economic strategies

As already mentioned, since 1990, a recreation area levy of AUS$1.80 per visitor collected by all reef tour operators to Green Island provides funding to QPWS for the ranger-in-charge, all capital works, interpretive signs and lifeguards at the swimming beach. This visitor levy generates an annual income

References

Access Economics (2009) *Economic Contribution of the Great Barrier Reef Marine Park, 2006–07*. Research Publication No. 98, Great Barrier Reef Marine Park Authority, Townsville, Queensland. Available at: http://www.gbrmpa.gov.au/corp_site/info_services/publications/research_publications (accessed 1 September 2010).

Aiello, R. (1998) Interpretation and the marine tourism industry, who needs it? A case study of Great Adventures, Australia. *Journal of Tourism Studies* 9, 51–61.

Anthony, D. (2008) Green Island Centenary of Parks. *Seagrass-Watch News* 33 (June 2008), 2. Available at: http://www.seagrasswatch.org/magazine.html (accessed 1 September 2010).

Baxter, I.N. (1990) Tourism. In: *Green Island Information Review*. Research Publication No. 25, 56–59. Great Barrier Reef Marine Park Authority, Townsville, Queensland. Available at: http://www.gbrmpa.gov.au/corp_site/info_services/publications/research_publications (accessed 1 September 2010).

Beaumont, N. (1997) Perceived crowding as an evaluative standard for determining social carrying capacity in tourist recreation areas: the case of Green Island, North Queensland. In: Hall, C.M., Jenkins, J. and Kearsley, G. (eds) *Tourism Planning and Policy in Australia and New Zealand: Cases, Issues and Practice*. Irwin Publishers, Sydney, pp. 168-180.

Cairns Sun (2009) Eco-friendly coaches. *Cairns Sun*, 12 August, p. 14.

Delaware North Australia Parks and Resorts (2010) Wilson Island, Great Barrier Reef. Available at: http://www.wilsonisland.com/ (accessed 1 September 2010).

DERM (2010a) Green Island National Park. Nature, Culture and History. Queensland Department of Environment and Resource Management, Brisbane. Available at: http://www.derm.qld.gov.au/parks/green-island/culture.html (accessed 1 September 2010).

DERM (2010b) Green Island National Park. Queensland Department of Environment and Resource Management, Brisbane. Available at: http://www.derm.qld.gov.au/parks/green-island/index.html (accessed 1 September 2010).

Dickson, R. (2009) Whales making waves in north. *The Cairns Post*, 1 August.

EAA (Economic Associates Australia) (1983) *Green Island Economic Study*. Research Publication No. 1. Great Barrier Reef Marine Park Authority, Townsville, Queensland. Available at: http://www.gbrmpa.gov.au/corp_site/info_services/publications/research_publications (accessed 1 September 2010).

EPA (1999) *Green Island National and Marine Park: Park Guide* (Brochure). Queensland Environmental Protection Agency, Brisbane.

EPA (2003) Green Island Recreation Area and Green Island National Park Management Plans. Queensland Environmental Protection Agency, Brisbane. Available at: http://www.derm.qld.gov.au/services_resources/item_details.php?item_id=200841 (accessed 1 September 2010).

EPA (2007) *Green Island National Park Visitor Guide*. (Brochure). Parks and Wildlife Service, Queensland Environmental Protection Agency, Brisbane.

Fuentes, M.M.P.B., Lawler, I.R. and Gyuris, E. (2006) Dietary preferences of juvenile green turtles (*Chelonia mydas*) on a tropical reef flat. *Wildlife Research* 33, 671–678.

GBRMPA (2006) *Marine Parks Permit Quicksilver Connections Limited*. Great Barrier Reef Marine Park Authority, Townsville, Queensland/Queensland Environmental Protection Agency, Brisbane.

GBRMPA (2007) *Great Barrier Reef Coral Reef Bleaching Surveys 2006*. Research Publication No. 87, Great Barrier Reef Marine Park Authority, Townsville, Queensland. Available at: http://www.gbrmpa.gov.au/corp_site/info_services/publications/research_publications (accessed 1 September 2010).

GBRMPA (2009) High Standard Tourism Programme. Great Barrier Reef Marine Park Authority, Townsville, Queensland. Available at: http://www.gbrmpa.gov.au/corp_site/key_issues/tourism/certification (accessed 1 September 2010).

Great Adventures (2010a) Reef and Fauna Information, Green Island, Great Barrier Reef, Cairns, Australia. Available at: http://www.green-island.com.au/reef-fauna.html (accessed 1 September 2010).

Great Adventures (2010b) History of Green Island, Great Barrier Reef, Cairns, Australia. Available at: http://www.green-island.com.au/history.html (accessed 1 September 2010).

Green Island Resort (2009) Green Island Resort Eco Facts. Available at: http://www.greenislandresort.com.au/eco-facts.html (accessed 1 September 2010).

Harriott, V.J. (2002) *Marine Tourism Impacts and Their Management on the Great Barrier Reef.* Technical Report No. 46, CRC Reef Research Centre, Townsville, Queensland.

Harris, R. and Leiper, N. (eds) (1995) Green Island Resort. In: *Sustainable tourism: An Australian Perspective,* Butterworth Heinemann, Chatswood, New South Wales, pp. 100–108.

Ilet, A., Aiello, R., Power, M., Recchia, C. and Sanders, L. (2000) The Great Barrier Reef World Heritage Area – ecotourism in the world's largest marine protected area. In: Charters, T. and Law, K. (eds) *Best Practice Ecotourism in Queensland.* Tourism Queensland, Brisbane, pp. 65–80.

Jenkin, C. (2009a) White meat, black market: poachers pillaging dugong and turtles. *The Cairns Post*, 28 August 2009, pp. 1–2.

Jenkin, C. (2009b) Dive in turtle stocks blamed on hunting. *The Cairns Post*, 13 October 2009, p. 3.

Koser, R. (2009) Reef turtles 'decimated.' *Port Douglas and Mosman Gazette*, 27 August 2009, p. 6.

Lady Elliot Island (2009) Great Barrier Reef Island Turns Green into Gold. Lady Elliot Island, Queensland, Australia (29 August 2009). Available at: http://www.ladyelliot. com.au/news/news_detail.asp?ID=103 (accessed 1 September 2010).

Lucas, A. (2008) Turtle soup. *Afloat* (May 2008). Available at: http://www.afloat.com.au/afloat-magazine/2008/may-2008/Turtle_Soup (accessed 1 September 2010).

MacPherson, A. (2007) A Different Kind of Fish Feeding Frenzy. Malaria, Bedbugs, Sea Lice & Sunsets Blog. Available at: http://coralnotesfromthefield.blogspot.com/2007/05/different-kind-of-feeding-frenzy.html (accessed 1 September 2010).

Martyn, J. (1993) *The History of Green Island: The Place of Spirits.* Author, Hidden Valley, Queensland.

Muir, F. (1993) Managing tourism to a sea-bird nesting island. *Tourism Management* 14, 99–105.

Orams, M. (1999) Management approaches. In: *Marine Tourism: Development, Impacts and Management.* Routledge, London, pp. 71–93.

Oxford Economics (2009) *Valuing the Effects of Great Barrier Reef Bleaching, August 2009.* Great Barrier Reef Foundation, Newstead, Queensland. Available at: http://www.apo.org.au/research/valuing-effects-great-barrier-reef-bleaching (accessed 9 September 2010).

Parkkali, S. (2006) Field trip Green Island. In: *Making a Difference National Training Workshop,* 11–14 September 2006, Cairns, Queensland. Interpretation Australia Association, Australia.

Seagrass-Watch (2008a) Gallery, Queensland Australia: 16–18 April 2008 – Green Island: 19 April. *Seagrass-Watch E-Bulletin* (28 April 2008), p. 4. Available at: http://www.seagrasswatch.org/publications.html (accessed 9 September 2010).

Seagrass-Watch (2008b) Wet tropics. *Seagrass-Watch News* 35 (December 2008), 4. Available at: http://www.seagrasswatch.org/magazine.html (accessed 1 September 2010).

Siebeck, U.E., Marshall, N.J., Kluter, A. and Hoegh-Guldberg, O. (2006) Monitoring coral bleaching using a colour reference card. *Coral Reefs* 25, 253–260.

Swartz, J. (2006) Green Island – tourist play-ground or something more? *Interpreting Australia* 33, 4.

The Cairns Post (2009a) Lucky few see turtles hatch. *The Cairns Post*, 26 February 2009, p.11.

The Cairns Post (2009b) Green Island bushwalk in top 10. *The Cairns Post*, 27 July 2009, p. 22.

TRRAC (Tourism and Recreation Reef Advisory Committee) (2002) *A Co-operative Framework for the Sustainable Use and Management of Tourism and Recreation Opportunities in the Great Barrier Reef Marine Park. Proposal of the Tourism and Recreation Reef Advisory Committee.* Available at: http://www.gbrmpa.gov.au/corp_site/info_services/publications/misc_pub (accessed 1 September 2010).

Wells, D. (2003) Wells *Approves Plan to Safeguard World-Class Tourist Attraction.* Ministerial Media Statement. Department of the Premier and Cabinet, Queensland Government, 5 December 2003.

5 Tourism and Sustainability in the Lakshadweep Islands

JITHENDRAN KOKKRANIKAL[1] AND TOM BAUM[2]

[1]University of Greenwich, London, UK; [2]University of Strathclyde, Glasgow, Scotland

Introduction

Islands offer unique attractions and have historically been one of the most popular tourism destinations. Most of them are small in size, and have a pristine environment, a blend of different lifestyles, indigenous cultures, unique land formations and flora and fauna (Sheldon, 2005). These unique features tend to attract a large number of visitors, and smaller islands offering a warmer climate have always been of particular interest to tourists on the lookout for the exotic. Pictures of sunny, green, white-sanded tropical islands with turquoise water are widely used by tourism marketers as the ideal escape for the modern-day tourists seeking a break from the mundane life (Baum, 1997). Islands in the Pacific, Mediterranean and Caribbean regions have become synonymous with modern-day mass tourism, consistently drawing large numbers of visitors.

Even though their geographical, cultural, ecological and economic features attract visitors, islands are also known for their fragile environment, geographical limitations and a culture that is less resilient to external influences. The small size of these islands and their relative lack of resources leave them with a range of development problems and dependent on the mainland for their survival (Kokkranikal *et al.*, 2003). Tourism, with its potential to contribute to the social and economic development of the destination communities, has been identified by many island communities as a strategy to deal with their development problems, and especially as an alternative source of income and livelihood diversification (Tao and Wall, 2009; Kokkranikal and Morrison, 2010).

Tourism development could offer a range of benefits to the destination communities, but it also entails a number of negative impacts (Wall and Mathieson, 2006), and island destinations, with their inherent characteristics, are probably more vulnerable to the negative impacts of tourism (Kokkranikal *et al.*, 2003). The fragility of the environment, limitations of resources and infrastructure, vulnerability of the indigenous societies, structural difficulties, and the lack of experience and expertise in tourism development and management make it more difficult for island communities to absorb and manage the inevitable impacts of tourism (Buhalis, 1999; Kokkranikal *et al.*, 2003).

Developing and managing tourism in a sustainable manner poses a major challenge in island tourism. The old Fordian forms of tourism are no longer sustainable for island tourism destinations, and many have been looking for ways to diversify away from the 'sun, sea, sand and sex' tourism to other more benign forms of tourism, such as those based on special interests, activities and business (Fayos-Sola, 1996; Ioannides and Holcomb, 2003; Bramwell, 2004; Aguilo *et al.*, 2005; Sharpley, 2007). With their natural limitations of size and geographical separation from the mainland, islands also offer the ideal setting for a better-planned and controlled development of tourism, and also to introduce corrective measures effectively.

Pointing to the growing concerns over the negative impacts of tourism in the islands, Kokkranikal *et al.* (2003) reported a number of planning and management measures for the sustainability-oriented development of tourism in islands; these include community-based tourism, strategic planning, insular and controlled tourism, segregated tourism, social impact assessment, carrying capacity assessment, environmental auditing, small scale tourism, eco-labelling, visitor management, and so on. Sheldon (2005) offers long-term stakeholder-involved planning, empowerment of the island community and culture, and environmental management, knowledge and information systems as approaches to deal with the challenges facing island tourism. This wide range of preventive and corrective measures also underlines the complexities and challenges involved in developing sustainable island tourism.

The aim of this chapter is to examine the issues and challenges in tourism development in the Lakshadweep islands with particular focus on its sustainability. The study is exploratory in nature and draws on data from secondary sources and key informant interviews, as well as on observations and findings of fieldwork carried out by the authors.

Lakshadweep – an Overview

Lakshadweep means 100,000 islands. It is an archipelago comprising 36 coral islands covering an area of 32 km², and is located in the Arabian Sea, off the south-west coast of India (Fig. 5.1). The islands have also been known as the Laccadive Islands.

Each island is fringed by coral sands, and is marked by a huge, shallow, calm lagoon on the western side which separates it from incoming swells of the outer sea by the coral reef. One of the smallest territories in India, Lakshadweep has a population of 60,595 people living on ten islands (Union Territory of Lakshadweep, 2009). The climate is tropical and the temperature varies from 20°C to 30°C. The islands are part of the Maldives group of islands and may be subject to the same effects of sea level rise resulting from climate change

Fig. 5.1. Location of Lakshadweep Islands. (Adapted from: http://schools.look4.net.nz/
geography/country_information/outline_maps/files_OM/india.jpg.)

(Ministry of Home Affairs, 2005). It is also located close to Kerala, which is a
major tourist destination in India (Fig. 5.2).

The first settlers are believed to have arrived on the islands of Amini,
Kavaratti, Andrott and Kalpeni during the 7th century AD from Kerala; the
islands of Agatti, Killtan, Chetlat and Kadmat were inhabited later (see the Fig.
5.2). The uninhabited islands were left alone because of the lack of potable
water. Having been under the control of several rulers from the mainland, the
islands came under the British rule in 1799 and became part of independent
India in 1947. Given its comparatively small size, the island archipelago was
ruled as Union Territory – governed directly by the central government of
independent India (George, 1997). Almost all the islanders are Muslims and
are classified as Scheduled Tribes, eligible for reservation in education and
employment, owing to the remote location of the islands. Hindus and Christians
form a very small minority. According to the 2001 national census, the

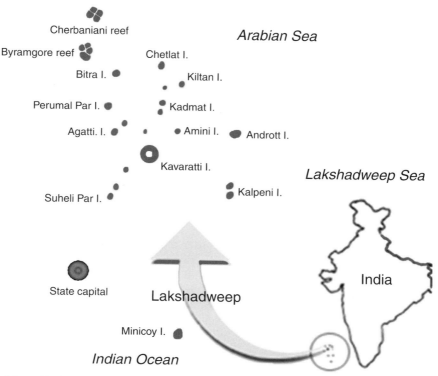

Fig. 5.2. Map of Lakshadweep Islands. (Adapted from: http://www.stayfinder.com/images/travelguide/india/destinations/islands/lakshadweep/lakshadweep_map.gif.)

population density of Lakshadweep is 1894/km². Because of the small size of the islands, developmental activities involving land are restricted, and only the islanders are allowed to buy and sell land, thus restricting migration from the mainland to control the island's population. Any investment in land-based businesses involve long-term lease of the land to outsiders.

Malayalam, the native language of Kerala, is spoken in all of the islands except for Minicoy, where Mahal, the language of the Maldives, is spoken. The society is matriarchal, with women playing an important role in the social and economic spheres of island life. They follow the *Marumakkathayam* system of inheritance, which used to be very common among the upper-cast Hindus in Kerala, under which the ancestral property is passed on to the female heirs. This system helps to safeguard the economic independence of women in the society. The predominance of women in all walks of life is a unique feature of Minicoy Island, where husbands take the wife's family name after marriage, and the women of the house manage all family affairs. This could be due to the fact that many of the islanders are seafarers and are away from the family most of the time. With 87.52% literacy (Union Territory of Lakshadweep, 2009), the islands are among the relatively better-developed regions in the country.

Alcohol is prohibited on all the islands, with the exception of Bangaram Island Resort. Despite the influence of Islam, there still prevails a caste system based on occupation, such as landowners, sailors and farmers. Well known for the simplicity and honesty of the people, Lakshadweep boasts a relatively crime-free society, with virtually no law and order problems (Planning Commission, 2008).

The administrative head of the Union Territory is the Administrator, who is normally a senior civil servant appointed by the central government of India. The island also sends an elected member to the Indian parliament. The island itself does not have a legislative body, leaving the Administrator as the head of the islands. A system of *Panchayati Raj* (village government) is followed in the island under the supervision of the Administrator, and is responsible for providing basic services on the islands. A total of 33 elected members representing the ten inhabited islands make up the District (Central) Panchayat, which is headed by an elected President. Individual islands have their own *Dweep* (village) Panchayat headed by an elected President. There are several departments dealing with law and order, civil supplies, public works, agriculture, finance and so on, that function under the Administrator. Agencies such as Lakshadweep Development Corporation Limited (LDCL), the Department of Tourism and the Society for Promotion of Nature Tourism and Sports (SPORTS) play key roles in implementing various development programmes.

With very few natural resources, economic activities on the islands are very limited. The economy is agrarian and for 90% of the population coconut farming is the principal source of livelihood. The islands produce 27.5 million coconuts per year (Lakshadweep Administration, 2010), which are converted into copra and sold to the coconut oil mills on the mainland. With territorial waters of 20,000 km^2 and a lagoon area of 4200 km^2, fisheries are another major economic activity of the islanders. There are over 500 mechanized boats on the islands. A tuna-canning factory, a handicraft production cum training centre and a number of coir (coconut husk fibre) product manufacturing centres constitute the industrial activities. There is also a hosiery factory on Kalpeni Island, a desiccated coconut powder unit on Kadmat Island and a smoked fish and fishmeal unit on Agatti Island. Coral mining, which used to be a major industry earlier, is now banned for environmental reasons. A large number of the islanders, especially from Minicoy Island, work as seamen all over the world. Four ships and two airline services provide the main transport link with the mainland. Speedboat and helicopter services are available for inter-island travel. Telecommunication facilities are available on all islands, and the islands also have their own intranet portal, called IntraLAK, which functions as a one-stop interface for e-Governance (IntraLAK, 2009). Electricity is generated by solar panels during the day and by diesel generators at night.

With a very limited resource base, the islanders are dependent upon the mainland for almost everything for their day-to-day life. The issue of dependence on the mainland is more pronounced when shipping services are disrupted occasionally as a result of mechanical breakdowns or inclement weather. Because of the distance from the mainland and lack of resources, infrastructure development on the island is very expensive. Owing to their remoteness, location and size, the islands are faced with a number of man-made and natural hazards (Box 5.1), and because of the high population density and range of human activities, the islands' environment is under constant pressure. Coral mining, dredging of navigational channels, unsustainable fishing practices, coastal development and souvenir collection are some of the major causes of environmental degradation (Ministry of Home Affairs, 2005).

Tourism in Lakshadweep

Often described as an exotic coral paradise, Lakshadweep does live up to this image. Coral colonies with a rich variety of marine fauna, and shallow lagoons with beautiful beaches fringe the islands. Tourism to the islands started with the introduction of regular transport services between the mainland and islands by ship in the 1970s and by air in the 1980s. The tourism activities on the islands range from deep sea-fishing, coral viewing, reef walking, diving and various other water sports, to visits to museums, aquaria, villages, Buddhist archaeological remains, and the handicrafts and coir-manufacturing centres. One of the uninhabited islands, Pitti, is a bird sanctuary.

Owing to the islands' fragile environment, high population density and physical limitations, tourism is organized in a very controlled manner. The

---

Box 5.1. Vulnerabilities and hazards for the Lakshadweep islands. (Source: Ministry of Home Affairs, 2005.)

- Geographical isolation.
- Insularity and remoteness.
- Small size of islands and population pressure.
- Communication and transport.
- Socio-economic vulnerability.
- Environmental vulnerability.
- Ecosystem vulnerability.
- Poor infrastructure.
- Scarcity of drinking water.
- Sanitation.
- Solid waste disposal.
- Energy requirement.
- Earthquakes.
- Storms.
- Rainfall inundation.
- Floods.
- Inundation of seawater in the islands.
- Coastal erosion.
- Sea level rise.
- Tsunamis.
- Oil spills.
- Marine pollution.
- Tourism.

islands follow a middle path between tourism promotion and environmental conservation, stressing high-value low-volume tourism (Kokkranikal *et al.*, 2003). There are restrictions on access, and permits are required even for Indian nationals to visit the islands. In order to ensure that the way of life of the islanders is not disturbed by external influences, only six islands are open to tourists – four inhabited islands (Kavaratti, Kalpeni, Minicoy and Kadmat) to domestic tourists, and two uninhabited islands (Bangaram and Agatti), to international tourists. These islands were selected on the basis of: (i) their geographical size; (ii) the availability of drinkable water in sufficient quantity; and (iii) proximity to transport routes (Kokkranikal *et al.*, 2003). With the setting up of a Water Sports Institute and Diving Centre, Kadmat is also now accessible to visitors from abroad. Until 2004, two passenger ships, MV Bharat Seema and Tipu Sultan, provided access for tourists to the islands. Two private companies were given licences – M/S Star Cruises in 2005 and M/S Ocean Cruises in 2007 – to operate cruise packages, which saw a sudden increase in tourism numbers in 2006/7 (see Table 5.1). Providing direct employment to more than 152 islanders, tourism generates in excess of 50 million Indian rupees (US$1 = 44 Indian rupees) in revenue to the islands (Lakshadweep Tourism, 2009). Jobs are found both in the skilled and semi-skilled category, with the public sector being the principal employer.

Tourism in the Lakshadweep islands is managed by the Department of Tourism, which formulates tourism policies and plans, and comes under the Lakshadweep Administration. SPORTS is a quasi-government organization functioning under the Department of Tourism and is responsible for the commercial operation and promotion of tourism in the islands. Started in

Table 5.1. Tourist arrivals in Lakshadweep. (Source: Union Territory of Lakshadweep, 2009.)

Tourist arrivals, 1992–2007	
1992/1993	3,437
1993/1994	3,373
1994/1995	4,225
1995/1996	4,680
1996/1997	4,861
1997/1998	4,123
1998/1999	2,735
1999/2000	2,120
2000/2001	3,863
2001/2002	3,798
2002/2003	5,004
2003/2004	4,703
2004/2005	2,588
2005/2006	15,203
2006/2007	21,522

1985, SPORTS organizes all package tours and operates most of the tourist facilities on the islands, as well as the information centres in the major cities of India. Until recently, tourism in Lakshadweep, with the exception of Bangaram Island, was organized around cruise trips, with day visits to the islands. During the 1990s, limited accommodation facilities – small tourist huts – were developed on the islands for domestic tourists. Some of the tourist huts on the islands, and the resort complex on Agatti Island, are owned and run by islanders (Table 5.2), with the majority owned by SPORTS. In 1998, SPORTS set up the first Water Sports Institute and the Laccadives Diving Centre on Kadmat Island; these were later leased out to a Mumbai-based company.

Bangaram, the only island catering for international tourists, has already become a well-known island resort, attracting celebrities and high-spending tourists. With tariffs ranging from US$400 to US$700 a day, the resort, with its 30 huts, is normally booked well in advance. It is run by the CGH group of hotels from the mainland, and is noted for its environment-friendly management practices and absence of amenities such as air conditioners, television, telephones and newspapers. The CGH group of hotels pays SPORTS about 5.5 million Indian rupees annually in rent. Further, as per the lease agreement, the resort has to employ 40% of its staff from the islands.

Issues and Challenges in Lakshadweep Tourism

Impacts of tourism on the physical environment have been well documented (Wall and Mathieson, 2006; Holden, 2008). With their very limited carrying capacity, smaller islands would find it difficult to absorb these impacts, necessitating a very careful and well-planned approach to tourism development. Limitations of infrastructure and resources, a major problem in island destinations, could exacerbate the pressure of tourism on their environments. However, these negative conceptualizations of tourism in small islands are challenged by Scheyvens and Momsen (2008), who argue that 'the vulnerability and dependence of small island states has been overstated in much of the tourism and general development literature', and identify a number of areas in

Table 5.2. Accommodation in the Lakshadweep islands. (Source: SPORTS, 2009.)

Islands	Tourist huts owned by		Number of beds
	The SPORTS	Private sector	
Bangaram		30	60
Kadmat	29		60
Agatti		10	20
Minicoy	10	3	26
Kavaratti	5		10
Kalpeni		4	8
Total	44	47	184

which the small islands are strong, which include high levels of cultural, social and natural capital, respect for traditional, holistic approaches to development, political strength, better economic governance and strong international linkages in the case of micro states. However, it is also argued that there is overwhelming evidence that points to the vulnerability of island destinations to the negative impacts of tourism (e.g. Gossling, 2003; Scheyvens, 2005; Campling and Rosalie, 2006; Bramwell, 2007; Connell, 2007; Sharpley, 2007; Sharma, 2009), and Lakshadweep is no exception. The Lakshadweep islands have a very fragile environment, and tourism development needs to be sensitive to its vulnerabilities (Ministry of Home Affairs, 2005). Given their small size and environmental brittleness, impacts are likely to occur instantly and intensely in Lakshadweep, adversely affecting the lives and the ecosystem of the inhabitants. Kokkranikal *et al.* (2003) have reported a number of issues and challenges confronting Lakshadweep tourism, which are summarized below.

Disposal of sewage is a major problem in Lakshadweep. Changing lifestyle and growing population have increased the generation of sewage and solid wastes. Most of the oceanic islands have no or a very limited supply of freshwater and so have to use saltwater extensively, and this can inhibit the bacterial breakdown of sewage (Wall and Mathieson, 2006). Like many islands all over the world, it is a common practice in Lakshadweep to dump sewage into the sea. In many islands, the untreated domestic wastes are discharged into the narrow shoreline, behind each household (Planning Commission, 2008). Most of the rubbish dumped into the sea may then be washed up on to the islands or the surrounding reefs, polluting the ecosystem. Sometimes the sewage is taken to the mainland for disposal. Neither system is environmentally very sensible, and an increase in the number of visitors and changing consumption patterns of the islanders would accentuate the ecological hazards.

Life in Lakshadweep is affected by a shortage of freshwater, which has been one of the factors responsible for limiting tourism to selected islands. The coralline nature of the islands make them highly porous, leading to salinity ingress, which affects the quality of the groundwater (Planning Commission, 2008). The major source of drinking water is rainwater, which is collected by rainwater harvesting, stored in tanks and then distributed through a network of pipes. The aquifers of Lakshadweep are highly sensitive and freshwater is seen floating as a thin lens over seawater (Dhiman and Thampi, 2009; Mondal *et al.*, 2009). The islanders are dependent upon one thermal desalination plant most of the year for drinking water. In a recent study by the Planning Commission (2008), it was found that the sole desalination plant is grossly inadequate for meeting the water requirements of the islanders, and construction of three more plants in other islands was recommended. With the islanders themselves experiencing drinking water shortage, visitors to the islands and their excessive demands for water can only exacerbate the situation.

The islands are vulnerable to oil spills from ships and oil tankers sailing close to them. Oil seepages from motor boats cause damage to corals and other marine life. Further, the propellers of the boats create pollution by stirring up mud from the seabed (Wall and Mathieson, 2006). With its major attractions and recreational activities based on the marine ecosystem, all these problems are very much present in Lakshadweep. Even though they have not yet become very serious, they are unlikely to remain in this state if there are no preventive and remedial systems in place. An increase in marine tourism and water sports would add to the existing pressures.

The coral reefs are important for the islanders, not only for their livelihood activities, but also for the survival of the islands (Syed Ismail Koya *et al.*, 2009). Fishes caught from the reefs and the lagoons are used for consumption by the local population, and the reefs also provide protection from erosion to the low-lying islands. Until the mid 1980s, coral mining was a major economic activity, with the government offering incentives to promote it as an industry. It has now been completely banned, saving the islands from certain ruin. The 1998 bleaching of the corals as a result of the El Nino effect affected almost 90% of the live coral in Lakshadweep. Coral used to be a major resource used by the islanders to build homes, and the high costs of bringing building materials from the mainland still pose a major threat to the coral reefs from the islanders. The release of untreated sewage, garbage and non-biodegradable solid wastes into the sea can cause further damage to the corals, and as these form a major attraction of the islands, and a number of recreational activities are based on them, tourism forms another major threat to their survival. Carelessness by tourists can disturb the habitat of corals as a result of walking on the reefs and anchoring boats. In addition, there is also the threat from souvenir-hunting tourists who pick up coral, despite the strict warning against doing so.

The 'simplicity' of the islanders, and a crime-free society, are very vulnerable to the influence of visitors, both domestic and international. Exposure to tourists and their different cultures can easily bring about sociocultural changes and may generate conflicts of values, communication problems, the development of unwelcoming attitudes of the islanders towards each other, isolation, separation and segregation (Reisinger, 2009). Such changes could also threaten the prevailing system of social hierarchy and cohesion, which helps the islanders to live and organize their lives as a mutually supportive social unit. All the islands have a social system according to which members belonging to different age groups are expected to carry out certain social duties, from running errands to taking decisions affecting the islands' society and economy (Kokkranikal *et al.*, 2003). Problems such as cultural shock, cultural conflict, cultural drift and demonstration effect are very real for the islands' traditional society, and can be very damaging to the island community (Fisher, 2004; Reisinger, 2009).

The dependence on the mainland is another factor that affects the economy and other commercial activities on the island tremendously. As the islanders primarily have fish and coconut as resources, economic leakage has always been very high. Even though no figures are available, considering the similarities between the Maldives and Lakshadweep, a conservative estimate of about 80% cannot be very wide of the mark. There are major questions on the extent of the economic benefits accruing to the islanders from tourism. Islanders are resentful towards ownership of tourism businesses by entrepreneurs from the mainland. With very limited economic activities available on the island, tourism could offer an alternative livelihood (Planning Commission, 2008; Tao and Wall, 2009), although it is doubtful whether an over-dependence on tourism would be healthy and sustainable (Kokkranikal, 2004). Further, almost all tourism-related planning and development decisions are taken by the Department of Tourism of the Indian government, based on the mainland, and the islanders do not have much say in these matters. SPORTS is just an agency to execute the decisions taken by the national tourism organization.

Evidently, sustainability is a major issue in Lakshadweep tourism. Its structural and geographical situation makes the islands highly vulnerable to a wide range of social, cultural, economic and ecological impacts, and tourism can exacerbate these (Kokkranikal *et al.*, 2003; Ministry of Home Affairs, 2005; Planning Commission, 2008).

Tourism and Sustainability in Lakshadweep

Owing to the resource constraints and consequent livelihood limitations, tourism offers of a viable option as an economic activity to the Lakshadweep islands. However, given its fragile environment and traditional society, Lakshadweep has to be careful to develop tourism in a sustainable manner. Conscious of the islands' environmental and sociocultural vulnerabilities, Lakshadweep tourism follows a 'philosophy of preservation' as its guiding principle (Lakshadweep Tourism, 2009). Significantly, as already mentioned, islands follow a policy of allowing only domestic tourists on the inhabited islands in order to avoid possible sociocultural problems. Contacts between the islanders and the visitors are kept to a minimum and there have not been any instances of social or cultural friction on the islands (Kokkranikal *et al.*, 2003; Lakshadweep Tourism, 2009). Besides the environmentally friendly policy initiatives, the main strategies being followed to address the sustainability concerns of tourism in Lakshadweep include 'controlled tourism', 'segregated tourism' and 'enclave tourism' (Guthunz and Krosigk, 1996; Kokkranikal *et al.*, 2003).

Tourism policy

Tourism policy initiatives are key to influencing the way tourism is developed and its consequent impacts (Dredge and Jenkins, 2007). Tourism policies that are rooted in sustainability ethics are essential to ensure that tourism is developed in harmony with the environment (Tribe, 2002; Jamal, 2004). Taking advantage of its geographical and physiographical limitations, Lakshadweep tourism has adopted a policy of promoting high-value and low-volume tourism in order to make tourism development environmentally sustainable and economically viable (Lakshadweep Tourism, 2009). However, the recent granting of licences to two companies to operate cruises has seen an abrupt increase in tourist arrivals (Table 5.1), and the impacts of this increase need careful examination. Key features of Lakshadweep's tourism policy are as follows (Box 5.2).

As part of the ninth five-year plan, the Lakshadweep Administration carried out an environmental impact assessment during 1997–2002. This resulted in the development of the following guidelines for tourism development projects on the islands (Box 5.3).

Some of the major sustainability-oriented tourism practices introduced on the islands include the following (Lakshadweep Tourism, 2009):

- Electricity is generated by solar plants.
- Islanders are educated to adopt an eco-friendly way of life.
- Biomass plants using coconut and other waste have been set up in Kavarati to generate electricity.
- A film is shown to tourists arriving on ships to inform them about the island, its environment, the coral reefs and their management, the ban on picking up corals, plastics, etc., and ways to keep the islands clean and enjoy the beauty without disturbing or destroying it.
- Islanders are trained in scuba-diving so that they not only know about marine wealth but also contribute to maintaining the ecology of the islands and work as the eyes and ears of the Administration.

These policy initiatives and guidelines have contributed to bringing about awareness regarding the importance of following environment-friendly

---

Box 5.2. Salient features of Lakshadweep tourism policy. (Source: Lakshadweep Tourism, 2009.)

1. Conservation of the fragile ecological and environmental structures.
2. Protection of the unique local culture and social fabric.
3. Promotion of high-value and low-volume tourism.
4. Promotion of sustainable tourism based on the islands' 'carrying capacity'.
5. Promotion of sea-based ship tourism for larger numbers of visitors.
6. Promotion of air-based tourism for high-value tourists.
7. Training of staff to upgrade tourism management skills and to develop local capacity and personnel to run the scuba-diving centres.
8. Privatization of facilities on stringent terms, such as land lease rent, royalties and percentage of gross turnover.
9. In order to protect the environment and culture the tourism policy also stresses:
    (i) no violation of prohibition;
    (ii) promotion of folk art and culture;
    (iii) eco-friendly water sports, mainly non-mechanized;
    (iv) promotion of scuba-diving;
    (v) promotion of solar power and biological toilets;
    (vi) collection of non-biodegradable waste for safe disposal;
    (vii) disposal of kitchen waste in the open sea;
    (viii) promotion of smokeless stoves;
    (ix) discouragement of diesel power generators; and
    (x) installation of silent power generators to avoid noise pollution.

Box 5.3. Guidelines for tourism projects. (Source: Lakshadweep Tourism, 2009.)

1. All proposed construction should have a thatched roof or tiled sloping roof.
2. Only biological toilets to be installed as far as possible.
3. Rainwater harvesting should be set up to conserve freshwater.
4. Use of pump sets should be minimized; any pump set used should have a cut-off mechanism to ensure that water below the minimum safe level is not drawn.
5. Waste disposal systems such as incinerators for non-recyclable/non-biodegradable waste should be installed and a system of returning (composting) all non-biodegradable waste must be in position.
6. Minimum cutting of trees/greenery and maximum planting of trees, plants, shrubs and creepers should be adopted.
7. A study of carrying capacity should be conducted before taking up development on any uninhabited island.
8. A system should be established to raise tourists' awareness of the ecosystem's fragility and vulnerability.

---

development and operation of tourism on the islands. However, it is important that the islanders maintain the present low-volume high-value approach to tourism and do not get swayed by the rush for more tourism which is found on the mainland.

Enclave tourism, which restricts visitors and their holiday activities to within specific tourist enclaves away from the local people, could be an effective strategy to limit the negative impacts of tourism, especially in societies that are vulnerable to the demonstration effect (Fisher, 2004). The enclaves make it possible to restrict and manage impacts to a limited area. The CGH resort on the Bangaram Island could be a very good example of enclave tourism (Kokkranikal *et al.*, 2003). Marketed as an upmarket and exclusive resort, Bangaram is the only island where foreign tourists are allowed to stay. Out of bounds to the islanders, alcoholic beverages are available on the island. Bangaram Island is a good example of price and structural enclavism (Jenkins, 1982). Known for its environment-friendly approach, the resort is completely insulated from other islands and provides a variety of water-based activities, such as kayaking, catamaran sailing, snorkelling, deep sea-fishing, and scuba-diving. Although 40% of the employees in the resort are from the islands, so far Lakshadweep appears to have been free from any social problems resulting from the demonstration effect (Fisher, 2004). Given the fact that the islands cannot supply many of the resources for the resort, except for the employment of the islanders, linkage between the resort and the island economy is limited. However, as the islands do not have resources to provide supplies to the resort, the issue of economic leakage is very real, but unavoidable. More importantly, owing to the separation between the locals and tourists, the enclave reduces the potential for local resentment towards affluent visitors to a minimum.

Segregated tourism is another strategy that helps to optimize revenue with a minimum number of tourists, who are kept as much away from the local society as possible, so that the possibility of distortion of the indigenous culture and lifestyle will be minimum (Guthunz and Krosigk, 1996; Salih, 2000). With its low-volume high-value quality tourism policy, Lakshadweep has been following this strategy right from the start. To begin with, only ship-based day visitors from the mainland were allowed on to the islands. Even the recently introduced island tourist huts are located as far away from the local community as possible. The interaction between visitors and the local society has been deliberately kept to a minimum. Moreover, according to tourism officials, cruise packages are still and will continue to be the major type of tourism organised by SPORTS. This strategy seems to be working well in Lakshadweep, as is evident from the fact that even 25 years after its introduction, tourism has remained relatively harmless to the economy, environment and society of the islands.

Controlled tourism is about limiting the number of visitors and tourist facilities and activities to a minimum, so that pressure on the resources and the undesirable consequences of tourism can be avoided (Kokkranikal *et al.*, 2003). The Lakshadweep Administration places a lot of importance on limiting tourism to within the islands' carrying capacity limits. Control can be exerted by various methods, such as entry restrictions, reducing the number of facilities and pricing, and also by introducing and enforcing behavioural guidelines for the visitors. By restricting access through a system of entry permits, confining tourism to only six islands, allowing only domestic tourists to the inhabited islands, limiting the number of tourist beds to a total of 184, organizing ship-based cruise packages and promoting sea-based tourism, the Administration controls the number, nature and activities of the visitors. The Administration has also introduced a set of behavioural guidelines (mentioned above), which the visitors are gently persuaded to adhere to with the assistance of a group of trained tourist guides from the local community. Box 5.4 contains a list of 'Dos and Don'ts' brought out by SPORTS.

Conclusion

Island tourism destinations experience a range of sustainability issues, which are difficult to prevent and manage, and the tourism literature is replete with strategies and policy measures to help develop island tourism sustainably (e.g.

Box 5.4. Dos and don'ts for the tourists in Lakshadweep. (Source: SPORTS, 2009.)

- Make sure of your reservation of tour in advance before leaving your station.
- Don't litter the land or the water. It pollutes.
- Do not pick up corals as souvenirs. It is a punishable offence.
- Do not use alcoholic drinks or intoxicants on the islands. There is prohibition on all islands except for Bangaram.
- Do not carry narcotics or drugs. It is a punishable offence.
- Do not swim or sunbathe nude. It is prohibited.
- Do not go out of your island lagoon without permission of the SPORTS authorities and without a proper escort. It can be risky.
- Don't pluck tender coconuts yourself. A fall can prove to be fatal. The coconut trees are privately owned and unauthorized plucking of coconuts is a theft.

Filho, 1996; Wong, 2001; Twinning-Ward and Butler, 2002; Sheldon, 2005; Garin-Munoz, 2006; Hampton and Christenson, 2007; Leslie-Ann, 2007; Roger *et al.*, 2007; Reddy, 2008; Seo *et al.*, 2009; Martin-Cejas and Sanchez, 2010; Robin and Haywantee, 2010; Yasarata *et al.*, 2010). The geographical, environmental, structural and political limitations of islands make them more vulnerable to the impacts of tourism. Many islands are very small and lack the capacity to withstand or absorb the impacts. Consequently, sustainable development of tourism assumes more importance in the case of island destinations. With its tremendous tourism potential, Lakshadweep has all the characteristics and shortcomings of a small island state that is part of a larger political entity. Any form of negative impacts from tourism can have a very pronounced effect on the island and can be fatal to its ecology and to the prevailing social cohesiveness (Kokkranikal *et al.*, 2003).

However, it is not unrealistic to develop and manage island tourism in an environmentally responsible manner, as is evident in the case of Lakshadweep. Tourism can be developed on islands in a balanced manner without the islands becoming victims of the problems of mass tourism. An analysis of the trends and practices in Lakshadweep tourism points to a sustainability-oriented development approach. Controlled, segregated and enclave tourism have been adopted as the foundations of Lakshadweep tourism, and have proven to be effective in minimizing, if not avoiding, the deleterious consequences of tourism. Lakshadweep provides a very good example to other island tourism destinations of possible strategies for achieving sustainability.

However, owing to various structural and political reasons, it is doubtful whether Lakshadweep has been able to realize its optimum potential as a tourist destination, a view that is shared by many people associated with the islands' tourism. It is also unlikely that the islands will be able to overcome these impediments in the foreseeable future. In a sense, those same restrictions that make Lakshadweep's tourism development a very slow process have contributed towards the sustainability of tourism in the islands. However, Lakshadweep tourism can take more measures to enhance both its orientation to sustainability and its competitiveness within the existing structural and political framework. Probably, a gradual development of tourism could be more desirable, and continued adherence to controlled, segregated and enclave tourism will be of great significance for the long-term sustainability of Lakshadweep tourism.

References

Aguilo, E., Alegre, J. and Sard, M. (2005) The persistence of the sun and sand tourism model. *Tourism Management* 26, 219–232.

Baum, T. (1997) The fascination of islands: a tourist perspective. In: Lockhart, D. and Drakakis-Smith, D. (eds) *Island Tourism: Problems and Perspectives.* Mansell, London, pp. 21–35.

Bramwell, B. (2004) *Coastal Mass Tourism. Diversification and Sustainable Development in Southern Europe.* Channel View Publications, Clevedon, UK.

Bramwell, B. (2007) Complexity, interdisciplinarity and growth management: the case of Maltese resort tourism. In: Agarwal, S. and Shaw, G. (eds) *Managing Coastal Tourism Resorts: A Global Perspective*. Channel View Publications, Clevedon, UK, pp. 73–89.

Buhalis, D. (1999) Tourism on the Greek islands: Issues of peripherality, competitiveness and development. *International Journal of Tourism Research* 1, 341–358.

Campling, L. and Rosalie, M. (2006) Sustaining social development in a small island developing state? The case of Seychelles. *Sustainable Development* 14, 115–125.

Connell, J. (2007) Islands, idylls and the detours of development. *Singapore Journal of Tropical Geography* 28, 116–135.

Dhiman, S.C. and Thampi, D.S. (2009) Ground *Water Management in Coastal Areas*. Central Ground Water Board: New Delhi. Available from: http://www.indiaenvironmentportal.org.in/files/Paper-Dhiman.pdf (accessed 20 March 2010).

Dredge, D. and Jenkins, J. (2007) *Tourism Policy and Planning*. John Wiley, Brisbane, Queensland.

Fayos-Sola, E. (1996) Tourism policy: a midsummer night's vision. *Tourism Management* 17, 405–412.

Filho, W.L. (1996) Putting principles into practices: sustainable tourism in small island states. In: Briguglio, L., Archer, B., Jafari, J. and Wall, G. (eds) *Sustainable Tourism in Islands and Small States: Issues and Policies*. Cassell, London, pp. 61–67.

Fisher, D. (2004) The demonstration effect revisited. *Annals of Tourism Research* 31, 428–446.

Garin-Munoz, T. (2006) Inbound international tourism to Canary Islands: a dynamic panel data model. *Tourism Management* 27, 281–291.

George, T.J.S. (1997) *India at 50*. Express Publications (Madurai), Chennai.

Gossling, S. (2003) *Tourism and Development in Tropical Islands: Political Ecology Perspectives*. Edward Elgar, Cheltenham, UK.

Guthunz, U. and Krosigk, F. (1996) Tourism development in small island states: from Mirab to Tourab? In: Briguglio, L., Archer, B., Jafari, J. and Wall, G. (eds) *Sustainable Tourism in Islands and Small States: Issues and Policies*. Cassell, London, pp. 18–35.

Hampton, M.P. and Christensen, J. (2007) Competing industries in islands: a new tourism approach. *Annals of Tourism Research* 34, 998–1020.

Holden, A. (2008) *Environment and Tourism*. Routledge, London.

IntraLAK (2009) Lakshadweep, the coral Paradise of India. Available at: http://intralak.nic.in/ (accessed 12 September 2009).

Ioannides, D. and Holcomb, B. (2003) Misguided policy initiatives in small island destinations: why do up-market tourism policies fail? *Tourism Geographies* 5, 39–48.

Jamal, T. (2004) Virtue ethics and sustainable tourism pedagogy: phronesis, principles and practice. *Journal of Sustainable Tourism* 12, 530–545.

Jenkins, C.L. (1982) The effects of scale in tourism projects in developing countries. *Annals of Tourism Research* 9, 229–249.

Kokkranikal, J. (2004) Tourism human resource development and sustainability in developing countries. In: *Tourism State of the Art –II, Proceedings*. Conference organized by The Scottish Hotel School, University of Strathclyde, 27–30 June 2004.

Kokkranikal, J. and Morrison, A. (2010) Entrepreneurial innovation in tourism: community networks and contributions in heritage tourism in Kerala. A conference paper for the Tourism Entrepreneurship Conference, organized by Wilfrid Laurier University, Ontario, Canada, 26–27 April 2010.

Kokkranikal, J., Baum, T. and MacLellan, R.L. (2003) Island tourism and sustainability: a case study of the Lakshadweep Islands. *Journal of Sustainable Tourism* 11, 426–447.

Lakshadweep Administration (2010) Department of Agriculture, Union Territory of

Lakshadweep. Developmental activities: Coconut Development Programme. Available at: http://lakshadweep.nic.in/depts/agriculture/Files/Scheme1.htm (accessed 18 March 2010).

Lakshadweep Tourism (2009) Lakshadweep Tourism. Available at: http://lakshadweeptourism.nic.in/web5.htm (accessed 12 September 2009)

Leslie-Ann, J. (2007) Interorganisational relationships in small twin-island developing states in the Caribbean – The role of the internal core-periphery model: the case of Trinidad and Tobago. *Current Issues in Tourism* 10, 1–32.

Martin-Cejas, R.R. and Sanchez, P.P.R. (2010) Ecological footprint analysis of road transport related to tourism activity: the case for Lanzarote Island. *Tourism Management* 31, 98–103.

Ministry of Home Affairs (2005) *Report of the National Task Force for a Special Study of Lakshadweep Islands to Assess Vulnerability to various Hazards and Suggest Mitigation/Prevention Measures*. Government of India, Ministry of Home Affairs, Disaster Management Division, New Delhi. Available at: http://www.ndmindia.nic.in/techAdvGroup/difexpgrp/LakshadweepReport.pdf (accessed 20 March 2010).

Mondal, N.C., Singh, V.S., Sarwade, D.V. and Nandakumar, M.V. (2009) Appraisal of groundwater resources in an island condition. *Journal of Earth System Science* 118, 217–229.

Planning Commission (2008) *Report on Visit to Lakshadweep – A Coral Reef Wetland Included Under National Wetland Conservation and Management Programme of the Ministry of Environment and Forests, 30th October–1st November 2008*. Planning Commission, Government of India, New Delhi. Available at: http://www.indiaenvironmentportal.org.in/content/report-lakshadweep-wetlandscoral-reefs (accessed 16 September 2010).

Reddy, M.V. (2008) Sustainable tourism rapid indicators for less-developed islands: an economic perspective. *International Journal of Tourism Research* 10, 557–576.

Reisinger, Y. (2009) *International Tourism Cultures and Behaviour*. Butterworth-Heinemann, London.

Robin, N. and Haywantee, R. (2010) Small island urban tourism: a residents' perspective. *Current Issues in Tourism* 13, 37–60.

Roger, S., Alistair, M.B., Maya, P., Arno, S. and Albert, W. (2007) National indicators of well-being: lessons from Pacific Island countries' tourism. *Asia Pacific Journal of Tourism Research* 12, 203–222.

Salih, A. (2000) Diver's perception – the Maldives. Unpublished dissertation, Postgraduate Diploma in Tourism, Centre for Tourism, University of Otago, New Zealand.

Scheyvens, R. (2005) Growth of beach *fale* tourism in Samoa: the high value of low cost tourism. In: Hall, C.M. and Boyd, S. (eds) *Nature-based Tourism in Peripheral Areas: Development or Disaster*. Channel View Publications: Clevedon, UK, pp. 188–202.

Scheyvens, R. and Momsen, J. (2008) Tourism in small island states: from vulnerability to strengths. *Journal of Sustainable Tourism* 16, 491–510.

Seo, J.H., Park, S.Y. and Yu, L. (2009) The analysis of the relationships of Korean outbound tourism demand: Jeju Island and three international destinations. *Tourism Management* 30, 530–543.

Sharma, A. (2009) Change should bring stability: an island community's perception of tourism. *Contours* 19 (4), 7–9.

Sharpley, R. (2007) A tale of two islands: sustainable resort development in Cyprus and Tenerife. In: Agarwal, S. and Shaw, G. (eds) *Managing Coastal Tourism Resorts: A Global Perspective*. Channel View Publications, Clevedon, UK, pp. 112–136.

Sheldon, P.J. (2005) *The Challenges to Sustainability in Island Tourism*. Occasional Papers 2005-1, School of Travel Industry Management, University of Hawaii.

SPORTS (2009) Society for Promotion of Nature Tourism and Sports (A society under Lakshadweep Administration). Available at: http://www.lakshadweep tourism.com/ (accessed 8 September 2009).

Syed Ismail Koya, M.S., Muley, E.V. and Wafar, M (2009) *Status of the Lakshadweep Coral Reefs, Indian Coral Reef Monitoring Network*. Available at: http://www.envfor.nic.in/icrmn/events/sr_lak.html (accessed 22 March 2010).

Tao, T.C.H. and Wall, G. (2009) Tourism as a sustainable livelihood strategy. *Tourism Management* 30, 90–98.

Tribe, J. (2002) Education for ethical tourism action. *Journal of Sustainable Tourism* 10, 309–324.

Twining-Ward, L. and Butler, R. (2002) Implementing STD on a small island: development and use of sustainable tourism development indicators in Samoa. *Journal of Sustainable Tourism* 10, 363–387.

Union Territory of Lakshadweep (2009) Home. Available at: http://lakshadweep.nic.in/ (accessed 10 September 2009).

Wall, G. and Mathieson, A. (2006) *Tourism: Change, Impacts and Opportunities*. Prentice Hall, London.

Wong, P. (2001) Small-scale tourism and local community development: the case of the Gili Islands, Lombok, Indonesia. In: *Proceedings of the WTO/UNEP Asia-Pacific Seminar on Island Tourism in Asia and the Pacific*. United Nations World Tourism Organization, Madrid.

Yasarata, M., Altinay, L., Burns, P. and Okumus, F. (2010) Politics and sustainable tourism development – can they co-exist? Voices from North Cyprus. *Tourism Management* 31, 345–356.

6 The Risk of Climate Change for Tourism in the Maldives

Susanne Becken, John Hay and Stephen Espiner

Lincoln University, Christchurch, New Zealand

Introduction

The Maldives has recently been well represented in the media headlines. In November 2008, the country's first democratically elected president, Mohamed Nasheed, announced that the Maldives will begin to use a portion of the country's tourist revenue to buy a new homeland. This initiative was explained as an insurance policy against the climate change that threatens to turn the 300,000 Maldivians into environmental refugees. Half a year later, the President made the bold announcement that the Maldives would be the first carbon-neutral country in the world by 2019. To this end, an environmental tax on tourists was proposed in order to help mitigate the carbon emissions associated with international air travel. Later in 2009, in an unprecedented publicity stunt, the President held the world's first underwater cabinet meeting, to raise awareness for sea-level rise and the risks it poses to the Maldives.

This case study of climate change and the Maldives provides insights into how multiple perspectives and scales of sustainability affect island destinations in regard to their long-term future. First, it unmistakably illustrates how unsustainable emissions of greenhouse gases around the world affect the very existence of some small island states – in this case as a result of sea-level rise that will eventually lead to widespread inundation of national (land) territory. Secondly, the case study shows how even small global players, like the Maldives, can make a difference in terms of climate change mitigation by reducing their own emissions and contributing to sustainable practices such as carbon sequestration. Finally, the wider implementation of local sustainable practices, such as proper waste management, biodiversity protection and community involvement, are discussed as essential for achieving effective adaptation to climate change.

Against this background, this chapter discusses the risks that face the Maldives as a result of global climate change, and contrasts these with the perceptions of climate change risks held by stakeholders in the tourism industry. Understanding how the public, and those with declared tourism interests, perceive climate change is critical for the successful development and implementation of political, economic and social action to address the potential impacts and consequences of climate change (Belle and Bramwell, 2005; Leiserowitz, 2007). Judgements, attitudes and beliefs held about the external environment are thought to have a significant influence on behaviour (Ajzen and Fishbein, 2005). Leiserowitz (2006), for example, noted that public support for or opposition to climate treaties, regulations, taxes or subsidies will be greatly influenced by people's perceptions of the risks and dangers of climate change. Lack of 'buy-in' is therefore likely to undermine wide implementation of sustainability strategies.

Background on the Maldives

The Maldives has long been recognized as one of the world's most vulnerable and least defensible countries to climate change (Barnett and Adger, 2003). The tropical island environment of the Maldives has proven to be a unique marketable asset in a country which is essentially devoid of any other commercially exploitable resources. The key factors contributing to the vulnerability of the Maldives are its low elevation (80% of the land area is less than a metre above sea level), fragile ecosystems, remoteness, geographical size and dispersion, lack of natural resources, small human resource base, highly limited internal market and extremely sensitive and competitive external market. The Maldivian economy is heavily dependent on just two main industries: fisheries and tourism. Both these industries face strong international competition and are vulnerable to a number of natural and human-related threats. For example, the total cost to tourist resorts and loss of government revenue from the tourism sector as a result of the 2004 Indian Ocean tsunami has been estimated to be in excess of US$300 million (Ministry of Planning and National Development, 2005).

Tourism in the Maldives is based on the beauty of its natural environment. The diversity of the reef ecosystems in the Maldives is among the richest in the world, covering a total area of 8920 km^2 and contributing 5% of the world's reef area. Of the tourists visiting the Maldives, an estimated 25–30% participate in scuba-diving and 75–80% go snorkelling (Ministry of Home Affairs, Housing and Environment, 2001). The coral reefs also show how tourism, when managed in an unsustainable way, can have a considerable impact on the natural environment. Coral reefs are not only economically important to the Maldives in terms of tourism, fisheries and other ecosystem services they provide, they also represent strategic natural offshore sea defence, acting to buffer shorelines from wave action and other oceanic forces.

The Maldives is highly dependent on tourism as a source of foreign exchange, employment and contribution to gross domestic product (GDP); in 2003, tourism accounted for 32.7% of GDP, arrivals numbered about 600,000 and the sector employed more than 17,000 people, or over 56% of the working population. Since tourism began in 1972, the sector has grown rapidly. International tourist arrivals have risen from 42,000 in 1980 to over 600,000 in 2004, an annual growth rate of over 9% (Ministry of Tourism and Civil Aviation, 2007). In 2009, 96 resorts and 14 hotels provided about 21,792 beds. More than 1200 overwater structures have been developed as guest rooms, spas and restaurants in tourist resorts. As part of the *Third Tourism Master Plan 2007–2011* (Ministry of Tourism and Civil Aviation, 2007), the Government has authorized an additional 1600 beds on 11 designated islands, with emphasis on environmental protection and preservation. Besides accommodation, the Maldivian tourism industry comprises activities (e.g. diving operators), tourist services and transport operators.

Despite a number of climate change adaptation projects and initiatives (including one on tourism), the Maldives (like most countries) has not developed tourism-specific strategies to deal with climate change. Among other reasons, this is because tourism in general consists of many different players, including small and large businesses, a range of public-sector stakeholders and communities (Becken and Hay, 2007). Additionally, it is driven by both domestic and international interests, especially in the Maldives, where only 57% of the employed workforce is local and considerable capital comes from overseas (Ministry of Environment and Construction, 2004). These circumstances make it challenging for tourism to develop a common approach to a complex problem such as climate change with its attributes of uncertainty, large temporal and spatial scales and irreversibility (Becken and Clapcott, in press).

Assessment of Climate Change Risks

A major challenge for the Maldives is that all climate projections for the country indicate an increasing likelihood of conditions detrimental to the tourism sector (Table 6.1). The consequences will be felt not only within tourism but also by the individuals, communities and enterprises that are dependent on it. Climate influences the viability and profitability of tourism, both directly and indirectly. In the sun-sand-and-sea tourism segment, which is the mainstay of tourism in the Maldives, climate is a key determinant in choosing a destination (Agnew and Palutikof, 2006). At the same time, adverse conditions have an impact on the tourist experience and, in extreme situations, on tourist health and safety and on the reputation of the country as a tourist destination (Pizam *et al.*, 1997; Sönmez and Graefe, 1998).

The tourism sector of the Maldives faces major risks related to climate change. These include accelerated shoreline and beach erosion, temporarily reduced water availability, interrupted supply chains, physical damage to property and warmer sea temperatures. Sea-level changes are of special significance to the Maldives. The Intergovernmental Panel on Climate Change (IPCC) projected globally averaged sea-level rise at the end of the 21st century to range from 0.19 to 0.58 m (Mimura *et al.*, 2007). Climate models indicate

Table 6.1. Climate risks, consequences for tourism and current coping strategies. (Source: Hay *et al.*, 2008.)

Climate risk events	Consequences of and significance to tourism	Coping strategies currently practised by the tourism industry
Elevated sea level, including high wave incidents	Coastal erosion, land loss, flooding, inundation	Moveable groynes, coastal revegetation, open-structured jetties, beach nourishment, wave breakers, sea walls, elevated structures
Elevated ocean and lagoon temperatures	Coral bleaching, algal blooms, fish morbidity	Coral gardens, beach and lagoon clean-up campaigns, changed marketing strategies
Changed ocean currents and/or wind patterns	Coastal erosion, land loss, changed surfing conditions, dangerous swimming conditions	Most of the above, plus strengthened early warning, awareness and safety programmes
Elevated air temperatures	Heat stress for humans, plants and animals, vector-borne diseases	Activity options, education and awareness raising, shade plants and structures, deep ocean water cooling systems, upgraded health-care facilities, mosquito fogging, vegetation and water body management
Increased rainfall variability and greater extremes	Drought, flooding	Water conservation, storage and reuse, rainwater harvesting, improved storm-water management
Extreme high winds	Outside activities curtailed, structural damage	Early warning, strengthened safety programmes, alternative activity options, building design

a geographical variation of sea-level rise resulting from non-uniform distribution of temperature and salinity and changes in ocean circulation. Local variations from this global average are also influenced by island tectonics and postglacial isostatic adjustment. For the Maldives, specifically, Woodworth (2005, in Mimura *et al.*, 2007) concluded that a rise in sea level of approximately 50 cm during the 21st century remains the most reliable scenario. In the meantime, the IPCC projections of sea-level rise have been discussed as being too conservative, and actual levels will depend especially on the rate of melting of the Greenland ice masses.

The effects of sea-surface warming on coral reefs in the Maldives are reflected in the increased incidence of coral bleaching and mortality events (Ministry of Environment and Construction, 2004). Coral bleaching events occurred in the Maldives in 1977, 1983, 1987, 1991, 1995, 1997 and 1998, with the last event being the most severe as almost all the shallow reefs in the country were affected. Average live coral cover before and after the bleaching was approximately 45% and 5%, respectively (Ministry of Home Affairs, Housing and Environment, 2001). Bleaching events, as well as slow recovery, have significant consequences for the tourism sector.

Hay (2006) has evaluated the likelihood (i.e. probability) components of climate-related risks in the Maldives for both present-day and future conditions. Changes over time reflect the influence of global warming. The risks evaluated are extreme rainfall events (both 3-hourly and daily), drought, high sea levels, extreme winds and extreme high air temperatures (Fig. 6.1). Projections of future climate-related risk are based on the output of global climate models, for given emission scenarios. All the likelihood components of the climate-related risks show increases as a result of global warming.

The observed long-term trend in relative sea level for Hulhulé, a resort island close to the Maldivian capital of Malé, is 1.7 mm/year, but the maximum hourly sea level has increased by approximately 7 mm/year, a rate far in excess of the observed local and global trends in mean sea level. For Hulhulé, an hourly sea level of 70 cm above mean sea level is currently a 100-year event. It will be likely to be at least an annual event by 2050. There is relatively high confidence in projections of maximum temperature. The annual maximum daily temperature is projected to increase by around 1.5°C by 2100. A

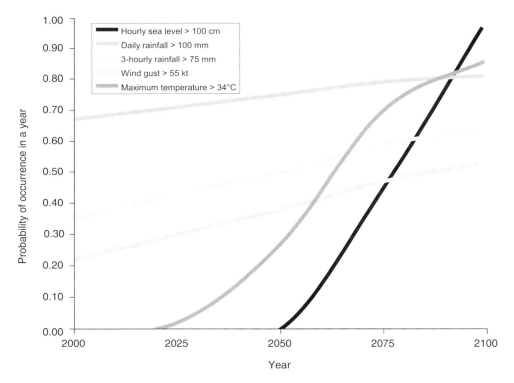

Fig. 6.1. Composite climate risk profile for Hulhulé (a resort island close to the Maldivian capital of Malé) showing the probability of listed climate events occurring in any one year, based on observed data for 2000 and projected to 2100 using best estimates of changes calculated from an average of the estimates for a multi model and emission scenario ensemble. (Source: Hay, 2006.)

maximum temperature of 33.5°C is currently a 20-year event. It will be likely to have a return period of 3 years by 2025.

No significant long-term trends are evident in the observed daily, monthly, annual or maximum daily rainfall. Currently, a daily rainfall of at least 160 mm is a relatively rare event at Hulhulé, with a return period of 17 years. There is large uncertainty in the rainfall projections, with one of the four global climate models indicating a decrease in rainfall in the future. An extreme daily rainfall of 180 mm is currently a 100-year event. It will be likely to occur twice as often, on average, by 2050. An extreme 3-hourly rainfall of 100 mm is currently a 25-year event. It will be likely to become at least twice as common, on average, by around 2050. A monthly rainfall below the tenth percentile is used as an indicator of drought. Drought frequency is likely to be lower in the first half of the present century, relative to the latter part of the last century and the second half of the present century. Currently, an extreme wind gust of 60 kt has a return period of 16 years. It is estimated that this will reduce to 9 years by 2025.

Perception of Climate Change Risks by Tourism Stakeholders

Theoretical background

Risk perception is the process through which individuals and communities form impressions about threats to the things they value. Unlike the assessments of climate scientists described above, risk perceptions are not technical calculations of likelihood and magnitude, but subjective evaluations formed through experience (both personal and vicarious) and personality dispositions which, within a cultural context, combine to direct attitudes and behaviour.

Common foci of the risk perception literature have been studies of how people characterize risk, of the accuracy of public perceptions of risk, of attitudes toward risk acceptability, and of how knowledge about risk perception can contribute to effective policy (Espiner, 2001). Among the conclusions drawn has been the claim that the public does not interpret risk in the same way as experts (Slovic, 2000; Gaskell and Allum, 2001; Sjöberg and Drottz-Sjöberg, 2008). Compared with technical experts, the public typically overestimate the threat of high-magnitude, low-frequency events and underestimate the threat of slow-to-accumulate risks (Slovic *et al.*, 1980). For members of the general public, the highest risk perceptions are held for those threats that involve severe, immediate and dreaded consequences (Slovic, 2000). The public–expert disparity is important to acknowledge because while the risk assessments of experts help to direct policy and risk-management decisions, the perceptions of the public reflect significant social and moral values and will direct behaviour, including willingness to adopt new management practices.

Multiple reasons have been suggested for the differences between public risk and expert risk assessments, including incomplete and sometimes contradictory data, complex theories and the unwillingness of some experts to understand public concerns (Leiss and Chociolko, 1994). While experts' assessments are made using algorithmic methods, the general public tends to rely on heuristic procedures such as the prominence or perceived frequency of events. If an event is easy to imagine or recall, its threat will be judged as more likely. This inferential strategy is known as the 'availability heuristic' and can help to explain why risk perceptions are sometimes inaccurate (Slovic, 2000; Tversky and Kahneman, 1982).

Risk perception is not purely a cognitive process; it is strongly influenced by emotional factors and images, as well as by experiential processes (Leiserowitz, 2006). Furthermore, understanding risk interpretations can be informed by knowledge of the sociocultural context, a feature acknowledged in the pioneering cultural theory work of Douglas and Wildavsky (1982), who emphasized that, in making judgements about risks, people act 'as social beings who have internalised social pressures and delegated their decision-making processes to institutions'. Hence, group membership and cultural values are likely to influence the ways in which people attend to some threats and ignore others.

Despite considerable academic literature on both the study of risk perception and that of climate change, few researchers have examined how climate change risks are perceived by the public (Leiserowitz, 2007). Siegrist (2008) suggested that the public's perception of climate change as a risk is likely to be moderated by the following challenges:

- Difficulties in thinking probabilistically;
- Difficulties in applying a systems-based approach;
- A lack of cultural discourse within which the debate can be placed; and
- Frustration, denial and apathy as a result of the perceived lack of scientific consensus.

Stakeholder interviews

To gain some understanding of how tourism stakeholders in the Maldives perceive the relative threat of climate change in the wider context of tourism sustainability, 16 interviews were undertaken in 2009. These were carried out face to face by a doctoral student from the Maldives. The interviewees represented different industry sectors (four accommodation, two activities, two services and four transport), three government organizations and the Maldives Association of Tourism Industry.

While exploratory in nature, the interviews highlighted a number of interesting aspects. Awareness of climate change was found to be high among stakeholders; however, actual concern about impacts on the Maldives was comparatively low. Almost all interviewees considered other risks to the tourism industry as being more important and urgent. The global economic recession and its potential repercussions on tourist arrivals was the main concern, followed by perceived over-investment in luxury resorts (at the expense of mid-range accommodation), shortage of skilled local labour, foreign influence on the ownership and operation of resorts and environmental issues (e.g. waste disposal and ecosystem degradation). Those who explicitly stated that climate change was not a risk provided explanations such as the degree of uncertainty ('It is all theory'), the long timescale of climate change ('It is a very long-term risk', 'We will survive for 100 years'), or justified their perspectives through reference to cultural values ('I strongly believe that the Mother Nature will compensate it somehow'). The latter statement was confirmed indirectly by a government representative stating that 'most people will give you a perfect text book answer, but their behaviour and habits will tell you that they do not actually believe it' as 'people consider this to be a divine act'. Reflective of their mandate, all the government representatives interviewed displayed higher levels of concern and knowledge than the industry representatives.

Two interesting perspectives emerged that reflect the specific nature of tourism as an industry that sells pleasure and – at the same time – is highly mobile. One interviewee pointed out that talking too much about climate change impacts in the Maldives 'may have negative impacts and people might not come here anymore' because they get scared. Just like tourists who may choose to visit other destinations, tour operators are also flexible in adjusting their destination portfolios. The resident manager of a large European tour operator noted that 'if all the islands are flooded we will not send any more clients; we will just divert them to another destination'. This operator's planning is for the next 5 to 10 years, which was also confirmed in other interviews with respect to the investment payback times for tourist resorts (about 5 years). Hence, tourism operators – especially those from outside the Maldives – are governed by very short time frames within which climate change is not considered a risk. Only a small number of the companies interviewed reported that they undertake formal risk assessments.

Despite the lack of initiatives to address climate change for their own businesses, operators interviewed were able to report 'perceived' impacts of climate change to date. These included the increasing unpredictability of the weather, in particular in relation to the monsoon, coral bleaching, warmer temperatures, stronger winds and beach erosion. The interview with the representative of the Ministry of Housing, Transport and Environment revealed that some of these impacts are not necessarily caused by climate change but by 'lack of knowledge' (e.g. with respect to coastal management and the building of structures) and poor environmental practices. It was also observed by other interviewees that the environmental standards are poorly implemented and insufficiently policed. When the interview addressed the implementation of measures to reduce vulnerability to climate change (adaptation), it became clear that respondents knew very little or nothing about what adaptation means and what could be done for tourism in the Maldives. Most interviewees immediately talked about sustainable tourism with a focus on environmental measures, 'green tourism', the announced carbon neutrality of the Maldives and the benefits for marketing an environmentally sound destination. Interestingly, there was wide support for these kinds of initiatives. All of the suggested measures relate to reducing greenhouse gas emissions (i.e. increasing sustainability within the Maldives) rather than addressing climate change impacts. Only one industry representative commented on the benefit of environmental protection with respect to increasing the destination's resilience (for climate change and other stressors), and another discussed the possibility of identifying those islands that might be better suited for development than others (e.g. in respect of elevation, erosion, wind).

The Maldives government was seen as the key player to address climate change ('Government has to do 90% of the work to solve this issue'), and most interviewees pointed to the need for more and better information, discussion forums and workshops, and demonstrations of practical measures. Trust in the government was generally high: 'If the government is telling us this is happening, then that means they have facts, and facts are collected by experts, if not they should not bring it up'. Government's role was also seen as one of coordination: 'the Tourism Ministry needs to play a very big role in linking tourism businesses and the other relevant government bodies'. Recognizing some of these responsibilities, the government representatives who were interviewed pointed consistently at barriers such as the lack of capacity and financial resources.

Policy Implications

The current success of tourism in the Maldives is the combined result of a clear vision and public–private partnership. The government and the tourist industry have agreed that the main tourism asset is the marine environment, and in order to manage it sustainably the government should set the industry very high standards. All resorts are required to have environmentally sound incinerators and sewage-treatment facilities. The resorts produce water for consumption through desalination technology, and in this way island groundwater is preserved. Mandatory environmental impact assessment is used to ensure that tourism development has minimal impact on the natural environment. Coral from the reefs cannot be used for any construction on a tourist resort; not more than 20% of an island may be cleared of bushes and other vegetation, and for construction and for building purposes a minimum setback limit of 5 m from the vegetation line of the island is required. The reality, as indicated by some interviewees above, may differ from the theoretical aspirations of environmental standards (see also Zubair *et al.*, 2010). This is likely to compromise the resilience of the Maldives' ecosystems to climate change.

The tourism sector in the Maldives is currently doing little to address the growing risks to the sector as a consequence of climate change. This becomes evident in the lack of concern among key stakeholders, limited (tourism-related) information on how to adapt and a lack of practical initiatives to illustrate adaptation. A mix of reef restoration and 'soft' coastal protection, for example, would do much to enhance the longevity of both resort islands and tourism-dependent communities. The main barriers are a lack of capacity (including awareness and knowledge), trained personnel and institutional support. These are exacerbated by the inability to finance measures that proactively reduce risks.

For a long-term sustainable tourism industry, and building on the many adaptation efforts in other sectors in the Maldives, tourism could engage in climate change adaptation through:

1. Development and implementation of national policies, regulation and coordination specifically for climate change adaptation.
2. Demonstration of effective adaptation initiatives for tourism operators.
3. Development of a risk communication strategy to ensure wide dissemination of knowledge on adaptation measures and mainstream these into everyday decision making.

The government's role is clearly seen as one of leadership and responsibility with respect to addressing climate change. The Tourism Master Plan already provides a useful framework for national tourism policy; however, currently it lacks specific consideration of climate change impacts. Operational procedures, such as tendering for new tourism investments and budget allocations to inhabited islands, could explicitly take into account future projections of sea-level rise, among other factors. The use of policy- and decision-support tools (e.g. strategic environmental assessment) could be beneficial. All of these require institutional strengthening for the Ministry of Tourism, the Ministry of Environment, Energy and Water, the Ministry of Atolls Development and other government agencies to improve coordination and support sound environmental management practices in the tourism sector. Longer term, the sector would benefit from improved projections of climate change, for example by working with the Meteorological Service of the Maldives.

Successful implementation of specific adaptation measures for tourism businesses would be facilitated by providing case-study findings for successful adaptation technologies and lessons learned (including costs), and good-practice guidelines for various sub-sectors. For example, safari boats are already seeking to reduce the adverse impacts of weather and climate extremes and variability, and different adaptation strategies could be shared more widely. Part of an operator-based approach to adaptation is a holistic perspective that seeks to strengthen the resilience of the natural resource base more widely. A key issue in the Maldives is the management of solid waste, and efforts to reduce, reuse and ensure sound disposal will contribute to more environmentally sound ecosystems. Similarly, the resilience of reef ecosystems can be enhanced through improved conservation practices, including deployment and use of mooring buoys, upgraded waste-water management (such as atoll transfer stations for receiving waste water from safari boats), coral restoration efforts (e.g. coral gardening), sustainable use of the reef fishery and related conservation activities.

The interviews reported above have shown that the concern about climate change among tourism stakeholders is low, a situation that must be addressed if adaptation measures are to be taken seriously within this crucial industry. A range of communication strategies are conceivable, for example public workshops, media releases and interactive internet websites (e.g. Facebook), the establishment of a 'national small islands knowledge centre', training courses or the inclusion of climate change into curricula, for example the curricula of the Maldives College of Higher Education. Given the general awareness about climate change, such initiatives are likely to meet fertile ground. Communication strategies for tourism stakeholders within the Maldives could build on the already successful campaigns that the President is running to raise awareness overseas. However, as observed by Patt and Schroeter (2008), it is critical to include people early on when seeking to promote the potential threats posed by climate change and designing strategies to respond to these risks. Early participation also increases the social sustainability of policy development and implementation.

Conclusions

The climate change risks for tourism in the Maldives are significant and adaptation measures are required to reduce the vulnerability of tourism businesses, infrastructure and communities. Adaptation measures need to be seen as an integral part of sustainable tourism development in the Maldives more generally, and win–win strategies that reduce climate risks and enhance sustainability are the preferred options. This is even more important given that the manifestations of climate change, in particular timescales, are characterized by uncertainty; it is this lack of scientific precision that contributes to the limited priority given to climate change by tourism stakeholders in the Maldives. In addition, it is likely that participants in the tourism industry are responding in a way similar to that we would expect from members of a non-scientific community when it comes to forming risk perceptions about outcomes which do not involve dreaded, immediately apparent consequences (Slovic, 2000). Awareness and risk perception among Maldivians' tourism stakeholders were found to be driven by economic agendas, perceived knowledge, environmental values, political agendas and world views (e.g. 'myths of nature') (Etkin and Ho, 2007). It also became apparent that some tourism operators perceive the risk of climate change in the light of the benefit they receive from tourism, rather than the potential harm that climate change might pose, thus confirming the findings of an earlier study that showed an inverse relationship between human benefits and perceived ecological risk (McDaniels et al., 1996). All of these factors may lead to a 'status quo bias', in which actors tend to take no action in the face of an uncertain mix of positive and negative effects, lack of control and perceived responsibility (Patt and Schroeter, 2008).

This lack of concern and initiative needs to be addressed because 'the failure of SIDS (small island developing states) to invest in policies to respond to climate change may leave them poorly prepared to cope with adverse changes and also increases the probability of severe consequences' (Belle and Bramwell, 2005). This present chapter demonstrates the gap between the scientific community and tourism stakeholders in the Maldives (with a few exceptions) in terms of understanding, awareness and perception of risks associated with climate change. In addition, there is a gap between policy makers, who are concerned about climate change and plan to address it, and other members of the tourism sector, including those related to marketing, who do not perceive the risk of climate change as an immediate one. This 'disagreement' is problematic and may pose a challenge for implementing climate change adaptation strategies (Patt and Schroeter, 2008). A participatory approach to communication, knowledge dissemination and strategy development is therefore highly recommended.

Acknowledgement

We acknowledge the effort by Irfan Zhaki in undertaking the 16 stakeholder interviews. The data informed this book chapter and complemented work undertaken by John Hay as lead consultant in an UNWTO (United Nations World Tourism Organization) project to develop a GEF (Global Environment Facility)-funded project on climate change and tourism in the Maldives.

References

Agnew, M. and Palutikof, J. (2006) Impacts of short-term climate variability in the UK on demand for domestic and international tourism. *Climate Research* 31, 109–120.

Ajzen, I. and Fishbein, M. (2005) The influence of attitudes on behavior. In: Albarracín, D., Johnson, B.T. and Zanna, M.P. (eds) *The Handbook of Attitudes*. Erlbaum, Mahwah, New Jersey, pp. 173–221.

Barnett, J. and Adger, N. (2003) Climate dangers and atoll countries. *Climatic Change* 61, 321–337.

Becken, S. and Clapcott, R. (2010) Developing public policy for climate change in the tourism sector. *Journal of Policy Research in Tourism, Leisure and Events* (in press).

Becken, S. and Hay, J. (2007) *Tourism and Climate Change – Risks and Opportunities*. Channel View Publications, Clevedon, UK.

Belle, N. and Bramwell, B. (2005) Climate change and small island tourism: policy maker and industry perspectives in Barbados. *Journal of Travel Research* 44, 32–41.

Douglas, M. and Wildavsky, A. (1982) *Risk and Culture: An Essay on the Selection of Technical And Environmental Dangers*. University of California Press, Los Angeles, California.

Espiner, S. (2001) The phenomenon of risk and its management in natural resource recreation and tourism settings: a case study of Fox and Franz Josef Glaciers, Westland National Park, New Zealand. Doctoral thesis, Lincoln University, New Zealand.

Etkin, D. and Ho, E. (2007) Climate change: perceptions and discourses of risk. *Journal of Risk Research* 10, 623–641.

Gaskell, G. and Allum, N. (2001) Sound science, problematic publics? Contrasting representations of risk and uncertainty. *Politeia* 63, 13–25.

Hay, J.E. (2006) *Climate Risk Profile for the Maldives. Report prepared for the Government of the Maldives*. Ministry of Environment, Energy and Water, Malé, Maldives.

Hay, J., Vereczi, G., Abdulla, A. and Saleem, A. (2008) *Integrating Tourism into Adaptation to Climate Change in the Maldives. Summary Report of the Initial Consultations*. Ministry of Environment, Energy and Water, Government of the

Maldives, Malé/United Nations World Tourism Organization, Madrid.

Leiserowitz, A. (2006) Climate change risk perception and policy preferences: the role of affect, imagery, and values. *Climatic Change* 77, 45–72.

Leiserowitz, A. (2007) *International Public Opinion, Perception, and Understanding of Global Climate Change.* Human Development Report Occasional Paper 2007/31, Human Development Report Office, United Nations Development Programme, New York.

Leiss, W. and Chociolko, C. (1994) *Risk and Responsibility.* McGill-Queens University Press, Quebec.

McDaniels, T., Axelrod, L.J. and Slovic, P. (1996) Perceived ecological risks of global change. *Global Environmental Change* 6, 159–171.

Mimura, N., Nurse, L., McLean, R.F., Agard, J., Briguglio, L., Lefale, P., Payet, R. and Sem, G. (2007). Small islands. In: Parry, M.L., Canziani, O.F., Palutikof, J.P., van der Linden P.J. and Hanson, C.E. (eds) *Climate Change 2007: Impacts, Adaptation and Vulnerability. Contribution of Working Group II to the Fourth Assessment Report of the Intergovernmental Panel on Climate Change.* Cambridge University Press, Cambridge, pp. 687–716.

Ministry of Environment and Construction (2004) *State of the Environment. Maldives 2004.* Malé, Maldives.

Ministry of Home Affairs, Housing and Environment (2001) *First National Communication of the Republic of Maldives to the United Nations Framework Convention on Climate Change.* Malé, Maldives.

Ministry of Planning and National Development (2005) *National Recovery and Reconstruction Plan: Programmes and Projects.* Malé, Maldives.

Ministry of Tourism and Civil Aviation (2007) *Maldives Third Tourism Master Plan 2007–2011.* Malé, Maldives. Available at:

www.tourism.gov.mv/downloads/ttmp. pdf (accessed 3 September 2010).

Patt, A.G. and Schroeter, D. (2008) Perceptions of climate risk in Mozambique: implications for the success of adaptation strategies. *Global Environmental Change* 18, 458–467.

Pizam, A., Tarlow, P.E. and Bloom, J. (1997) Making tourists feel safe: whose responsibility is it? *Journal of Travel Research* 36, 23–28.

Siegrist, M. (2008) *Public Risk Perception of Climate Change.* Swiss Federal Institute of Technology, Zurich. Available at: http://www.sec.ethz.ch/education/HS2008/701151000L/StDo/Presentation_risk_perception_CC.pdf (accessed 3 September 2010).

Sjöberg, L. and Drottz-Sjöberg, B. (2008) Risk perception by politicians and the public. *Energy and Environment* 19, 455–483.

Slovic, P. (2000) Informing and educating the public about risk. In: Slovic, P. (ed.) *The Perception of Risk.* Earthscan Publications, London, pp. 182–198.

Slovic, P., Fischhoff, B. and Lichtenstein, S. (1980) Facts and fears: understanding perceived risk. In: Schwing, R.C. and Albers, W.A. (eds) *Societal Risk Assessment: How Safe is Safe Enough?* Plenum Press, New York, pp. 181–214.

Sönmez, S.F. and Graefe, A.R. (1998) Influence of terrorism risk on foreign tourism decisions. *Annals of Tourism Research* 25, 112–144.

Tversky, A. and Kahneman, D. (1982) Availability: a heuristic for judging frequency and probability. In: Kahneman, D., Slovic, P. and Tversky, A. (eds) *Judgment Under Uncertainty: Heuristics and Biases.* Cambridge University Press, New York, pp. 163–178.

Zubair, S., Bowen, D. and Elwin, J. (2010) Not quite paradise: inadequacies of environmental impact assessment in the Maldives. *Tourism Management*, doi:10.1016/j.tourman.2009.12.007.

II Socially Sustainable Perspectives of Island Tourism

7 Host and Guest Perceptions of Tourism Impacts in Island Settings: a Malaysian Perspective

FATHILAH ISMAIL[1], BRIAN KING[2] AND RANJITH IHALANAYAKE[2]

[1]University Malaysia, Terengganu, Malaysia; [2]Victoria University, Victoria, Australia

Introduction

Malaysia is located in South-east Asia and consists of two major parts, namely Peninsular Malaysia and East Malaysia. With a land area of over 330,000 km^2, it includes hundreds of islands, of which six are considered to be large islands. Malaysia is culturally diverse and its population of 27 million (2007) is made up of several ethnic groupings, including Malays (50.4%), Chinese (23.7%), indigenous (11%), Indians (7.1%) and others (7.8%). Islam is the predominant religion, though there are numbers of other groups, including Buddhists, Taoists, Hindus, Christians and Sikhs.

Malaysia's economy is one of the fastest growing in South-east Asia and according to the International Monetary Fund, its gross domestic product (GDP) was ranked 39th in the world in 2008. The economic system may be described as an open state-oriented market approach. Services and manufacturing account for 51% and 36% of the economy, respectively, with agriculture accounting for a further 13%. Major industries include rubber and palm oil, manufacturing, petroleum production and refining, electronics, tin mining, and logging and timber processing. Tourism has played an increasing role within Malaysia's services sector since the establishment of the first government Department of Tourism in 1959.

The government has actively developed tourism as a potential source of foreign exchange, employment and other economic and non-economic benefits. This process has been assisted by Malaysia's endowment of a variety of natural, cultural and man-made attractions, which attract domestic and international tourists. These attractions include beaches, tropical islands surrounded by pristine coral reefs, 19 national parks, jungles, hill resorts and South-east Asia's highest mountain, Mount Kinabalu (in East Malaysia). In terms of cultural appeal, Malaysia incorporates a blend of centuries-old cultures, arts and traditions, and of multi-racial, multi-ethnic and multi-religion communities. Ethnic diversity is well established and is manifest through the wide range of languages, costumes, festivals, cuisine and crafts. The recent expansion of commercial and industrial activity has diversified Malaysia's appeal by providing a basis to position the destination for shopping, sport and health tourism, and as a hub for the meetings, incentives, conventions and exhibitions (MICE) market. Malaysia is also a price-competitive destination.

The first major expansion of Malaysian tourism occurred during the 1980s. During this decade Malaysia recorded an average growth for international arrivals of 12.7% annually, although growth stagnated over the following 5 years (1991–1995) (see Table 7.1). This setback can be attributed to the Asian financial crisis and to health scares (e.g. from Coxsackie viruses). During the latter 1990s (1996–2000) international arrivals staged a recovery and an average growth rate of 6% was reported. Despite recent threats to tourism such as the 11 September 2001 terrorist attacks, the Iraq War and bird flu, Malaysia's tourism sector demonstrated resilience during the period 2001–2006, with international arrivals registering double-digit annual growth (10%). Table 7.1 indicates that income from international tourism grew much faster than international arrivals. During the 1990–1995 period, international tourism receipts grew at an average annual rate of 16.5%, while international arrivals were restricted to growth of 0.1%. Similar growth was reported during the period that followed, and international tourism receipts exceeded US$10 billion in 2006.

As indicated in Table 7.1, the Association of Southeast Asian Nations (ASEAN) has been the dominant tourism source market over recent years. ASEAN countries accounted for almost 74% of total international arrivals in 1990 and this increased to almost 79% in 2006. This large share is indicative of Malaysia's reliance on short-haul markets. Of the ASEAN countries, Singapore accounted for 61% of total arrivals to Malaysia in 1990. Although this share had declined to 55% by 2006, Singapore remains the most prominent source of international arrivals. Outside the ASEAN countries, Japan is the second source of international arrivals, with a share of almost 7% in 1990, followed by Taiwan with slightly under 3% of total arrivals. By 2006, the share of these markets had declined considerably. Contrary to the prevailing trend in many developing regions of the world, traditional long-haul markets such as the UK, USA and Australia have shown less interest in Malaysia as a destination. Each of these source markets accounted for a market share of 2–3% of international arrivals in 1990, but this declined over the period to 2006.

Despite the growth of international arrivals during recent decades, the tourism sector faces two major challenges. The first is its reliance on a single generating market, namely ASEAN countries (in general) and Singapore (in particular). Such market concentration is unhealthy from both an economic and a political perspective. The economic impact of tourism is lower from short-haul source markets, and Malaysia has lagged behind its major competitors in terms of tourism receipts, compared with arrivals. A second factor has been

Table 7.1. Economic significance of international tourism in Malaysia, 1990–2006. (Source: Ismail, 2009.)

Country/Region	1990 Arrivals		1995 Arrivals			2000 Arrivals			2006 Arrivals		
	Number	%	Number	%	AAGR (%)[a]	Number	%	AAGR (%)	Number	%	AAGR (%)
ASEAN countries[b]	5,495,150	73.8	5,537,312	74.1	0.2	7,190,421	71.7	5.4	13,824,631	78.8	11.5
Singapore	4,569,127	61.4	4,537,347	60.7	(0.1)	5,420,200	54.1	3.6	9,656,251	55.0	10.1
Thailand	514,691	6.9	530,254	7.1	0.6	940,215	9.4	12.1	1,891,921	10.8	12.4
Indonesia	139,896	1.9	233,996	3.1	10.8	545,051	5.4	18.4	1,217,024	6.9	14.3
Brunei	214,985	2.9	189,657	2.5	(2.5)	195,059	1.9	0.6	784,446	4.5	26.1
Philippines	56,451	0.8	46,058	0.6	(4.0)	81,927	0.8	12.2	211,123	1.2	17.1
Vietnam	–	–	–	–	–	7,969	0.1	–	63,866	0.4	41.5
Japan	507,764	6.8	330,725	4.4	(8.2)	455,981	4.5	6.6	354,213	2.0	(4.1)
China	6,895	0.1	103,130	1.4	71.8	425,246	4.2	32.8	439,294	2.5	0.5
Taiwan	193,575	2.6	293,896	3.9	8.7	213,016	2.1	(6.2)	181,829	1.0	(2.6)
Hong Kong	103,102	1.4	146,603	2.0	7.3	76,344	0.8	(12.2)	89,577	0.5	2.7
India	108,411	1.4	27,701	0.4	(23.9)	132,127	1.3	36.7	279,046	1.6	13.3
Australia	149,136	2.0	136,300	1.8	(1.8)	236,775	2.4	11.7	277,125	1.6	2.7
UK	196,320	2.6	164,489	2.2	(3.5)	237,757	2.4	7.7	252,035	1.4	1.0
USA	174,986	2.4	136,405	1.8	(4.9)	184,100	1.8	6.2	174,336	1.0	(0.9)
Other countries	510,569	6.9	592,188	8.0	3.0	870,815	8.8	8.0	1,674,777	9.6	11.5
Total	7,445,908	100.00	7,468,749	100.00	0.1	10,022,582	100.00	6.1	17,546,863	100.00	9.8
Tourism receipts (US$ bn)	1.4		3.0		16.5	5.2		11.6	10.9		13.1

[a]AAGR, Average annual growth rate.
[b]ASEAN, Association of Southeast Asian Nations.

the slow growth and decreasing market share of the traditional long-haul markets.

Malaysia urgently needs to diversify its markets and attract more visitors from long-haul sources such as Europe, the UK, the USA, Australia and New Zealand. As it pursues a policy of market diversification, one of Malaysia's greatest assets is its wide range of attractive smaller islands which are replete with natural resources. If marketed properly, small island tourism offers the prospect of providing Malaysia with a competitive advantage in long-haul markets, thereby assisting the longer-term sustainability of the sector. However, to achieve a successful outcome, it will be critical to understand the needs and expectations of visitors from these markets.

Across the world, for many small island destinations, economic development has proved elusive as a result of factors such as resource deficiencies, isolation, high transportation costs, constrained exports and an absence of economies of scale. However, in the case of islands with abundant natural attractions, tourism may offer the best prospects for economic growth and may even be needed to ensure community survival. To achieve economic viability and to minimize any potential damage to fragile island systems, such destinations need to be planned, developed and managed sustainably. Along with economic and ecological concerns, sociocultural factors play an important part in the pursuit of sustainability, because destinations need to accommodate the needs of both hosts and guests and to reconcile any diverging expectations. The interactions between local communities and tourists that occur in small island settings tend to be quite intense, leading to either positive or negative impacts. Irritation among local residents as a result of unsatisfactory interactions may undermine their willingness to participate in the pursuit of sustainable tourism and may reduce the prospects of economic benefits. Unsatisfactory interactions may also prompt visitors to choose other destinations that offer similar characteristics.

The importance of cross-cultural tourism settings has been increasingly acknowledged as tourism activity has expanded globally. Most islands in Malaysia have attracted some international tourists from different parts of the world, notably from Europe, North America, Australia and New Zealand. Visitors from these markets often come from cultural backgrounds that differ substantially from those of the local residents. In light of such differences, it is important to understand the potential impact of cultural differences on perceptions towards tourism development within a destination. The research described here investigates cross-cultural exchanges between hosts and guests, and the prospective impact of cultural differences on perceptions of tourism development in island settings. The study aims to determine whether:

1. There are differences in the socio-demographic profiles of host and guest communities in island settings within Malaysia.
2. Different perceptions of tourism are evident between host and guest communities in the case of small island destinations.
3. Different perceptions of tourism are evident across hosts and guests who have different cultural backgrounds.

Literature Review

Culture is a complex concept and many definitions have been proposed within the literature (Reisinger and Turner, 2003). In understanding the relationship between tourism and culture, it is important to consider the role played by values. Values are derived from culture and may be directly attributable to influences and controls evident within the cultural environment (Reisinger and Turner, 2003). Values and rules of behaviour have been summarized by Reisinger and Turner (2003) as being critical for comparing the cultural characteristics of hosts and guests. It may be argued that values play an important role in determining the prevailing rules of behaviour (Samovar and Porter, 1988), and they have been described as guiding and ranking behaviour (Peterson, 1979; Fridgen, 1991). As noted by Rokeach (1973), different values have different behavioural manifestations. Rules of behaviour help to define what is or is not socially acceptable, and such rules may differ substantially across cultural groups, including at the level of national subcultures (Harre and Secord, 1972). Within the literature, values and rules have been identified as exhibiting the greatest dichotomies in the case of comparisons between eastern and western cultures (Nakamura, 1964; Foa *et al.*, 1969; Hofstede, 1980).

It is important to understand cultural differences between hosts and guests in island tourism settings because such distinctions influence behaviours such as the consumption of goods, activities, preferences, eating habits and, ultimately, satisfaction and repeat visitation. Compatibility between and across cultural groups will influence whether tourism can be sustained, in that it may minimize negative interactions that undermine the host culture. Reisinger and Turner (1997) have noted the critical importance of identifying the cultural distinctions between hosts and guests for the development of marketing strategies and segmentation. Tourists appear more likely to visit a destination when the hosts understand the cultural backgrounds of tourists and when the tourists understand the host culture (Reisinger and Turner, 1998). Sensitivity to cultural differences will also determine the effectiveness of a destination when it attempts to compete in the increasingly global marketplace.

Much of the earlier tourism literature stressed the economic and physical impacts of tourism and placed less emphasis on its social aspects (Pizam, 1978). Although acknowledgement of the social, psychological and economic effects of tourists on host communities is not new (Jafari, 1973; Young, 1973; Pizam, 1978), recent studies have given greater attention to negative tourism impacts on the host community. It has been well documented that communities which have been negatively affected by tourism may retaliate by exhibiting hostile behaviour towards tourists, thereby reducing destination attractiveness. Tourism earnings and employment opportunities may also be affected. This experience suggests that tourism development should incorporate the opinions of host communities in order to build community support.

Resident perceptions are influenced by a range of factors, including cultural values, rules of behaviour, dependency on tourism spending and employment, host–guest interactions and the level of development (Murphy, 1985; Madrigal, 1995). Research has increasingly shown that negative perceptions of tourism are associated with higher tourist densities, greater length of residency at the destination and native-born status (Pizam, 1978; Murphy, 1985; Liu *et al.*, 1987; Um and Crompton, 1987; Davis *et al.*, 1988; Canan and Hennessy, 1989; Madrigal, 1993, 1995). Positive perceptions of tourism are associated with distance travelled from the source market and economic reliance. Socio-economic variables appear to have little effect on resident perceptions of tourism (Pizam, 1978; Liu and Var, 1986; Madrigal, 1993). An inverse relationship is evident between the level of tourism development and host perceptions of the impacts of tourism. Lower-to-moderate levels of tourism development appear to be more beneficial for the local population. However, resident perceptions show a downwards trend when development continues beyond a certain point (Doxey, 1976; Butler, 1980; Allen *et al.*, 1988; Gunn, 1988). If a tourism destination is to thrive in an ecologically sustainable manner, adverse impacts need to be minimized and overall impacts need to be viewed favourably by residents (Ap, 1992).

Considerable research has been undertaken on resident perceptions towards tourism generally, but relatively fewer studies have examined small islands, particularly in the case of Malaysia. When the significance and growth potential of tourism in Malaysia's small islands is considered, it is clear that a study of resident and guest perceptions of tourism is timely. This chapter identifies the positive and negative impacts of tourism as perceived by both parties. The approach addresses the concern that previous studies on tourism impacts in island settings have focused primarily on the views of hosts and have neglected the views of tourists.

Scope of Study

The primary aim of this study is to investigate the different cultural backgrounds of host and guest communities in small island settings and the influence of culture on perceptions of tourism impacts. It is anticipated that relationships between cultural diversity and perceptions will be more complex in the case of smaller, close-knit communities relative to those in larger and more dispersed communities. A mix of smaller and larger destinations has been selected within Malaysia in order to measure such differences. Data were collected at three island locations off the coast of Peninsular Malaysia, namely Perhentian, Redang and Langkawi. Two of the islands, Perhentian (13.92 km^2) and Redang (10.32 km^2), are smaller and one is relatively larger Langkawi (478.47 km^2). Perhentian and Redang Islands are the most visited small islands in Malaysia relative to other small islands in Peninsular Malaysia and were selected because:

- Physical isolation has meant that relative to other larger island communities, the residents of these islands appear to be more committed than others to their customs and culture and more sensitive to cultural concerns.

- Because tourism is the major economic activity, the host communities are likely to be concerned about issues of sustainability and about impacts on resident welfare.
- Residents interact with tourists frequently and intensely and must share the limited island facilities. Tourist–host differences are likely to be more obvious in such contexts.
- Most Perhentian and Redang Island residents are Muslim and follow more traditional belief systems than is the case with their counterparts on other Malaysian islands. Thus, attributing the influence of a single predominant religion on tourist interactions should be easier in these settings than in islands where the coexistence of various religions is commonplace.
- Perhentian and Redang are Malaysia's most popular small island destinations and attract international tourists from diverse cultural backgrounds. The conspicuous juxtaposition of tourists from a variety of different cultural and national backgrounds should assist the task of measurement.

The name 'Perhentian Island' (or Pulau Perhentian) is used here to refer to two islands, Perhentian Besar and Perhentian Kecil. These islands form part of a small archipelago located approximately 19 km off the coast of north-eastern Malaysia in the state of Terengganu (refer to Fig. 7.1). The main tourist accommodation consists of chalets and resorts, with most of these located on Perhentian Besar. The largest local community (2000 Malays) is a small village on Perhentian Kecil. Perhentian Island is only accessible by boat via Kuala Besut, Terengganu. Before the onset of tourism development, the main economic activity was fishing. When the island was declared a marine park, fishing was prohibited and the fishing industry proceeded to disappear. Today, tourism is the dominant source of employment and of economic activity.

Redang Island (or Pulau Redang) is located (about 45 km) off the coast of Terengganu in East Peninsular Malaysia (Fig. 7.1). It forms part of a small archipelago consisting of nine islands with Redang being the biggest and the only one to offer resort and chalet facilities. About 1000 people (mostly Malays) live on this island and tourism is the major economic activity. Fishing is prohibited and Redang is an important turtle conservation site. There is small airport on the island with direct services from Kuala Lumpur. The island is also accessible by boat via two jetties located at Kuala Terengganu and Merang in Terengganu.

Langkawi Island (Pulau Langkawi) is located off the north-western coast of Peninsular Malaysia in the state of Kedah (Fig. 7.1), and is the largest island within an archipelago of 99 islands. The population of 65,000 is predominantly Malay, with Chinese, Indians and Thais comprising small minorities. Langkawi can be reached by air through Kuala Lumpur and Singapore, or by sea from Satun (Thailand) and Belawan (Indonesia) via Penang. Before the development of tourism, the economy of Langkawi was primarily agricultural (rice and rubber production), with fishing also playing a part.

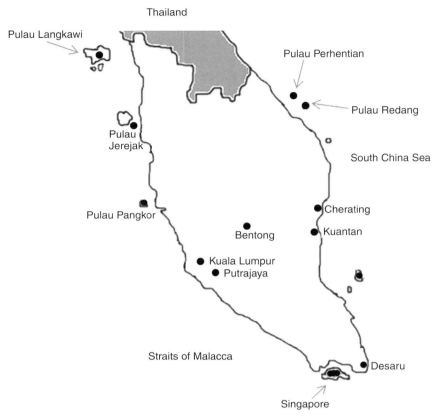

Fig. 7.1. Map of Peninsular Malaysia. (Source: Adapted from Holiday Inc. website, accessed 8 October 2007).

For the purposes of the present investigation Langkawi represents Malaysia's larger islands. It receives in excess of 2 million domestic and international tourists annually compared with Perhentian and Redang Islands, which receive about 40,000 each. Blessed with a variety of sea- and land-based activities and attractions as well as modern facilities and infrastructure, Langkawi has been actively marketed both locally and internationally. Langkawi attracts tourists from diverse market sources for a variety purposes, including holidaying, shopping, attending official events and business. Most tourists to Perhentian and Redang Islands visit for holiday purposes.

Arrivals to Perhentian and Redang are more seasonal because their location off the east coast of Peninsular Malaysia is affected by the monsoon season which runs from October to March. Unlike Langkawi, where tourists can visit all year round, Perhentian and Redang are closed to tourism during the monsoon season. Given the diminutive size of Perhentian and Redang compared with Langkawi, and the limited period of operation (6 months), annual arrivals of 40,000 may be considered as substantial. These two islands receive the highest number of arrivals of all smaller islands located off Peninsular

Malaysia. However, it is important to note that in contrast to Langkawi, which is managed by a single agency (Langkawi Development Authority, LADA) which takes responsibility for data gathering, complete and accurate arrival data is not available for the two smaller islands.

A small island may be defined as an island with a population less than one million or land area less than $1000 \ km^2$ (Bass and Dalal-Clayton, 1995), so all of the three islands investigated in the present study may be classified as small islands, though Langkawi is considered to be a larger island for comparison purposes.

Findings of Study

The following section reports the survey findings under three headings, namely host demographic profiles, tourist demographic profiles and principal components analysis.

Host demographic profiles

Occupation was the major demographic difference evident between host respondents on the smaller and larger islands. As they live on smaller islands with a narrower economic base, the Perhentian and Redang respondents expressed a heavier reliance on tourism for earning a living, with most being directly employed in tourism. The Langkawi respondents were involved in a wider range of economic activities that included agriculture and fishing as well as tourism. As residents of the biggest and most developed island off Peninsular Malaysia, with preferential duty-free status, the hosts on Langkawi are generally younger. The Langkawi hosts are engaged primarily in roles related to selling. Langkawi also attracts service providers from outside Malaysia, many from across the Thai border. These providers are largely engaged in restaurant-related roles.

Tourist demographic profiles

The demographic profiles of the tourist respondents on the two smaller islands and on Langkawi were distinguishable on the basis of age. More than 57% of the tourist respondents on Perhentian and Redang Islands were younger, and typically between 21 and 30 years old. In the case of Langkawi, only 33% of tourists were from this age group, indicative of an older age profile. In many small island destinations across Malaysia, water-based activities such as diving and snorkelling are major attractions and appeal to younger visitors. This may account for the higher number of younger respondents on Perhentian and Redang Islands. Tourists to Langkawi are attracted for a greater diversity of purposes, including holiday, shopping, attending official events and business.

Consistent with its broader appeal, Langkawi attracts a wider range of age groups.

The larger and smaller island destinations are distinguishable by the primary country of origin of tourists (European, English and Chinese). Langkawi attracts tourists from a wider range of source markets than Perhentian and Redang Islands. The major sources of European tourists to both destinations are Denmark, France, Germany, Italy, Netherlands, Sweden and Switzerland. In the case of Langkawi, tourists from the former Eastern Europe (e.g. Estonia and Hungary) are also prominent. The diversity of source markets may be explained by Langkawi's positioning as Malaysia's premier island destination and its diverse attractions which include both sea- and land-based activities. Langkawi has been extensively promoted in the domestic and international markets by both the private and by the government sectors. It is an important venue for meetings, courses and conferences, and hosts public and private sector organizations from both Malaysia and overseas.

Principal components analysis

Principal components analysis (PCA) was used to explore the relationships between the variables (perceptions of tourism impacts) that were explored by the survey, and identified perceptual groupings towards tourism development from among the respondents. The PCA approach identifies underlying structures across a large set of variables by focusing on a smaller set of components (Hair *et al.*, 2006). The survey instrument used in the present investigation incorporated 19 perceptions of tourism impacts. Various of the attributes have been used in previous studies (Belisle and Hoy, 1980; Brougham and Butler, 1981; Sheldon and Var, 1984; Liu *et al.*, 1987; Milman and Pizam, 1988; King *et al.*, 1993; Akis *et al.*, 1996). Table 7.2 presents the list of 19 perceptions of tourism impacts and provides an indication of whether the impact was perceived by respondents as being positive or negative.

The PCA provides a summary of the 19 perceptions of impacts grouped into constructs. The results are more readily interpretable when presented in this form than is the case when individual variables are compared. Table 7.3 presents the PCA analysis outputs from the perspective of both hosts and guests at the two destination types (smaller and larger islands) and outlines the constructs in terms of explained variance, rank order in terms of importance and positive or negative perceptions. Rotation selection was based on an eigenvalue of one, and VARIMAX rotation was undertaken to maximize the differences between constructs. The Kaiser-Meyer-Olkin measures of sampling adequacy (KMO) were above 0.6 for all sample groups, and Barlett's Sphericity Test was significant ($p = 0.000$), indicating that the data were suitable for the PCA (factor loadings of above 0.5 are deemed to be significant on the basis that there is a strong correlation between a particular group of variables; Tabachnick and Fidell, 2007).

Five components were extracted from the Perhentian and Redang host samples, comprising 63% of the explained variance. Only four components

Table 7.2. Perceptions of positive and negative tourism impacts.

Economic	Sociocultural	Environmental
Attracts investment (+)	Meeting locals/tourists is a valuable experience (+)	Improves the transportation system (+)
Increases standard of living (−)	Increases in recreational facilities (+)	Provides an incentive for the restoration of historic buildings (+)
Increases price of land and housing (−)	Undesirable impacts on local culture (−)	Provides an incentive for the conservation of natural resources (+)
Increases cost of living (−)	Local residents are exploited by tourists (−)	Results in unpleasantly crowded tourism locations (−)
Generates employment opportunities (+)	Increase in the crime rate (+)	Adds to pollution (−)
Increases the variety of goods for sale (+)		Destroys natural environment (−)
Improves public infrastructure (+)		
Increases price of goods and services (−)		

were extracted in the case of the Malay tourist samples, representing 67% of the explained variance. The PCAs for the other two groups generated five components, explaining 66% and 70% of the total variance respectively. The PCA for the Langkawi host sample also resulted in five components, with a similar explained variance of 64%. The PCA for the other three Langkawi tourist groups generated four components with total explained variance of above 60% (64% and 65%, respectively), except in the case of the English group (just below 60%).

Positive and negative perceptions towards the impacts of tourism are evident among respondents in both destinations. Negative perceptions are more evident (reporting a higher explained variance) in the smaller islands (Perhentian and Redang) than in Langkawi. English respondents had the strongest perceptions that tourism contributes to negative impacts (particularly price and environment), followed by Chinese respondents. Malays were generally more positively disposed, though they did express concern about the environmental impacts (e.g. litter, pollution, damage to coral reefs and overcrowding). Malay tourists on Langkawi identified some negative impacts of tourism on the local culture, including alcohol consumption and prostitution. Positive perceptions were more closely identified with economic prosperity, while negative perceptions were more strongly associated with social and environmental problems.

These findings confirm previous literature by Pizam (1978), Belisle and Hoy (1980), Sheldon and Var (1984), King, Pizam and Milman (1993) and Lankford (1994). The literature has asserted that hosts tend to form views of

Table 7.3. Perceptions of the impacts of tourism.

Sample group	Perthentian and Redang Islands			Langkawi Island		
	Factor	Impact	% of variance	Factor	Impact	% of variance
Hosts	1. Infrastructure	Positive	14.7	1. Economic opportunity and infrastructure	Positive	22.1
	2. Environment and culture	Negative	13.5	2. Environment and price	Negative	13.3
	3. Price	Negative	12.5	3. Conservation	Positive	10.1
	4. Economic opportunity and experience	Positive	11.6	4. Infrastructure and experience	Positive	10.0
	5. Conservation	Positive	10.4	5. Culture	Negative	8.9
Malay tourists	1. Environment	Negative	20.6	1. Environment and culture	Negative	29.0
	2. Conservation and infrastructure	Positive	16.4	2. Infrastructure	Positive	18.3
	3. Price	Negative	16.2	3. Price	Negative	10.5
	4. Economic opportunity	Positive	13.7	4. Conservation	Positive	6.5
Chinese tourists	1. Infrastructure	Positive	16.7	1. Economic opportunity and infrastructure	Positive	21.0
	2. Environment	Negative	15.3	2. Environment	Negative	18.7
	3. Price	Negative	14.5	3. Price	Negative	15.2
	4. Conservation	Positive	10.7	4. Conservation	Positive	9.6
	5. Economic opportunity	Positive	9.3			
English tourists	1. Price	Negative	19.8	1. Environment and culture	Negative	18.0
	2. Environment	Negative	17.3	2. Price	Negative	17.2
	3. Conservation	Positive	14.1	3. Infrastructure	Positive	13.5
	4. Infrastructure	Positive	11.0	4. Conservation	Positive	11.1
	5. Experience	Positive	7.7			

tourism based on their personal employment and welfare experiences. Host respondents in the current study appeared to view and articulate the positives more explicitly than guests, though they were less consistently positive in the case of smaller islands than in Langkawi.

Respondents on the smaller islands expressed concerns about exploitation and about the negative impacts on local culture. English tourists at both destinations (smaller and larger islands) expressed concern about price increases. Unlike the more self-contained Malay and Chinese respondents, the English welcomed opportunities for encounters with local residents. This finding supports the general hypothesis that perceptions towards tourism differ across cultural groups.

Culture-based perceptions can be used as a guideline in the planning and management of small islands. Unlike the other cultural groups, the host respondents in both the smaller and the larger islands expressed concern about the negative impacts of tourism on local culture. In responding to this finding, the Malaysian government should give consideration to such views when developing island tourism. Sensitive issues such as alcohol consumption and prostitution should be managed and monitored to avoid unnecessary impacts on local hosts. This should enhance the willingness of local hosts to accept tourists at the destination over the longer term.

The research findings revealed that English tourists are more concerned about environmental impacts than the other two tourist groups (Malays and Chinese). In order to sustain small island tourism and increase tourism earnings, different marketing strategies should be undertaken. Promotion activities need to be strengthened in long-haul markets such as Europe, the UK, the USA, Australia and New Zealand, while Malay and Chinese tourists could be encouraged to focus on destinations in mainland Malaysia where the environment is less fragile.

Gaining the goodwill of local communities is important for enhancing sustainable tourism growth on small islands. Offering activities that expose tourists to local culture and customs would be helpful. English tourists in particular seem to value the experience of meeting local people. Encouraging home-stay programmes on Malaysia's smaller islands may be worthwhile, given the importance of young independent travellers as a major source market for such destinations. A home-stay programme could benefit local hosts through income generation and assist younger tourists to travel cheaply. At the same time, it would safeguard the environment by lessening the need for new chalet and resort development to meet the demand for accommodation.

Tourism development on the smaller islands in Malaysia is occurring at a slow rate relative to the other larger island destinations generally and relative to Langkawi in particular. However, it is worth noting that information about the smaller islands is quite limited. One of the important aspects of destination planning and marketing is the availability of a comprehensive database of tourist arrivals. Unfortunately, data availability on arrivals to small islands in Malaysia is limited, and the reliability and validity of the available data is questionable. As reported in the research findings presented here, distinct tourist groups will have their own behavioural characteristics. In recognizing the role played by cultural diversity in tourism, information on tourist arrivals would be useful for developing island tourism in a sustainable manner. Serious effort is needed on the part of the Malaysian government to establish a complete and accurate database of tourist arrivals for small islands throughout Malaysia. One option would be to establish a single agency along the lines of the Langkawi Development Authority to manage small island tourism across Malaysia.

Concluding Remarks

This chapter has investigated the perspectives of hosts and guests towards tourism development in small island settings within Malaysia. It has been found that hosts generally responded favourably towards tourism, while expressing some awareness of the negative impacts. This finding is significant because, to date, tourist attitudes towards development have not been given serious consideration in Malaysia. The present chapter has provided evidence that both domestic and international tourists are concerned about the impacts of tourism in island settings. Impacts such as upward pressure on prices and pollution may affect tourist experiences and satisfaction in different ways. Dissatisfied tourists may shift their preferences towards alternative destinations that offer an equivalent climate and better products and services, and may encourage others to do the same via word-of-mouth communication. An understanding of the perceptions of tourism development from the different cultural perspectives of hosts and guests should be useful for developing applicable destination strategies, and a better understanding of cultural distinctions in different destination settings should enable the development of more tailored services and enhance host and guest satisfaction.

The research findings among hosts and guests suggest that tourism planning in fragile island settings should give close consideration to environmental protection. Both of these key audiences should receive regular notification that conservation is occurring and be reassured that strategies are in place to manage the potential impacts of tourism. Natural assets should be managed carefully in the interests of the longer-term survival of the destination. The average length of stay for travel to island destinations is typically short, and this provides only a brief window of opportunity to communicate the longer-term benefits of tourism to the island community. Some of the communication options include pamphlets, tour guide information and signs located at key tourist sites. Such information provision should explain how tourism contributes to preservation and protection, and provide the context of longer-term development issues. Conservation practices should address the concerns that have been expressed by both hosts and guests. Communications should explain why conservation is occurring and how it can be compatible with market-based tourism. Such communication can occur verbally or be incorporated into brochures and information booklets. Tourists can also be involved in the process of sustainability by being asked to provide suggestions, ideas and inputs about appropriate development. Relevant information could also be provided in response to the interest expressed by longer-haul tourists to have opportunities to meet with local residents.

Several constraints were applicable to the present investigation. Sample selection was a limitation. The research focused on cross-cultural exchanges between hosts and guests in small island settings and how cultural differences affect their behaviour and perceptions of tourism development. In light of the focus on cultural differences, the identification of sample groupings was based exclusively on language spoken. The grouping together of the English and Chinese respondents into single language groups was undertaken irrespective of country of residence. As the findings are based on these broader groupings, they may not represent the real behaviour of visitors from particular source nations, and any generalization of the findings therefore needs to be handled with caution. It is suggested that future research should be conducted on the basis of country of origin. The host respondent sample is a further limitation. During the data collection phase, approaches to older hosts were generally avoided because of the prevailing perception among this group that survey-based research is unfamiliar and of limited value. Owing largely to such selectivity, over 70% of the host respondents at both destinations (the smaller islands and Langkawi) were in the younger age groups. Given the skewed age range, respondent opinions may not be representative of the views that are prevalent within the wider community. On this basis, it is suggested that future research includes a wider range of respondent age groups. Notwithstanding these limitations, it is clear that the study contributes to the literature in the under-researched field of island tourism in Malaysia.

References

Akis, S., Peristianis, N. and Warner, J. (1996) Residents' attitudes to tourism development: the case of Cyprus. *Tourism Management* 17, 481–494.

Allen, L.R., Long, P.T., Perdue, R.R. and Kieselbach, S. (1988) The impact of tourism development on residents' perceptions of community life. *Journal of Travel Research* 27, 16–21.

Ap, J. (1992) Residents' perceptions on tourism impacts. *Annals of Tourism Research* 19, 665–690.

Bass, S. and Dalal-Clayton, B. (1995) *Small Island States and Sustainable Development: Strategic Issues and Experience.* International Institute for Environment and Development, London.

Belisle, F.J. and Hoy, D.R. (1980) The perceived impacts of tourism by residents: a case study in Santa Marta, Columbia. *Annals of Tourism Research* 7, 83–101.

Brougham, J.E. and Butler, R.W. (1981) A segmentation analysis of resident attitudes to the social impact of tourism. *Annals of Tourism Research* 8, 569–590.

Butler, R.W. (1980) The concept of a tourist area cycle of evolution: implications for management of resources. *Canadian Geographer* 24, 5–12.

Canan, P. and Hennessy, M. (1989) The growth machine, tourism and selling culture. *Sociological Perspectives* 32, 227–243.

Davis, D., Allen, J. and Cosenza, M. (1988) Segmenting local residents by their attitudes, interests and opinions toward tourism. *Journal of Travel Research* 27, 2–8.

Doxey, G. (1976) When enough is enough; the natives are restless in old Niagara. *Heritage Canada* 2, 26–27.

Foa, U.G., Mitchell, T.R. and Lekhyananda,

D. (1969) Cultural differences in reaction to failure. *International Journal of Psychology* 4, 21–26.

Fridgen, J.D. (1991) *Dimensions of Tourism.* Educational Institute, American Hotel and Motel Association, East Lansing, Michigan.

Gunn, C. (1988) *Tourism Planning.* Taylor and Francis, New York.

Hair, J.F., Black, W.C., Babin, B.J., Anderson, R.E. and Tatham, R.L. (2006) *Multivariate Data Analysis*, 6th edn. Pearson Education International, Upper Saddle River, New Jersey.

Harre, R. and Secord, P. (1972) *The Explanation of Social Behavior.* Blackwell, Oxford, UK.

Hofstede, G. (1980) *Culture's Consequences: International Differences in Work-related Values.* Sage Publications, Beverly Hills, California.

Ismail, F. (2009) The development of small island tourism in Malaysia. PhD thesis, Victoria University, Melbourne, Australia.

Jafari, J. (1973) Role of tourism on socioeconomic transformation of developing countries. MSc thesis, Cornell University, New York.

King, B., Pizam, A. and Milman, A. (1993) Social impacts of tourism: host perceptions. *Annals of Tourism Research* 20, 650–665.

Lankford, S.V. (1994) Attitudes and perceptions toward tourism and rural regional development. *Journal of Travel Research* 32, 35–43.

Liu, J.C., Sheldon, P.J. and Var, T. (1987) Resident perception of the environmental impacts of tourism. *Annals of Tourism Research* 14, 17–37.

Liu, J.C. and Var, T. (1986) Resident attitudes toward tourism impacts in Hawaii. *Annals of Tourism Research* 13, 193–214.

Madrigal, R. (1993) A tale of tourism in two cities. *Annals of Tourism Research* 20, 336–353.

Madrigal, R. (1995) Residents' perceptions and the role of government. *Annals of Tourism Research* 22, 86–102.

Milman, A. and Pizam, A. (1988) Social impacts of tourism on Central Florida. *Annals of Tourism Research* 15, 191–204.

Murphy, P.E. (1985) *Tourism: A Community Approach.* Routledge, New York.

Nakamura, H. (1964) *Ways of Thinking of Eastern Peoples.* East-West Center Press, Honolulu, Hawaii.

Peterson, R.A. (1979) Revitalizing the culture concept. *Annual Review of Sociology* 5, 137–165.

Pizam, A. (1978) Tourism impacts: the social costs to the destination community as perceived by its residents. *Journal of Travel Research* 16, 8–12.

Reisinger, Y. and Turner, L.W. (1997) Cross-cultural differences in tourism: Indonesian tourists in Australia. *Tourism Management* 18, 139–147.

Reisinger, Y. and Turner, L.W. (1998) Cultural differences between Mandarin-speaking tourists and Australian hosts and their impact on cross-cultural tourist-host interaction. *Journal of Business Research* 42, 175–187.

Reisinger, Y. and Turner, L.W. (2003) *Cross-cultural Behaviour in Tourism; Concepts and Analysis.* Butterworth-Heinemann, Oxford.

Rokeach, M. (1973) *The Nature of Human Values.* Free Press, New York.

Samovar, L.A. and Porter, R.E. (1988) *Intercultural Communication: A Reader*, 5th edn. Wadsworth Publishing, Belmont, California.

Sheldon, P.J. and Var, T. (1984) Resident attitudes to tourism in North Wales. *Tourism Management* 5, 40–47.

Tabachnick, B.G. and Fidell, L.S. (2007) *Using Multivariate Statistics*, 5th edn. Pearson Education, Upper Saddle River, New Jersey.

Um, S. and Crompton, J.L. (1987) Measuring resident's attachment levels in a host community. *Journal of Travel Research* 26, 27–29.

Young, G. (1973) *Tourism, Blessing of Blight.* Penguin Books, Harmondsworth, UK.

8

Island Casino Development: an Antithesis of Socioculturally Sustainable Tourism. The cases of St Croix and Christmas Island

JANNE LIBURD[1] AND JACK CARLSEN[2]

[1]University of Southern Denmark, Esbjerg, Denmark; [2]Curtin University, Western Australia

Introduction

Sustainable tourism development cannot be understood in isolation from the socio-political context in which it was born or from the spatial context in which it is adopted as a managerial philosophy (Liburd, 2010). As a socially constructed and contested concept (Bramwell, 2004), sustainability is often framed by the type of tourism development that is proposed and the interests of those affected by the development. One of the most contentious forms of tourism development on islands involves casinos and gambling, and the sociocultural impacts on island communities have been well documented. This chapter commences with a critical review of the literature on island casino development which demonstrates that tourism impact studies often rest on binary oppositions and a judgemental bias, in which one term not only becomes privileged at the expense of another (Bruner, 1994) but is at odds with the principles of sustainability. This may in part be the result of the lack of knowledge as to what forms of island tourism development are culturally acceptable to host communities and the absence of any clear guidelines on how to apply sustainability principles to the social and cultural dimensions of tourism development (Scott, 2004).

According to the Global Development Research Centre (2010) sustainable tourism 'in its purest sense is an industry which attempts to make a low impact on the environment and local culture, while helping to generate income, employment and the conservation of local ecosystems. It is responsible tourism which is both ecologically *and culturally* sensitive' [our italics].

This chapter sets out to facilitate an understanding of the sociocultural complexities at stake in island casino development and sustainability in the contexts of St Croix of the US Virgin Islands and Australia's Christmas Island (CI). Over the past three decades, casino gaming facilities have been proposed as a 'quick-fix' solution to stagnant economies in various settings. Inspired by the tourism impact studies of the 1970s (Smith, 1977, 1989; Hsu, 2000), considerable attention has been paid to residents' positive and negative perceptions of casino development in their communities (Ap, 1990; Long *et al.*, 1990; Lee and Back, 2003, 2006; Lee *et al.*, 2010). Harrison (1996) identified the tenuous links between the 'quasi-paradigm' of sustainability and the sociocultural impacts of tourism development, and suggested that it can apply to levels of social cohesion, cultural boundaries and the interpretation of traditions (Scott, 2004).

Demographic analyses are also routinely performed to understand the sociocultural impacts of tourism, but segments and clusters are more often formed on the basis of other characteristics such as attachment to the visitor industry, the perceived benefits to locals, or general attitudes towards development and the environment. Andereck *et al.* (2005) found significant differences among communities in Arizona regarding tourism as an economic development strategy. They found that attitudes were not necessarily a good predictor of the actual future support of a proposed tourism attraction, and recommended combining qualitative and quantitative research methods to explore these issues. Moreover, a caveat with all resident attitude surveys is that they are a snapshot in time; thus, events during the timespan of the data collection period could sway public opinion. Consequently, a few studies have explored the changing attitudes of gaming residents using a longitudinal approach (Carmichael *et al.*, 1996; Hsu 2000; Lee *et al.*, 2003). Others have conducted cross-cultural research in order to compare differences in residents' perceptions of casino development in South Korea and Colorado (Lee *et al.*, 2010). In general, quantitative impact studies are not designed to capture in-depth sociocultural aspects, such as identity, cultural or moral values that inform perceptions about casino and tourism development. Such qualitative and internalized values are difficult to measure, understand and compare, especially if couched in the realm of economics.

Spatial context is also known to influence resident attitude surveys. Many resident attitude studies are conducted statewide, or as regional analyses. McCool and Martin (1994) identified a potential division between those who promote and benefit from tourism and those who live somewhat separately from the tourism community. These relationships are less obvious in relatively mature destinations, and in the case of small islands, including St Croix and Christmas Island, the separation is less likely. Yet the extant literature on casino gambling and development impacts has failed to address the vulnerable and most fragile of tourism destinations, namely small islands. In small islands, economic, sociocultural and environmental changes are more likely to affect the whole country than is the case in large land-based countries. For example, the economies of small islands tend to be based on a single or narrow range of activities (e.g. tourism, mining, particular cash crops). The population is relatively small and hence represents a limited pool of skills. Distances across individual islands are short so that ecological and sociocultural impacts may be felt across the island (e.g. chemical discharge, sea level rise, crime). Countries of many islands may face different problems of perceived and spatial distance which emphasize the importance of contextual analysis and in-depth understandings in order to facilitate sustainable development (Bass and Dalal-Clayton, 1995; Liburd 1999). In short, findings from resident attitude studies vary widely as a result of the community context, the theoretical orientation and the applied survey method. Furthermore, findings by Moscardo and Pearce (1999) indicate that those conducting attitude surveys have too often imposed their own perceptions of the impacts of tourism on respondents. They assert that resident attitude studies are particularly concerned with the *content* rather than the *context* in and of which the study takes place and form. Impact studies generally espouse an understanding of culture as difference and a commodity. This is a functionalist and highly prescriptive approach that reduces culture to a static, place-bound entity commonly addressed as 'clashes of difference' or 'differences for sale' (Liburd and Ren, 2009). Consequently, culture becomes either an exotic backdrop to help promote tourism or a vulnerable property of a disempowered 'other' to be protected from the exploitation of tourism (Burns, 2005).

The notion that the sociocultural dimensions of tourism development can somehow be categorized as 'positive' or 'negative' is somewhat of a fruitless exercise as tourism development can take many forms and host communities typically display a wide spectrum of attitudes based on diverse sets of values, beliefs and knowledge. Moreover, the ranges of stakeholders, networks and actors in island tourism destinations are multiple, as are their aspirations and needs. What may constitute socially beneficial tourism development to some may be considered detrimental to others. The challenge for island communities seeking a path to sustainability is to identify which sociocultural, environmental and economic changes are acceptable in order to determine what is to be sustained, and for whom and how, by the people whose habitat the object of tourism development is, or may become (Liburd, 2007).

Casino development is one such form of tourism that requires detailed understanding of how cultural values are put to work, and how they are negotiated and internalized, in particular in island contexts.

The two case studies presented in this chapter are prefaced by a clearer explication of the research methods used. In addressing the sociocultural sustainability of island casino development, the first case study, of St Croix, focuses on how policy processes, identity constructions and power work in multiple sites that are informed by values and context. In the second case study, the sociocultural impacts of the casino development on CI on the local community are described. Lessons learned from the two case studies then identify and focus on the sociocultural sustainability perspectives that emerge from this form of island tourism development. Finally, we tease out some of the predicaments for management and for future research into the sociocultural sustainability of island casino development.

Research Methods

The case study from the Eastern Caribbean island of St Croix draws on longitudinal studies, interviews and anthropological fieldwork conducted by the first author of this chapter in the US Virgin Islands (1995–1998, 2000, 2001 and 2006). Findings reported are based on a combination of qualitative methodologies of participant observation and in-depth interviews with casino stakeholders, government officials and potential investors, as well as informal interviews and conversations with local residents. Discourse analysis was applied to uncover the transformative power and recontextualization of different elements of tourism and casino development, policy-making processes, identity and belonging within an overarching framework of sustainable tourism development. Widely acknowledged within discourse studies, an analysis of linguistic elements presupposes a proper appraisal of their context and processes of production and reception (Drew and Heritage, 1992; van Dijk, 1997; Wodak, 2006; Krzyzanowski and Oberhuber, 2007), and of power and knowledge relations (Foucault, 1980). By tracing discourses and translating connections in multiple sites and contexts we can uncover how casino development works, and what it does in specific island contexts, findings which have implications for transitions towards or indeed away from sustainable development.

The second case study is based on interviews and discussions with CI residents during multiple field visits in the 1990s. This case study reviews the forces of change that led to the development and establishment of the casino resort complex, and the impacts that this had on CI between 1990 and 1995. While most of the impacts became evident after the opening of the resort in 1993, the historical and cultural setting into which the development was introduced determined the subsequent extent of the impacts. The most significant impacts that resulted from the closure of the CI Resort in 1998, just 5 years after opening, are also described. Widely accepted definitions of sustainable tourism particularly refer to respect for sociocultural aspects of host communities and reducing or mitigating any undesirable cultural or social impacts. The case study of CI resort development demonstrates that casino development can represent the antithesis of socioculturally sustainable tourism development in island settings, as it neither respects host communities nor is cognizant of undesirable impacts.

Casino Development on St Croix

St Croix is the largest island in the USA Virgin Islands of the Lesser Antilles, immediately East of Puerto Rico. With 19 ethnic groups in a population of approximately 125,000 (Liburd, 1999) sociocultural perspectives on local values, identity, equity and control are highly varied. Sprauve (1990) suggests that these groups be ordered into sociolinguistic groups (rather than groups by origin) of which he defines 15, or, more simply, 'Blacks', 'Whites' and 'Others', or 'Natives', 'Aliens' and 'Others'. The latter grouping is consistent with the antagonisms underpinning the casino development process, which will be further discussed in the recontextualisation of local ownership and empowerment as central tenets to sustainability.

Although not a cruise destination like the sister island of St Thomas, St Croix relies heavily on income from various types of tourism. These include golf, diving, fishing, historical tours, and stays at resorts and a recently built casino. Gambling, including lotteries, cockfighting, car racing, horse races, dominoes, cards, bingo and crap games (craps), is a favoured leisure activity in St Croix. In 1979, a referendum 'On Casino Gambling and Cock Fighting' was proposed in the 13th Legislature, but without any outcome. Other pieces of legislation specifically focusing on casino development were introduced at government level without any outcome until the early 1990s. Central to all of the formal gaming initiatives is the argument that St Croix is in 'dire need of development', unlike the sister island of St Thomas. Located only 44 miles apart, dominating perceptions of animosity and divergence between the two islands are profound (Liburd, 1999). St Croix residents, referred to as Crucians, frequently mention the 'congestion of St Thomas' with its population of approximately 60,000 on 'only' 24 mountainous square miles, compared with the St Croix population of 125,000 in 84 square miles of rolling hills and flat land. In St Thomas, which is dominated by a highly successful cruise industry, tourism arrival statistics are similarly deployed to underscore the 'under-development' of St Croix.

On 8 November 1994, 58% of votes were cast in favour of the referendum and 42% against, which led to the passing of *Act No. 6069, Bill No. 21-0027*, entitled *The Virgin Islands Casino and Resort Control Act of 1995* (hereinafter the casino bill). Exclusively legislated for the island of St Croix, and contrary to common practice, the casino bill defines an exhaustive set of social, cultural, economic and environmental regulations. In stipulating four categories of casino development, the land zoning regulation is of particular interest (Section 228a, the casino bill). Specifically, 'at least fifty one per cent (51%) of a Tier III hotel must be owned by a Native Virgin Islander' (Section 435b, the casino bill), defined as follows:

> Notwithstanding any law to the contrary 'Native Virgin Islander' shall be defined as any person born in the Virgin Islands prior to 1927; any person who is an offspring of parent(s) born in the Virgin Islands prior to 1927; or any person outside the Virgin Islands to Native Virgin Islands parent(s) while parent(s) was studying abroad, employed abroad, or in active military service.
>
> (Section 402, the casino bill)

Setting judicial precedence, a native of the USA Virgin Islands, and hence a potential Tier III Casino Resort owner, was qualified through ancestral birthplace up to 1927. The year 1927 marks the first decade from the 1917 transfer of the former Danish West Indies to the USA, following which island residents were given 10 years to choose whether to remain Danish or become American citizens. Further illustrating the connectivity of this case, the regulations and motives of the casino bill were strongly inspired by the success of (native) American Indian gaming, especially the case of the Mashantucket Pequot of the Foxwoods Resort Casino in Connecticut (Carmichael *et al.*, 1996). The *Indian Gaming Regulatory Act of 1988*, Section 20, stipulated that Indians may conduct gaming on 'newly acquired lands'. To explore the commercial and collaborative possibilities in St Croix, a number of meetings were held in 1995–1996 between the Mashantucket-Pequot tribe and the St Croix Senator sponsoring the 1995 casino bill. Historic oppression and ethnic minority status in their own place of origin emphasized the need for local control and empowerment. Common socio-economic problems between the Mashantucket Pequot and native Crucians were articulated. Once a classic Caribbean planter society, St Croix has attracted workers from abroad under various imperial forms, notably enslaved Africans and European planters. Post emancipation, St Croix became the home for a number of Puerto Ricans, and the construction of two considerable transnational corporations alongside a growing tourism industry during the 1950s and 1960s attracted continental Americans and thousands of workers from the Eastern Caribbean islands. At the same time, many Virgin Islanders (and West Indians of the Eastern Caribbean) migrated to urban areas of the American mainland and Europe, following which foreign-born 'aliens' outnumbered Virgin Island natives. Legal documents favouring native Virgin Islands workers over 'aliens' and their children, not to mention round-ups of illegal residents blamed for the increase in violent crimes and drug abuse, blemish recent US Virgin Islands history. Thus, it was hardly surprising that a majority of St Croix residents, many of whom are second- and third-generation immigrants and USA citizens, strongly objected to the casino bill, which favoured only those whose offspring were traceable to the US Virgin Islands before 1927. Illustrating the highly emotional debate also captured by local radio and newspapers, a letter to the editor stated:

> Whereas this process of immigration has been greatly accelerated in the past 10 years so that our tourism industry, building construction and sugar cane industry would collapse if it were not for the services of workers from other parts of the West Indies. Whereas even before the arrival of these immigrants on our shores the US Virgin Islands was closely linked to other parts of the West Indies by bonds of culture, African heritage and common background. And yet Senator Bryan and his gang would turn those who have made such significant contribution to the US Virgin Islands, their children and grandchildren into second class citizens.
>
> (Lloyd, 1996)

The casino bill rules and regulations, as adopted from New Jersey and the Foxwoods Casino Resort, were consequently amended to fit the US Virgin Island context. On 8 March 1996, the revised definition of a 'Native Virgin Islander' became 'Anyone who was born in the Territory'. Two years later, the increasingly negative perceptions of casino development, expatriate ownership and local control were altered following pop star Michael Jackson's visit to St Croix in May 1998. Mr Jackson was promised concessions to build a casino resort and a theme park despite seeking 20 years tax exemption and rezoning of beach property. The economic and environmental stipulations of the casino bill stipulated a maximum of 10 years tax exemption and adherence to existing, strict land-zoning laws. None the less, local politicians stated: 'We should do whatever is necessary. Michael Jackson is a big name. He would be an asset to our community' (Bryan, 1998). Although Michael Jackson never filed for a casino license in St Croix, the visit of the popular celebrity reported on global USA news stations instantaneously exposed St Croix as an interesting place to play, visit and reside.

Summary

More than a decade after passing the casino legislation in St Croix, a multinational corporation now runs the only casino establishment, which enjoys patronage from a predominantly local clientele. Tracing the legislative processes behind casino development in St Croix, the transformative power of the applied development discourse was related to issues of nativity and local control. This implies that the work of carefully designed development strategies, policy-making ideals, coincidences, conflicting interests and 'local' identities can be accounted for. By understanding how these discourses and power relations work, how they include and exclude, they can, consequently, also be unmade. It appears that rather than reducing or mitigating undesirable impacts on the natural, historic, cultural and social environment of St Croix, in accord with the objectives of sustainable tourism, the St Croix casino development further polarized the multi-ethnic resident community based on historical, spatial, socio-economic and political differences.

The Christmas Island Resort Development

Christmas Island was first named on Christmas Day 1643 by Captain William Mynors of the British East India Company. Two hundred and fifty years later, this remote Indian Ocean island located 2600 kilometres from Perth, Western Australia, was recognized as a significant source of a highly valued commodity, phosphate of lime. The Cocos (Keeling) Islands-based Clunies-Ross Estate first settled the island in 1888, and in 1897, with the Christmas Island Phosphate Company, began extracting the phosphate for supply to the market gardens of Britain for use as a powerful fertilizer.

Politically, CI has been administered as a Crown colony of Britain through the colonial government in Singapore, and consequently inherited the legal regimes imposed on all of the Straits Settlements. As a result of the declining fortunes of Britain after World War Two, the governance of the Crown colony was transferred to Australia in 1958, and CI, along with the Cocos (Keeling) Islands, became the Australian Indian Ocean Territories. Since that time, the Australia government and the Australian-New Zealand owned Christmas Island Phosphate Company have shared responsibility for the welfare of the 2500 to 3000 inhabitants of CI. This predominantly private administration created a socio-economic system that encouraged a strong work ethic, a complex social hierarchy based on race and religion, and an economic pluralism in which the interests and fortunes of the phosphate mine operators, the Christmas Island Phosphate Company and the community of CI were indistinguishable. Historically, the main economic activities on CI are phosphate mining and the provision of government services.

In 1987, the Australian government announced that mining on the island would be wound up. This essentially political decision came after years of industrial unrest, substantial operating losses and unsatisfactory government subsidization of island public services. The Union of Christmas Island Workers and secretary Gordon Bennett pushed for the transfer of mine operations to a locally owned company, but the Australian government's preferred option seemed to be the depopulation of the troublesome territory and the granting of a lease to a private company, Elders Resources, which would supply its own workforce from the mainland.

Amid all of this political, social and commercial upheaval on CI, plans to establish a casino resort complex and a major upgrade of airport facilities were announced in December 1986 by the Australian government. The CI resort developers experienced major delays and it was several years before the AUS$80 million project would actually commence. Plans to establish a casino resort complex were bought to fruition in the early 1990s when a casino operator's licence was granted to an Australian property developer and a consortium of Singaporean and Indonesian businessmen. During the period of construction – from December 1990 to the commencement of operations in December 1993 – the project was plagued by disputes and disagreements between the construction management company and the developers (Christmas Island Resort (CIR) Pty Ltd). Financial disputes partly resulted from cultural differences in conducting business with contractors. Progress payments are an accepted means of conducting business transactions in all Australian building projects. However, the Singaporean and Indonesian businessmen involved in the CIR project were against making progress payments to contractors before the contract was completed, in case the contractor disappeared without completing the work. The legal and financial difficulties associated with this project not only provided a lesson in building in a remote location, but also in conducting business in a multi-cultural business environment.

The CI Resort was operated by the Europe-based Casinos Austria International. They employed about 300 workers, about two-thirds of whom originated from the Australian mainland. These workers occupied the skilled positions associated with the casino operation, including croupiers, supervisors and management positions. The remaining 100 positions were unskilled (cleaners, ground staff, bus drivers, etc.), and these were made available to CI residents. Local residents openly expressed their dissatisfaction with the allocation of these menial positions when the more highly skilled and rewarding positions were allocated to non-residents. The indirect employment generated by the CI Resort was difficult to estimate, but the casino workers and their families accommodated in the settlement at Poon San would provide considerable business for local retailers, restaurants and clubs. Most of the local businesses are owned and managed by CI residents, and a number of new businesses opened to cater for the increased population. The direct economic benefits to the community and the Australian government of the first year of operation of the resort were estimated to be around AUS$10 million (Carlsen, 2000). The majority of this (AUS$9 million) accrued to the Australian government as company tax, with the remaining funds deposited separately in a Community Benefit Fund (CBF), for community use.

The CI Resort was highly dependent on a specific group of 'high roller' gamblers from Jakarta, Indonesia, who arrived by charter flight and spent the majority of their time gambling. In mid-June 1998, after a series of legal disputes, discontinuance of northern charter airline services, casino closure and job losses, CIR was given '21 days to show good cause why its license should not be cancelled' (Drummond, 1998). The casino licence was subsequently revoked, leaving former CIR employees without an income or a means of leaving the islands, and CI residents without employment and income. The resort operators, Casinos Austria International, were able to relocate many of their trained staff to a new casino in Cairns, Queensland, but the local CI employees and the businesses that were established to service the CI Resort guests were left with very few prospects.

During the 5 years of its operations, the social costs associated with the CI Resort included crimes against persons and property, family breakdowns due to excessive gambling and the use of illegal drugs. Potential social impacts from attempts by organized criminals to spread their interests in extortion and prostitution were also identified during interviews and discussions with CI residents in 1995. The Australian Federal Police have had only a limited presence on CI, and there has been no real identifiable trend in personal and property crime associated with the CI Resort development. However, there were some serious charges laid over the period 1994/1995, including assaults, sexual assaults and drug-related charges. There were also a number of less serious crimes, including criminal damage, theft, burglary and car stealing (Table 8.1), which all have a more profound impact in a small island community than in larger mainland communities.

There was also some evidence of organized crime associated with the casino, with attempts by local members of the Hong Kong-based triad group 27K to stand over casino security staff, resulting in a brawl at the resort in

Table 8.1. Criminal offences by type 1994/1995. (Source: Carlsen, 2000).

Type of criminal offence	Number of charges
Criminal damages	8
Theft	56
Burglary	15
Car stealing	6
Drug related	1
Assaults	7
Sexual assaults	3

January 1995. There are also reports of organized prostitution operating out of Jakarta to CI. These activities exposed members of the community to the health risks and social problems that accompany increased promiscuity and changes in morals.

The social impacts of excessive gambling by CI residents are less well documented, but none the less form another set of social costs of the CI Resort development. There are three subcultures of the CI community, the CI Malay community, the mainland expatriate community and the CI Chinese community. Of these, the CI Chinese gamblers have a higher propensity to gamble to excess. This problem is exacerbated by the fact that the CI Chinese control most of the businesses on CI, indicating that they have more accessible capital which can be used for gambling. Gambling by one CI Chinese businessman led to the loss of a business, domestic violence and subsequent family breakdown. Other CI residents also have access to large amounts of capital as a result of the capital gains from the purchase and resale of residential property on CI. The release of land and housing on to the commercial property market gave CI residents priority to purchase their seaside homes at very favourable prices. Some took advantage of the interest in CI real property from speculators in Indonesia and Australia to make substantial capital gains. Unfortunately, it was reported that in some cases these funds had been lost through excessive gambling, leaving those residents in a difficult personal situation.

It was evident from discussions with CI residents and croupiers at the casino that there is use of hard drugs by the resort patrons. It is believed that these drugs keep gamblers awake and alert for long periods, allowing for extended gambling activity. The social costs associated with the increase in drug use by casino patrons relate to the potential of these drugs to infiltrate the community, creating problems of addiction among CI residents. While some drug addiction, historically opium use, is not foreign to CI, the introduction of newer 'designer' drugs, such as crack and ecstasy, can only exacerbate a serious social problem on CI, and result in increased health and policing costs.

Another dimension of the social impact of the casino is the effect that it has on the existing social clubs on CI. There were a number of social clubs where controlled gambling was conducted, which served an important role in the socialization and recreation of CI residents. The CI Resort had a substantial impact on the patronage of these clubs, as CI residents were drawn to the casino by the opportunity of larger winnings. Scott (2004) found that gambling in the Turkish–Cypriot culture has undergone a transformation from its social origins in coffee shops, cinemas and town centres through increasingly larger money wagers in commercial casinos developed on the island.

On a positive note, one interviewee reported a noticeable increase in the level of community pride and an improvement in the racial attitudes of CI residents after the casino opened. There seemed to be a shift away from the colonial attitude of some community members, towards a more integrated community on CI. This could also be the result of a number of other factors, such as community ownership of the mining operation and the demise of the old working-class structures.

Summary

Discontinuance of the casino licence, together with the cessation of charter services and the ongoing legal disputes between CIR and the building company led to the closure of the CI Resort in 1998, just 5 years after it had commenced operations. The CI Resort building and grounds were left to fall into disrepair and the location of the main building in a fragile coastal area of the island has only accelerated the decay. Part of the building had been leased by the Australian government in 2002 to accommodate illegal immigrants detained in Australian territory. A Sydney-based entrepreneur currently owns the CI Resort and is negotiating with the government regarding ongoing use of the CI Resort facilities to accommodate staff of a controversial Immigration Detention Centre on CI.

Implications for Casino Development and Island Tourism Sustainability

While individual case studies, by their nature, have limited generalizability, the themes and sub-themes that they capture can be related to the wider body of theory and practical knowledge on sustainable tourism development (Carlsen *et al.*, 2008). Lessons learned from these two cases will identify and further analyse the sociocultural sustainability perspectives that emerge from this form of island tourism development. However, rather than pinpointing socio-economic and cultural differences, or accepting 'culture' and 'ethnicity', or 'local' versus 'foreign', as predefined, grounded bases for social relations, cultural misconceptions and difference (cf. Lew and Kennedy, 2002; Andereck *et al.*, 2005; Lee *et al.*, 2010), the following discussion will illustrate how casino development is used and integrated through tourism legislation and local performances. This means that differences, whether cultural, ethnic, economic or spatial, are not analytical taken-for-granted points of departure, but are seen as ongoing performances and social-material production (Law, 2004; Ren, 2009). This implies that the transition towards sustainability should be informed by values in and of the context in which the journey unfolds. The case studies demonstrate that, by their very nature, casino developments can be a socioculturally divisive and destructive force that in many ways represents the antithesis of sustainability.

It is evident from the CI Resort case study that Australian government policy in the Indian Ocean Territories is to retain control over land use and over the tourism development approvals process, and through using its legal powers and licensing arrangements. This desire for control could be related to the strategic location of CI as the north-western extremity of Australian territory. The power of veto over land alienation has delayed a number of developments in the past, and will continue to frustrate the journey towards sustainability if clear guidelines are not devised in relation to CI tourism development. Similarly, the first case study exposed how casino legislation aimed to develop the island of St Croix, and how it was used as a process to enact and potentially regain control by 'old' Crucian natives through which the meaning of belonging and identity were renegotiated. The two cases both illustrated how such values and networks are informed by and constructed in the local context. They also exist through global relations which should be included to account for intertwined networks, discourses and interactions that extend beyond the geographical boundary.

In both cases, the plan to develop casino resorts caused significant social disruption in the islands. Contrary to a ubiquitous notion of the capillary power of development while infusing lifeworlds through more-or-less concealed mechanisms, cultures, knowledge and power are subject to change and meanings attributed in various contexts, which are traceable through empirical investigations of how the casino development processes worked. Social clubs were in charge of small-scale gambling, a favoured pastime activity in both islands. When the casinos opened, residents were attracted to the casinos by the opportunity of larger winnings, which in some cases led to excessive gambling and family breakdowns. Similar to the findings by Przybylski *et al.* (1998) the concept that gambling operations are necessarily tourism attractions can therefore be challenged, as many smaller casinos are merely local services.

Motivated by the Foxwoods Casino legislation featuring native ownership, training and fiscal control, residents in St Croix had to explicate what it meant to belong and to be a local, native Virgin Islander. The legislative process further divided and disintegrated the multi-ethnic population, of whom a majority traced their sense of belonging and identity to other Caribbean islands – despite having lived on St Croix for several generations. In these connected contexts, it is not altogether clear how the process altered residents' quality of life, and especially their subjective well-being. Spillover effects of satisfaction in major life domains such as leisure on overall life fulfilment are widely recognized in the literature (Neil *et al.*, 1999; Liburd *et.al.*, 2011). Greater emphasis could feasibly have been placed on aspects of mobility and transnational relations directed away from the island context of St Croix.

In CI, an inadequate labour supply and lack of training provisions led to the importation of workers, and thus lost salary and tax income. Residents were only offered menial, unskilled jobs, making meaningful interaction with the 'high roller' gamblers even less likely. This type of enclave tourism could be justified as having very little impact on local culture, which subsequently is preserved. But this line of argument, based on cultural clashes and misconceptions, fails to understand that these are effects of the socio-material workings within the destination as the casino development is used to point to and perform cultural (and socio-economic) differences. It further explicates how semi-romantic notions of local control and local ownership must be empirically qualified in order to ensure equity and democratic rights, both of which are central tenets of sustainable development (World Commission of Environment and Development, 1987).

Conclusion

The two case studies presented in this chapter provide insights into the casino development experiences of communities on the islands of St Croix and Christmas Island from a social and cultural sustainability perspective. They have also stimulated reflections on the predicaments involved in the process and offered contextual perspectives on sociocultural sustainability. Arguably, the role of government and desire for control in this type of tourism development not only runs contrary to the notion of local empowerment, it also challenges the very meaning of sustainable development in the respective island contexts. The case studies demonstrate that casino development can be a socioculturally divisive and destructive force that in many ways represents the antithesis of sustainability in island settings, as it neither respects host communities nor is cognizant of undesirable impacts, including resident perceptions of subjective and social well-being.

Large-scale resort and casino proposals are commonly met by very 'investment friendly' conditions by Caribbean governments in exchange for marketing opportunities (Holder, 1993; Patullo, 1996) based on 'top-down' development strategies, which was also the case in CI. Understanding how casino development is used at multiple levels, here as a policy process, in identity building and tourism/leisure innovation, we arrive at deeper and richer sociocultural notions. These insights allow us to move beyond traditional functionalist theories and notions of cultural clashes and stereotypical misconceptions, which again can be used to inform more sustainable solutions and management of island destinations. Translating the broader aims and values of sustainable development to a specific island location, on a sectoral base sustainable tourism must contribute to the specific development needs and quality of life in the destination. Only thus is one able to judge whether specific practices are likely to be transformative and facilitate the interests and needs of a group of people.

Still, critical reflections are needed upon the following if island casino development is to support the social dimensions of sustainable development. Key questions should ask first, who in the local community benefits from island casino development and who is adversely affected? Secondly, the question of how competing interests of the local, heterogeneous community can be met and managed in the long-term must be addressed. Finally, the political question of the determination of sociocultural values and practices that should be preserved, and for whom and how, must be resolved. In order to potentially provide richer, broader and, hence, culturally more sustainable notions of destination cultures, not only in research but also in the communication, marketing and managing of destinations (Ren, 2011), island destinations and tourism researchers need to engage in dialogue to critically address the underlying issues of stewardship. This involves examining the kind of tourism to be developed (by whom and how it should be governed) and what the end objectives behind these activities should be in order to facilitate a transition towards sustainable tourism development.

References

Andereck, K., Valentine, K.M., Vogt, C.M. and Knopf, R.C. (2005) Residents' perceptions of community tourism impacts. *Annals of Tourism Research* 32, 1056–1076.

Ap, J. (1990) Residents' perceptions research on the social impacts of tourism. *Annals of Tourism Research* 17, 610–616.

Bass, S. and Dalal-Clayton, B. (1995) *Small Island States and Sustainable Development: Strategic Issues and Experiences*. Environmental Planning Issues No. 8, International Institute for Environment and Development, London.

Bramwell, B. (2004) (ed.) *Coastal Mass Tourism: Diversification and Sustainable Development in Southern Europe*. Channel View Publications, Clevedon, UK.

Bruner, E.M. (1994) Abraham Lincoln as authentic reproduction. a critique of post-modernism. *American Anthropologist* 96, 397–415.

Bryan, A.B. (1998) Do whatever is necessary. *St. Croix Avis*, 11 May 1998, p. 3.

Burns, P.M. (2005) Social identities, globalisation and the cultural politics of tourism. In: Theobald, W.T. (ed.) *Global Tourism*. Elsevier Butterworth-Heinemann, Oxford, pp. 391–405.

Carlsen, J. (2000) Population-development-environment interactions on the Cocos (Keeling) Islands. PhD thesis, University of Western Australia, Perth, Australia.

Carlsen, J., Liburd, J.J., Edwards, D. and Forde, P. (2008) *Innovations for Sustainable Tourism. International Case Studies*. University of Technology, Sydney.

Carmichael, B.A., Peppard, D.M. and Boudreau, F.A. (1996) Megaresort on my doorstep: local resident attitudes toward Foxwoods Casino and casino gambling on nearby Indian Reservation land. *Journal of Travel Research* 34, 9–16.

Drew, P. and Heritage J. (1992) *Talk at Work: Interaction in Institutional Settings*. Cambridge University Press, Cambridge.

Drummond, M. (1998) WA tycoon faces casino share loss. *The West Australian*, 23 June 1998, p. 30.

Foucault, M. (1980) *Power/Knowledge: Selected Interviews and Writings*. Pantheon, New York.

Global Development Research Center (2010) Sustainable Tourism Info-Sheets: Defining Sustainable Tourism. Available at: http://www.gdrc.org/uem/eco-tour/sustour-define.html (accessed 9 September 2010).

Government of the US Virgin Islands (1995) The Virgin Islands Casino and Resort Control Act of 1995. Act No. 6069, Bill No. 21–0027.

Harrison, D. (1996) Sustainability and tourism: reflections from a muddy pool. In: Briguglio, L., Archer, B., Jafari, J. and Wall, G. (eds) *Sustainable Tourism in Islands and Small States, Volume 1: Issues and Policies*. Pinter, London, pp. 69–89.

Holder, J.S. (1993) The Caribbean Tourism Organisation in a historical perspective. In: Gayle, D.J. and Goodrich, J.N. (eds) *Tourism Marketing and Management in the Caribbean*. Routledge, London/New York, pp. 20–27.

Hsu, C.H.C. (2000) Residents' support for legalized gaming and perceived impacts of riverboat casinos: changes in five years. *Journal of Travel Research* 38, 390–395.

Krzyzanowski, M. and Oberhuber F. (2007) *(Un)Doing Europe: Discourses and Practices of Negotiating the EU Constitution*. Sage, London.

Law, J. (2004) *After Method. Mess in Social Science Research*. Routledge, London.

Lee, C.-K. and Back, K. (2003) Pre and post-casino impact of residents' perception. *Annals of Tourism Research* 30, 868–885.

Lee, C.-K. and Back, K.J. (2006) Examining structural relationships among perceived impact, benefit, and support for casino development based on a 4 year longitudinal data. *Tourism Management* 27, 466–480.

Lee, C.-K., Kim, S.S. and Kang, S.K. (2003) Perceptions of casino impacts – a Korean longitudinal study. *Tourism Management* 24, 45–55.

Lee, C.-K., Kang, S.K., Long, P. and Reisinger, Y. (2010) Residents' perceptions of casino impacts: a comparative study. *Tourism Management* 31, 189–201.

Lew, A. and Kennedy, C. (2002) Tourism and culture clash in American Indian country. In: Krakover, S. and Gradus, Y. *Tourism in Frontier Areas*. Lexington Books, Lanham, Maryland.

Liburd, J.J. (1999) Sustainable tourism development. Case studies from the Eastern Caribbean. PhD thesis, Faculty of Arts, Aarhus University, Denmark.

Liburd, J.J. (2007) Sustainable tourism, cultural practice and competence development for hotels and inns in Denmark. *Tourism Recreation Research* 32, 41–49.

Liburd, J.J. (2010) Sustainable tourism development. In: Liburd, J.J. and Edwards, D. (eds) *Understanding the Sustainable Development of Tourism*. Goodfellow Publishers, Oxford, pp. 1–18.

Liburd, J.J. and Ren, C. (2009) Selling difference: conceptualising culture in tourism education and management. In: Blacso, M. and Zoelner, M. (eds) *Teaching Cultural Skills: Adding Culture in Higher Education*. Samfundslitteratur, Copenhagen, pp. 71–90.

Liburd, J., Benckendorff, P. and Carlsen, J.C. (2011) Tourism and quality of life: how does tourism measure up? In: Uysal, M., Perdue, R. and Sirgy, J. (eds) *Handbook on Tourism and QoL Research*. Springer, Berlin/New York/London (in press).

Lloyd (1996) Immigrants' blood, sweat and tears build US Virgin Islands. *St. Croix Avis*, 5 January 1996, p. 3.

Long, P., Perdue, R.R. and Allen, L.L. (1990) Rural resident tourism perceptions and attitudes by community level of tourism. *Journal of Travel Research* 28, 3–9.

McCool, S. and Martin, S. (1994) Community attachment and attitudes towards tourism development. *Journal of Travel Research* 32, 29–34.

Moscardo, G. and Pearce, P.L. (1999) Understanding ethnic tourists. *Annals of Tourism Research* 26, 416–434.

Neil, J.D., Sirgy, M.J. and Uysal, M. (1999) The role of satisfaction with leisure travel/ tourism services and experience in satisfaction with leisure life and overall life. *Journal of Business Research* 44, 153–163.

Patullo, P. (1996) *Last Resorts: The Cost of Tourism in the Caribbean*. Cassell, London.

Przybylski, M., Felsenstein, D., Freeman, D. and Littlepage, L. (1998) Does gambling complement the tourist industry? Some empirical evidence of import substitution and demand displacement. *Tourism Economics* 4, 213–231.

Ren, C.B. (2009) Constructing the tourist destination. A socio-material description. PhD thesis, Faculty of Humanities, University of Southern Denmark, Esbjerg.

Ren, C.B. (2011) Beyond hosts and guests: translating the concept of cultural misconception. *International Journal of Culture, Tourism and Hospitality Research* (in press).

Scott, J. (2004) Coffee shop meets casino: cultural responses to casino tourism in northern Cyprus. In: Bramwell, B. (ed.) *Coastal Mass Tourism: Diversification and Sustainable Development in Southern Europe*. Channel View Publications, Clevedon, UK, pp. 307–320.

Smith, V.L. (1977) *Hosts and Guests. The Anthropology of Tourism*. Blackwell, Oxford.

Smith, V.L. (1989) *Hosts and Guests. The Anthropology of Tourism*, 2nd edn. University of Pennsylvania Press, Philadelphia.

Sprauve, G. (1990) Fission and fusion and creole, calypso and cultural survival in the Virgin Islands. Available at: http://www.stx.k12.vi/KRAAL/fission.htm (accessed on 9 September 2010).

van Dijk T.A. (1997) *Discourse as Social Interaction*. Sage, London.

Wodak, R. (2006) Mediation between discourse and society: assessing cognitive approaches. *Discourse Studies* 1, 179–190.

World Commission of Environment and Development (1987) *Our Common Future*. Oxford University Press, Oxford.

Yanow, D. and Schwartz-Shea, P. (2006) *Interpretation and Method. Empirical Research Methods and the Interpretative Turn*. M.E. Sharpe, Armonk, New York.

9 Social Sustainability of Tourism in a Culture of Sensuality, Sexual Freedom and Violence: Trinidad and Tobago

JOHNNY COOMANSINGH

Minot State University, North Dakota, USA

Introduction to Rainbow Country

Trinidad and Tobago can be considered as two treasured pearls in the string of island gems that form the Caribbean archipelago. Christopher Columbus claimed these beautiful islands for Spain in 1498, but after several wars among European colonial powers, Britain took control of Trinidad in 1797. After more than 30 wars between the Dutch, French and British, Tobago likewise fell to the British in 1802. In 1886, Britain annexed Tobago to Trinidad (Williams, 1964). The islands obtained independence in 1962.

Geologically, the islands of Trinidad and Tobago are part of the Andean mountains. Tobago's Main Ridge forms the last vestige of the Andes. Because of its equatorial climate, the country supports many species of South American flora and fauna. Apart from its abundant and diverse flora and fauna, Trinidad has a world-famous asphalt lake. History records that Sir Walter Raleigh, while on his quest to find El Dorado, caulked his ships with the asphalt from this lake. The site, 40 ha (99 acres) in area, is a tourist attraction, complete with all the folklore that surrounds the formation of the lake.

Labelling itself as a rainbow country, Trinidad and Tobago continues to advertise to the world the notion that the people of every resident ethnic group are treated equally. Trinidad and Tobago could also lay claim to the title 'land of festivals' in the Caribbean Basin. Among other activities, this multi-religious, multi-ethnic, polyrhythmic and feting state celebrates several festivals, including Divali, Holi, Parang, Siparee Mai, Fisherman Fete, Tobago Heritage, Hosay and, above all, the Trinidad Carnival. All celebrations and festivals play their part in maintaining the beliefs, religious persuasions and cuisine that congeal to frame the island society. Nevertheless, it is the pre-Lenten carnival that gives to Trinidad and Tobago its sense of place, and the primary platform upon which tourism is promoted. In terms of tourism development, the Trinidad Carnival is, most probably, the goose that laid the golden egg (InternetExpress,

2000). The Trinidad Carnival continues to attract tourists, primarily from Europe and North America, because carnival as a celebration of freedom from slavery is one of the greatest street spectacles in the world (Mason, 1998), not to mention the attendant precursors to the carnival itself, for example, the Dimanche Gras Show. Against this backdrop of festivals, and in particular the Trinidad Carnival itself, an analysis of the barriers and threats relevant to the development of the tourism industry in terms of its sustainability is necessary.

No True History of Tourism

Trinidad has never had a true history of tourism owing to its hydrocarbon-based economy and the development of the industrial sector after its independence in 1962. There was little growth, and even stagnation, in the tourism sector during 1977–1987. Moreover, there was no real need to develop a tourist industry because exploitation of petroleum and natural gas had become the economic driver. The abundance of oil and gas money engendered an anti-tourist nationalism. In fact, Eric E. Williams, the first prime minister of Trinidad and Tobago, did not concentrate on the development of the tourism industry for fear that the country would breed a generation of janitors and busboys (Henry-Kunzel, 1994). However, the money obtained from the petroleum industry was short lived. During the late 1980s and early 1990s, soft prices for petroleum on the world market ruffled the takings of the treasury, and in view of the situation, the government sought for a solution to bolster the flagging economy.

Although not a panacea for the country's economic woes during the world oil crisis, the nascent tourism industry proved beyond doubt that it had the potential to replace the financial shortfall caused by unstable oil prices. According to Scher (2007), tourism 'has slowly gained momentum as a potentially lucrative alternative to the petroleum and agricultural base of the country's economy'. Today, Trinidad has a literal bonanza with respect to the inflows of tourists, especially during carnival time. Visitor arrivals have increased at an average rate of 6.4% per annum. In 2000, more than 360,000 European and North American tourists visited the republic. Over the 5-year period of 1995–1999, visitor expenditure rose from US$70 million to US$162 million (Global Newswire, 2001). For the ventures involving tourism development via cruise ship visits, the government had hopes of raking in a minimum of US$175,000 per annum in head taxes alone (Richards, 2001).

The pre-Lenten Trinidad Carnival also generates jobs for hundreds of people who design and construct costumes, prepare feting venues, shape, tune and blend steel-pan instruments, organize fetes (carnival parties), arrange calypso and steel-pan music and vend food as the celebration approaches. Overall, the costume construction industry of the celebration injects more than US$1 million into the economy (Potter, 2001). A CNN report states that a great part of the local economy in Trinidad is dependent upon the annual carnival. According to Dr Keith Nurse, economic researcher at The University of the West Indies, in the 2001 carnival visitors spent an estimated US$150 million (Associated Press, 2005). All of this carnival activity is enveloped in the 'carnival mentality', a way of life, riveted in the psyche of the majority of the population.

Carnival Mentality

The world-famous pre-Lenten carnival staged annually in the republic is the most photographed, the most copied and the most imitated of all carnivals (Mason, 1998). Regardless of political or economic oppression, the annual ritual of carnival reveals the true sinew of Trinidad and Tobago in terms of its power of place. The Trinidad Carnival is in fact a kind of superorganic entity (Zelinsky, 1992; Mitchell, 2000), the basic value system, the glue that directly or indirectly sustains or holds the society together. Among the Caribbean states, and possibly within the entire world, it is the carnivalesque landscape that gives to Trinidad and Tobago its cultural distinctiveness (Coomansingh, 2008). Tied firmly to the carnival is Trinidad and Tobago's national identity (Green, 1998). Therefore, intimately linked to the carnival is the social sustainability of tourism. According to Green (1998), the people of Trinidad and Tobago are well known to possess the 'carnival mentality' (a live-for-the-moment attitude). As a corollary to the carnival mentality, Birth (1999) explains that when it comes to time management, 'anytime is Trinidad time'. The 'anytime is Trinidad time' syndrome in itself could be a threat to social sustainability because of the lackadaisical attitude that is inherent in many Trinidadians. In spite of the carnival mentality, the business approach to carnival generates substantial income throughout the carnival season for both rich and poor. The Trinidad Carnival is a product packaged not only for local masqueraders, but also for tourists who wish to participate in the bacchanal. Bacchanal in Trinidad and Tobago suggests feting, partying excesses, the possibility of ultimate inebriated debauchery and, in some cases, confrontation.

The celebration of carnival provides citizens with fresh opportunities for new forms of exchange and confrontation (Koningsbruggen, 1997) that are reminiscent of the battles between slaves and slave masters in the former British colony (Hill, 1972). Confrontation is still visible on the carnival landscape of Trinidad and Tobago in relation to the social differentiation of the masses, and is highly observable in the quality of masquerade bands during carnival days. The affluent tend to gravitate to expensive specialized masquerading bands, a cultural barrier that is a bit difficult to breach. Status and the class structure are still visible at carnival time. Indeed, carnival in Trinidad and Tobago could be viewed as a sensory relief for those who are most blinded by the spectrum of supposed 'civilized' white colonialism and its 'respectability'; yet, it is, at the same time, the heart and soul of true cultural freedom and a reaffirmation and celebration of positive identity for those who were most affected by colonialism (Sampath, 1997). Regardless of the country's present psycho-social ramifications, the carnival is constantly undergoing cultural sanitization.

Cultural Sanitization

The Trinidad Carnival continues to experience cultural sanitization on its way to becoming a cultural product designed for tourists, with the concomitant loss to some of its masquerading originality. Many would suggest that the loss of masquerading originality could be a barrier to carnival's sustainability because there are gatekeepers who would prefer to maintain the 'historical' aspects of carnival. Despite the fact that some of its originality has been lost, the carnival continues to grow and survive in more imaginative ways. An aspect of such growth is exemplified in the domination of the carnival landscape today by thousands of skimpily clad women who 'wine dong di place' (dancing sensuously and provocatively) to the music of steel pan and calypso in large masquerading bands ('wine' here refers to a sensual, vulgar dance in which the hips are lewdly gyrated in time with the rhythm of steel-pan music). Although the dances are sensual in nature, women who 'wine' for the 2 days of carnival are simply expressing their sexuality in a different way, and not necessarily as invitations to sexual intercourse. Almost all women who desire the stamina to wine at carnival exercise at gyms to get in shape 3–6 months before the carnival. Involved in this process are participating tourists who have added more texture to the tapestry of the event.

From the descriptions mentioned here, Trinidad and Tobago seems like paradise. Moreover, with all its natural beauty, variety of cuisine, rich resources and festivals, one would imagine that all would be well in the wonderland of calypso and steel band. However, all is not as pleasant as it seems in this little piece of paradise. To examine whether tourism could be socially sustained, we must also look at the people who came, and what is the present scenario on the landscape regarding such a population.

The People

With the arrival of Europeans in the New World, much of the Amerindian population died because of the oppressive nature of the Spanish (Clawson, 2006). Having decimated the Amerindian population, the Spaniards and the other Europeans after them found a new source for supplementing the needed labour. In the year 1606, Dutch merchants brought 407 African slaves to Trinidad, and by 1813, the slave population had risen to 25,696 (John, 2004). Slave trading eventually ended in 1834, but as early as 1845, the British Crown began importing East Indians (from India; cf. West Indians) to the colony as indentured servants to offset the shortfall in the labour supply involved with sugar production. Importation of East Indians ceased in 1917. The first shipload of East Indians comprised 225 immigrants, who disembarked on the shores of Trinidad on 30 May 1845. During the period 1845–1917, 143,939 East Indian indentured servants sailed to Trinidad (Munasinghe, 2001). Today, in such a self-governed, plural society, the two major ethnic groups (Afro and Indo-Trinidadians) jostle each other for state control and power (Ryan, 1972).

According to Bissessar (2002), the so-called equality of all people is far from reality because 'electoral outcomes have reflected ethnic cleavages'. The disagreement between the races, especially on the island of Trinidad, has manifested itself not only in every election, but also in calypso lyrics and the carnival masquerade. There is abundant evidence that a serious social problem exists. Social sustainability is difficult to achieve while such cleavages persist but, with time, there is hope that the people will become more agreeable and understanding.

The Place

Although Trinidad is blessed with asphalt deposits, many roads, especially in the rural areas, are riddled with potholes and landslides. Bridges, barriers and road signs are in dire need of repair. Apart from the poor roads (Coomansingh, 2005), the hostility of drivers on such narrow roads leaves much to be desired in terms of road safety. Noisy vehicles with their huge booming speakers constantly pierce the silence of residential neighbourhoods; some of them with speeds of up to 100 to 120 km/h. Historic buildings are abandoned, and left to rot away. Because of the denuded hillsides in the Northern Range, flash flooding with its attendant mud and debris plagues Port of Spain and several adjacent cities (Alexander, 2009).

Homeless people continue to squat, even in government forest reserves earmarked for scientific research, for example the Aripo Savannah. Feral dogs roam the landscape, while vagrants make their homes on the pavements and constantly rummage through garbage bins for food. Piles of garbage litter the landscape. Pavements are broken, jagged and uneven. Manholes are sometimes left uncovered. Soap and paper towels are always in short supply in the airport lavatories. Used paper cups and plates, plastic bags, bottles and other detritus litter some of the beaches. After a 'river lime' ('lime' means to hang out, party, 'shoot the breeze' – have a chat) the rivers become polluted with the entrails of animals and feathers. In some religions, after certain rites are performed, human hair and other foreign matter are thrown into the rivers. It is difficult not to see young strong youth literally ravaging a garbage truck on the Beetham Highway as it slows down to enter the Port of Spain dump. Traffic jams are endless, and long lines at the banks or other service institutions (public or private) are unavoidable. This brief description brings to the fore a snippet of an image of Trinidad and Tobago that many ignore.

Tourists need a modicum of security and safety when they visit any country. Entertaining tourists under conditions such as those described here is simply abhorrent. The question is: how sustainable is such a scenario? The solutions to some of the problems raised are easy to fix, while others are not so simple to deal with. It might sound a cliché, but total quality management on the part of the political directorate is required if the country is to move towards social sustainability. Education of the masses about their role in protecting the environment, in holding and accepting the environment as a personal concern, is an imperative if the tourism product is to pay dividends.

The Product and the Problem

Although celebrated throughout the main cities, the carnival dominates in the nation's capital, Port of Spain. As the dominant city in the nation, Port of Spain attracts more participants and tourists (Coomansingh, 2006), giving rise to serious capital leakage from smaller populated communities. Smaller communities (villages) and even some bigger cities, such as San Fernando, Chaguanas, Sangre Grande and Arima, have been trying to offset this barrier by staging their own calypso shows and carnival parades. These communities have had some success, but Port of Spain continues to hold the monopoly. However, if the carnival commodities offered by these other communities should continue and develop, tourists will invariably enjoy a richer experience.

Tourists come to Trinidad not only for the Mardi Gras (Fat Tuesday) carnival parade, they also come with the intention of attending attractions such as calypso shows, the Steelband Panorama and the grand Dimanche Gras (Fat Sunday) Show. The Dimanche Gras Show features the kings and queens of the several masquerade bands throughout the country, and it is at this show that the judges crown the year's calypso monarchs. The Dimanche Gras heralds the Lundi Gras (Fat Monday) J'Ouvert (Jouvay) masquerade. Participants in the Jouvay masquerade parade through the streets of Port of Spain from around 2:00 am until about 11:00 am on Carnival Monday. However, amid the music and wanton partying excesses, there are cultural dark and violent patches that continue to leave indelible stains on the festivity. Murders, rapes and callous banditry have tainted the carnival celebrations every year. Many of the gangs involved in these acts come to Port of Spain from places deemed dangerous and violent, where not even citizens born in Trinidad and Tobago dare to visit. This is a barrier to sustainability that is difficult to overcome because of the history of the country. There is no escaping the truth that there are places in the Port of Spain hillside suburbs that are considered dangerous and rife with violence, but this is where the Trinidad Carnival, calypso and the steel band found a home and slowly developed to what it is today. Trinidad and Tobago needs the beauty of the calypso, the steel band and the carnival masquerade to maintain the tourism product, but inherent in this trio is an underlying current of violence and decadent behaviour.

Dangerous Places and Violence

Calypso music, steel-band music and the pre-Lenten carnival became the most important aspects of Trinidadian culture after Trinidad's emergence from British colonial domination. As a means of expressing their freedom from slavery, African descendants who inhabit the hillside suburbs of Port of Spain continued to develop the steel band, and annually stage the carnival (Liverpool, 1994; Mangurian, 2002). Steel bands (bands of people beating steel or iron implements) eventually became steel-pan orchestras. These bands, strewn all over the landscape of both islands, became centres of musical creativity for people judged as undesirables by the more 'cultured' members of the society.

During the early development of Trinidad, French plantation owners staged large masked balls or *fêtes champêtres* (festive balls/garden parties) that lasted from Christmas to Ash Wednesday. Depicted in the fetes was a reversal of roles; slaves mimicked their masters, and masters mimicked their slaves. Although the Trinidad Carnival engenders fun and gaiety, the celebration also promotes activities that directly or indirectly involve the use of alcoholic beverages, illegal drugs and the stimulation of sexual overtures.

Copying the carnival from the French plantation owners, with the concomitant reversal of roles, these undesirables, including *jamettes* (from *diameter* – women who live below the level of respectability) and men from violent steel bands or 'badjohns' finally forged the Trinidad Carnival. For them, the carnival not only provided the stage for celebrating their freedom from slavery, it also gave voice to the establishment of their identity (Cowley, 1996; Koningsbruggen, 1997; Green, 1998; Mason, 1998). The carnival celebration as it is known today developed in locations known to be hostile and dangerous; places such as Hell Yard, Belmont, Laventille, Gonzales, Morvant, St James and John John, poverty-stricken suburbs ('behind the bridge') of the capital city, Port of Spain (Koningsbruggen, 1997; Mason, 1998).

Many honourable and respectable people still reside within the milieu of these depressed neighbourhoods, but the cultural landscape of these dangerous hillside suburbs is one fraught with severe unemployment, illegal drug running, drug addiction, gun-toting bandits, murder, gang warfare and untold violence (Hutchinson-Jafar, 2005). These overcrowded, slum landscapes in the Port of Spain periphery are very similar to those of the *favelas* in Brazil, and the *barrios* in Caracas, Venezuela (Rowntree *et al.*, 2002; Clawson, 2006). Many of these citizens consider the annual pre-Lenten carnival a money-making opportunity in terms of the legal and illegal earnings extracted from the celebrations.

A Time for Making Money

In the literature on tourism, the focus is primarily on the amount of money generated by the tourism product. The Trinidad Carnival could be considered a landscape to which some monetary value could be assigned. Everything in the carnival has value. Mas' camps, the locations at which costumes for masqueraders are designed and created, can be found in Port of Spain, San Fernando, Point Fortin, Arima, Chaguanas and Sangre Grande. These camps charge their members a fee for their costumes, which may range from US$125 to upwards of US$1000. However, not everyone involved in the Trinidad Carnival has the opportunity to make 'big' money. Certainly, it is a threat to the social sustainability of tourism when some people of the population only see the carnival as a means to illegally extract income from carnival celebrants through violent means.

The carnival season, which extends from Boxing Day to Ash Wednesday in Trinidad and Tobago, in several ways helps to financially assist many people during this time of the year. In economic terms, the *New York Times* labelled

Trinidad as a 'tiger in the sea of pussycats' because of its petroleum and natural gas deposits (Rohter, 1998). However, for many citizens, a high standard of living in the slums and shanties of Port of Spain is not a reality. Such dwellers living in the suburban hillsides of Port of Spain and on the adjacent Caroni River flood plain (Beetham and Sea Lots) depend on the downstream employment that the annual festival provides. The profits accrued at this time will probably be the only income they might realize for the entire year (Mason, 1998). In almost all instances, the vendors are only interested in the money they can gouge from the system. They are not too enamoured with the tourist because they never see tourism as return business; this is a definite threat to the tourism industry.

The Crime Situation

As anywhere else, Trinidad and Tobago is dealing at present with increased crime partially generated by illicit drug peddling. It is known worldwide that Trinidad and Tobago is a transshipment point for illegal drugs coming out of South America. There is a literal war over drug turf 'behind the bridge' in Port of Spain. As far as possible, tourists should avoid these areas. This is not a good sign for any kind of venture in tourism, and is probably the most serious threat to social sustainability. Many foreign countries have already posted travel warnings about the situation in Trinidad and Tobago, although the republic is not singular in this respect. Although the situation in Trinidad and Tobago is not justifiable, many other countries more dependent on the tourism product, for example in the Caribbean region, suffer the same fate.

There is no excuse for any kind of violence during carnival time, but whether we like it or not, carnival celebrations represent the dethronement of the sacred (Mitchell, 2000). Even though the pre-Lenten Trinidad Carnival instituted by the French eventually took to the streets, it still occurred in a 'world apart' (Mitchell, 2000). Thus, as any other pre-Lenten carnival, the Trinidad Carnival is an inversion of normal social order, a cathartic tension between social controls and social protest, a temporary spectacle of inversion of a more permanent revolution of the social order. Carnival or no, the licentiousness, this 'inversion of social order', this 'cathartic tension between social controls and social protest', happens every day somewhere in Trinidad and Tobago. Carnival-based behaviour is part of the culture, and the accommodation of tourists is not really part of the mentality of the Trinidadian masses, although maybe it is to a small extent of the people of Tobago. People in Trinidad and Tobago were never educated to appreciate tourists; indeed a threat to the sustainability of tourism.

Violent behaviour of any kind is unwarranted, but it appears that this is a problem associated with the Trinidad Carnival. Nevertheless, the same is true for the several pre-Lenten carnivals studied around the world. Security forces in Trinidad boasted of a 'safe' celebration in 2004, but the level of violence associated with the annual carnival is difficult to forecast in subsequent celebrations. Censorship of the mass media is a common political ploy, and oftentimes reporting institutions provide reports that are more positive in order to safeguard the carnival. The carnival forms a major part of the tourism product. Even the maps produced by the Tourism and Industrial Development Corporation of Trinidad and Tobago (TIDCO) have been 'sanitized'. These maps exhibit the so-called safe areas of Port of Spain, but simultaneously omit directions to the slums and shanties on the periphery of the city. In other words, tourists receive indirect warnings in such documents to avoid these areas. It is quite possible that middle-class tourists are seen as representative of authority, colonialism and oppression, as vestiges of domination; their presence alone puts them at risk in certain situations. The rebellion exhibited by the underclass during the era of slavery in Trinidad did not go away. That selfsame rebellion manifests itself today in one form or another against tourists.

Conclusion

In Trinidad and Tobago, there will always be the bourgeoisie and the proletariats. With the arrival of emancipation and independence, a proclamation arose across the state that 'massa day done' (the era of the slave master has ended) but the element of repression is still present in more sophisticated ways. Economic independence is lacking in certain areas of the country. Persistent poverty and high unemployment is obvious. The covert Afro–Indo racial war brewing politically and otherwise in the system will continue indefinitely, and the inequality that envelops the masses will be a constant shroud over the landscape. Many people will remain in economic bondage. Reaction to this economic situation engenders to some extent the violence expressed against tourists as well as against domestic participants during carnival celebrations. Carnival from its very beginnings in Trinidad has always been rife with 'warfare'. It is a fact that carnival celebrations serve as pressure valves that seek to release the feelings and grievances of a population in song, music, dance, gastronomy and masquerade. Indeed, the Trinidad Carnival is unique in the sense that it is internalized by the masses as they go about their daily lives. Regardless of ethnicity, creed or class the carnival culture affects everyone directly or indirectly.

Many are the threats and barriers that Trinidad and Tobago must overcome on the road to the social sustainability of tourism. Some of the barriers are more difficult to overcome than others, for example, social class and status; hence, some people from the ranks of the destitute and impoverished who exist on the carnivalesque landscape will continue to commit violent acts during the carnival season. It is a matter of history, culture and politics. If any kind of sustainability is to be attained, changes in the concept of the masses concerning the views they hold of their natural environment must occur. This can only be achieved through proper and intense education programmes. In order for the tourism product to survive, the peoples of Trinidad and Tobago must embark on a programme to truly appreciate tourists; this is an imperative. Unless the illicit drug war ceases, the true prognosis is that amid the sensuality and sexual freedom, violence in all its forms will continue to proliferate on the landscape;

this, in turn, will negate the social sustainability of tourism in Trinidad and Tobago. Much more surveillance is required by the armed forces on land and sea to control or eliminate the drug-running activity. Although 'anytime is Trinidad time', time management is a very serious issue, and a new approach should be entertained if there is to be any hope for social sustainability in the tourism sector. All is not lost, for despite a few isolated violent acts committed annually against participating tourists by citizens of Trinidad and Tobago, tourists continue to immerse themselves in the 'carnival mentality' and participate with glee in the bacchanal.

References

Alexander, G. (2009) Construction main cause of downtown flooding – Imbert. *Trinidad and Tobago Guardian*, 7 August 2009. Available at: http://guardian.co.tt/news/general/2009/08/07/construction-main-cause-downtown-flooding-imbert (accessed 7 August 2009).

Associated Press (2005) Lose yourself at Trinidad's Carnival. Available at: http://www.cnn.com/2005/TRAVEL/DESTINATIONS/01/19/trinidad.carnival.ap/index.html (accessed 20 January 2005).

Birth, K. (1999) *Anytime is Trinidad Time*. University Press of Florida, Gainesville, Florida.

Bissessar, A. (2002) Addressing ethnic imbalances in the public services of plural societies: the case of Guyana and Trinidad and Tobago. *International Journal of Public Sector Management* 15, 55–68.

Clawson, D.L. (2006) *Latin America and the Caribbean: Lands and Peoples*. McGraw Hill, New York.

Coomansingh, J. (2005). The commodification and distribution of the steelpan as a conflicted tourism resource. PhD thesis (Geography), Kansas State University, Manhattan, Kansas.

Coomansingh, J. (2006) The intersections of tourism, culture and society in the creation of a temporary reality in the Trinidad Carnival. *eRTR (e-Review of Tourism Research)* 4, 85–91.

Coomansingh, J. (2008) Eye-food: an exhibition of sexuality and sensuality in the pre-Lenten Trinidad Carnival. In: *Proceedings, Annual Meeting of the Association of American Geographers*, Boston, Massachusetts, 15–19 April, 2008, p. 288.

Cowley, J. (1996) *Carnival, Canboulay and Calypso*. Cambridge University Press, Cambridge.

Global Newswire (2001) Moves to develop tourism. *Financial Times*, 14 February 2001, p. 1.

Green, G.L. (1998) *Carnival and the politics of national identity in Trinidad and Tobago*. PhD thesis, The New School for Social Research, New York.

Henry-Kunzel, G. (1994) Tobago expects tourism to spur economy. *Hotel and Motel Management* 209, 21.

Hill, E. (1972) *The Trinidad Carnival: Mandate for a National Theater*. University of Texas Press, Austin, Texas/London.

Hutchinson-Jafar, L. (2005) Crime wave swamps Caribbean tourist destinations. CDNN (Cyber Diver News Network) Travel News, 13 October 2005. Available at: http://www.cdnn.info/news/travel/t051013.html (accessed 17 September 2010).

InternetExpress (2000) Carnival goose an endangered species. In: *Trinidad and Tobago Express*. Available at http://trinidadexpress.com (accessed 13 August 2000).

John, M. (2004) *The Plantation Slaves of Trinidad 1783-1816: A Mathematical and Demographic Enquiry*. Cambridge University Press, Cambridge.

Koningsbruggen, P. (1997) *Trinidad Carnival:*

A Quest for Identity. Macmillan, London.

Liverpool, H.U. (1994) Researching steelband and calypso music in the British Caribbean and U.S. Virgin Islands, *Black Music Research Journal* 14, 179–201.

Mangurian, D. (2002) A short history of the shiny drum. *IDBAmérica Magazine*, June 2001. Available at: http://iadb.org/idbamerica/English/MAY01E/may01e2.html (accessed 27 May 2002).

Mason, P. (1998) *Bacchanal: The Carnival Culture of Trinidad*. Temple University Press, Philadelphia, Pennsylvania/Latin American Bureau (Research and Action), London/Ian Randle Publishers, Kingston, Jamaica.

Mitchell, D. (2000) *Cultural Geography: A Critical Introduction*. Blackwell, Oxford.

Munasinghe, V. (2001) *Callaloo or Tossed Salad: East Indians and the Cultural Politics of Identity in Trinidad*. Cornell University Press, Ithaca, New York.

Potter, A. (2001) Costumes big business, as revelers get ready for Trinidad's pre-Lenten carnival. *Associated Press* (International News).

Richards, P. (2001) Trinidad and Tobago finds its tourism groove. *Interpress Service, English News Wire*, 25 January 2001. Available at: http://www.highbeam.com/doc/IPI-40361245.html (accessed 17 September 2010).

Rohter, L. (1998) A tiger in a sea of pussycats: Trinidad and Tobago bids goodbye to oil, hello to gas. *New York Times*, 4 September 1998, p. 1.

Rowntree, L., Martin, L., Price, M. and Wycoff. W. (2002) *Diversity Amid Globalization: World Regions, Environment and Development*. Prentice Hall, Englewood Cliffs, New Jersey.

Ryan, S. (1972) *Race and Nationalism in Trinidad and Tobago: A Study of Decolonization in a Multicultural Society*. University of Toronto Press, Toronto, Ontario.

Sampath, N. (1997) Mas' identity: global and local aspects of Trinidad Carnival. In: Abram, S., Waldren, J. and Macleod, D. (eds) *Tourists and Tourism: Identifying with People and Places*. Berg, Oxford/New York, pp. 149–171.

Scher, P. (2007) The devil and the bed-wetter. *Western Folklore*, Winter and Spring 2007, pp. 107–126.

Williams, E.E. (1964) *History of the People of Trinidad and Tobago*. Praeger, New York/Andre Deutsch, London.

Zelinsky, W. (1992) *The Cultural Geography of the United States: A Revised Edition*. Prentice Hall, Englewood Cliffs, New Jersey.

10 Sustainable Host–Guest Interactions on Islands: Bruny and Magnetic Islands

BRENT MOYLE, GLEN CROY AND BETTY WEILER

Monash University, Victoria, Australia

Introduction

With more than 100,000 islands scattered across the globe, approximately one in ten people in the world is an islander (King and Connell, 1999). Islands are also popular destinations for tourists, in part because of their inhabitants, who are seen by outsiders as being unusual, and even unique, with respect to their cultures and lifestyles (Carlsen, 1999). On many islands, tourism planners and policy makers attempt to capitalize on these distinct social and cultural elements of island life and use tourism as a tool for economic development and job creation (Carlsen, 1999; Scheyvens and Momsen, 2008).

Although tourism is recognized as having a number of benefits for island inhabitants, inappropriate development and visitor behaviour can result in adverse environmental, social and cultural impacts (Hall, 1994). Competition for space, infrastructure and key resources can also create resentment towards visitors, all of which can threaten the sustainability of the tourism industry and the islands themselves. On islands, the potential for friction is magnified by the temporal and spatial boundaries within which locals and visitors interact. It is, thus, essential that the sustainable management of tourism, perhaps more so on islands than in other contexts, incorporates active consideration of, and planning for, opportunities for host–guest interactions that are designed to respect the culture, lifestyle and traditional community values of local inhabitants and local environments. Arguably, attention to host–guest interactions is key not only to ensuring that visitors are aware of appropriate behaviours on the island, but also to optimizing the experience of island visitors, and thereby enhancing the sustainability of island tourism. This research proposes that managing host–guest interactions can optimize the positive impacts and the longer-term sustainability of island tourism interactions.

The chapter explores the perceptions of locals and visitors of facilitators of host–guest interactions, and discusses the implications of these perceptions for tourism sustainability for island communities. To do this, interaction is first conceptualized through the lens of social exchange theory, and the method of analysis used for the case study is outlined. Secondly, a brief introduction to the case study islands (the Australian Bruny Island and Magnetic Island) is presented. Thirdly, the facilitators of sustainable host–guest interactions are discussed and these are then linked back to the literature on sustainable tourism development. The chapter concludes with discussion of the implications for tourism planners and policy makers, and recommendations for future research.

Sustainability and Social Interaction

As social interaction is proposed as an avenue to enhancing island tourism sustainability; it is important to identify what it is. Social interaction is the personal and immediate aspects of exchange in everyday life, more simply, the actual encounters between people (Layder, 1994). Unsurprisingly, micro-sociology, the study of ways that individuals act and react to one another, has social interaction at its heart (Cerulo, 2009). Within micro-sociology, it has been widely acknowledged since the book *The Gift* (Mauss, 1954), that some form of exchange takes place during social interactions. The exchange interaction approach has led to the development and application of a variety of theories, with the most prominent approach labelled social exchange theory (Blau, 1964; Emerson, 1976). Social exchange theory incorporates a family of related conceptual models, all of which share a coherent social exchange perspective (Cropanzano *et al.*, 2001). In this perspective, social structures and processes impinge on and emerge from resource transfers between individuals and/or collectives (Markovsky *et al.*, 1988). Taken as a whole, social exchange theory conceptualizes the exchange of resources between individuals and groups, and provides a framework for understanding and fostering what can be sustainable relationships, interactions and transactions (Ap, 1992).

The interaction between hosts and guests has also received considerable attention in the tourism sphere, with many using social exchange theory to frame their studies (Sirakaya *et al.*, 2001). The form of social exchange theory most commonly applied in tourism conceptualizes the process of interaction as four key stages: the initiation of an exchange, the exchange formation, the exchange transaction evaluation and the evaluation of exchange consequences (Ap, 1992). In tourism, social exchange theory has been used primarily as a framework for understanding residents' collective perceptions of the consequences of interaction and, specifically, the economic, environmental and sociocultural impacts of tourism on communities (Jurowski *et al.*, 1997; Andereck *et al.*, 2005; Chhabra, 2007). In extreme cases, it has been found that inappropriate tourism development leads to harassment and even violence towards visitors by disgruntled facets of the local population (McNaughton, 2006; McElroy *et al.*, 2007; Moyle *et al.*, 2010a). This impact literature has aided the understanding of community attitudes towards tourism, and of how communities contribute to or inhibit support for tourism development. Consequently, importance has been placed on host–guest relations, with studies emphasizing the need to implement holistic approaches to ensure that tourism operates in a sustainable manner (Kuo, 2007; Uriely *et al.*, 2009). Importantly, these studies have provided the impetus to enhance the understanding of the process of the social interactions of tourism.

In the process-focused context, the second stage of host–guest interaction, the exchange formation, before actual interaction occurs, is core. The exchange-formation stage presents the antecedent conditions representing opportunities for an exchange, as perceived by at least one actor (Ap, 1992). At this stage, an actor predicts whether an exchange will result in rewards or benefits. Importantly, the resources exchanged do not need to be tangible nor economic. If the prediction is for rewards, the actor will attempt to maximize the possible rewards and benefits, though also seek to ensure that the exchanged resources are roughly equivalent. If either actor predicts the antecedents as unfavourable, they have the option to withdraw before the actual exchange of resources. If both actors view the conditions as favourable, then an exchange relationship usually forms. As such, this chapter examines the exchange-formation stage and, importantly, the hosts' and guests' perspectives of the facilitators for mutually beneficial social interaction. The focus on mutually beneficial interactions informs sustainable tourism development decisions for island communities. As a result of this focus, the conceptual contribution of this chapter is twofold. First, the chapter contributes to how hosts' perceptions of interactions with visitors inform the community's understanding and acceptance of tourism. Secondly, the chapter contributes to the underdeveloped, yet critical, sustainable tourism development dimension of guests' perceptions of interactions with island community locals. These contributions are made through the application of holistic social exchange theory to explore hosts' and guests' perceptions of the facilitators of interaction.

In-depth interviews were conducted with 15 key community and tourism stakeholders and 20 visitors on each of the two islands studied in order to uncover the facilitators of social interaction in a tourism context. In total, 70 interviews were completed, 30 with locals and 40 with guests. The interviews guided participants through the holistic social exchange theory process of interaction. The same set of questions was used to elicit responses from hosts and guests on the islands, with minor modifications to the beginning of the interviews to provide an appropriate background. Site observations and secondary data are also used to inform the analysis, which focuses on high-lighting the complex series of host–guest interactions that occurs on islands.

Qualitative analysis, through the lens of social exchange theory, enables an in-depth focusing on the antecedent conditions that facilitate sustainable host–guest interactions, the second stage in the process. None the less, because the interviews guided locals and visitors through every stage of the holistic interaction process, links are also explored between the facilitating antecedents of host–guest interaction and sustainable tourism outcomes.

Bruny and Magnetic Islands

Bruny Island is located off the east coast of Tasmania, in the southernmost and coolest part of Australia (Fig. 10.1). At over 100 km in length, Bruny Island is deceptively large, but has a small permanent population of 620 locals (Davis, 2004). The main tourist activities on the island centre on the community and the island's natural and historical attributes, including the South Bruny National Park (Moyle *et al.*, 2010a). There is a definite summer peak season of visitors to Bruny Island (Moyle *et al.*, 2010b); however, there are no island specific visitor numbers available, with the ferry claiming commercial-in-confidence status on their passenger numbers. The island is a small part of a large data-collection region, attracting approximately 330,000 domestic overnight visitors and 110,000 international visitors per annum (CD MOTA, 2009), though, again, it is difficult to identify how many of these actually visit the island. Indications from the island's residents are that Bruny Island largely attracts domestic tourists, predominantly from mainland Tasmania, including a number with holiday homes on the island. All the same, there is a small but growing number of interstate and international visitors to the island, mostly as part of a greater Tasmania visit. Caravans and camping are the main accommodation options on the island, though a small number of bed and breakfasts also cater for visitors. Again, there are also a number of holiday homes on the island, some of which are also rented to visitors.

Magnetic Island is located off the coast of Queensland, in subtropical northern Australia (Fig. 10.1). The island is on the iconic Great Barrier Reef and blends a World Heritage-listed National Park with a permanent population

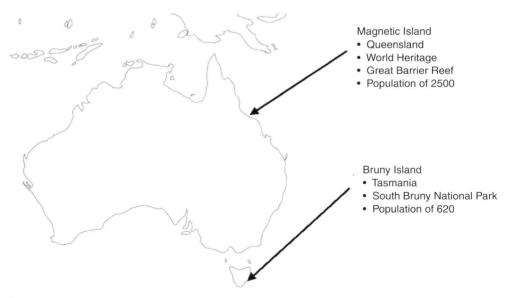

Magnetic Island
• Queensland
• World Heritage
• Great Barrier Reef
• Population of 2500

Bruny Island
• Tasmania
• South Bruny National Park
• Population of 620

Fig. 10.1. Location map of Magnetic and Bruny Islands, Australia.

of 2500 residents (Magnetic Island Holidays, 2008). Community events, the reef and the other natural features of the island are the main attractors, as well as a break from the close-by city of Townsville (Moyle *et al.*, 2010a,b). Compared with Bruny Island, Magnetic Island attracts a broader range of domestic interstate and international visitors, owing to its better accessibility and weather, and its position on the Great Barrier Reef. The larger region attracts approximately 1,100,000 domestic overnight and 150,000 international visitors per annum (CD MOTA, 2009). In comparison with Bruny Island, residents note that Magnetic Island attracts a large proportion of the visitors to the region, with peak periods during summer school holidays and Easter. There is a range of accommodation available on the island, including hotel resorts, apartments, a number of bed and breakfasts and, again, holiday homes available for rent to other visitors.

Magnetic Island is much more developed for tourism than Bruny Island. Although the islands are at opposite ends of Australia, both have an established tourism industry driven by a demand for natural experiences, and intersecting with vibrant local communities. Together, they offer an opportunity to explore how host–guest interactions can be harnessed for the social and cultural sustainability of islands.

Facilitators of Sustainable Host-Guest Relations

On Bruny Island (BI) and Magnetic Island (MI), hosts and guests viewed a number of conditions as favourable to social interaction. A chief facilitator of host–guest interaction emerging from the interviews was the festivals and events that take place on Bruny and Magnetic Islands. Many locals consider events, such as the annual International Jazz Festival on Magnetic Island, as important for the quality of life of the island inhabitants, and also in creating a forum where the community could interact with visitors without a major intrusion on their lifestyle, with friendships often emerging during events:

> Festivals are a great opportunity where we can choose to interact with tourists, we are not forced; it is all authentic. Heaps turn out from the community and all intermingle. Plenty of new friendships and even relationships have developed during the festivals on the island.
>
> (Local, MI)

Guests also reported events as having a considerable role to play in harnessing host–guest interaction, thereby enhancing the preservation and awareness of the culture, heritage and lifestyles of island communities. For example:

> we've met some amazing characters over the years at functions over long weekends, especially the Easter Wood Chopping festival. ... The atmosphere is amazing ..., every year we learn something new about the island. I've spoken to people about early explorers all the way through to the problems they're facing on the island today. The people we have met here are priceless, that's why we come over here every chance we get.
>
> (Visitor, BI)

As illustrated by this quote, festivals and events can induce repeat visitation, and add another dimension to the experience of visitors who come to feel welcomed into the community, so enhancing the potential sustainability of the island.

Connected to festivals and events, hosts and guests regarded community markets as a key facilitator of host–guest interaction. On both islands, there are multiple markets dispersed over the settlements. In addition to the opportunity to interact with visitors, these markets deliver much needed economic benefits to the community and counteract the seasonal variations in visitor numbers, and thus foster sustainable island tourism:

> Without the trickle of extra income we get from markets over the summer it would be very difficult for many people to stay on the island over the winter.
>
> (Local, BI)

On Magnetic Island, there is a weekly market in Arcadia and a monthly market at Horseshoe Bay. On Bruny Island, the markets rotate around the key settlements on the island. On both Bruny and Magnetic Islands, community groups, clubs and societies, and coast-care community-led environmental groups, run largely by volunteers, organize the majority of the festivals, markets and other events, including theatre performances, art exhibitions, music concerts and sporting events. The festivals, markets and events provide opportunities for locals to socialize, and in many instances are to attract visitors and harness host–guest interaction:

> The hard work of a dedicated few makes life here more liveable for everyone that's already here … but also gives people a reason to keep coming back and discovering something new.
>
> (Local, MI)

Thus, existing community groups on islands have a fundamental role in organizing the festivals, events, markets and the many other associated host–guest forums that facilitate host–guest relations. These events and other forums additionally facilitate sustainable host–guest interactions, as residents choose to participate, and, in this antecedent stage, have the inherent ability to evaluate the potential outcomes. Based on the choice to participate, residents perceive ownership of the interaction and are consequently more receptive to and positive about interactions with visitors (Moyle *et al.*, 2010b). It has also been identified that when the interaction is 'imposed' on the residents, some react very negatively, affecting the sustainability of the interactions, and island tourism sustainability generally (Moyle *et al.*, 2010a). The committed individuals within these groups, clubs and societies, who sustain many host–guest interactions, are also key facilitators to beneficial host–guest interactions. Many of these individuals invest themselves in the events to celebrate the culture, heritage and environment of islands:

> I know all of us are doing something worthwhile for future generations, as well as the people visiting now … it is important to conserve the culture and history here just as much as the environment.
>
> (Local, BI)

Another facilitator of sustainable interaction emerging from the interviews on Bruny and Magnetic Islands was the role of the local business owners and their employees. Visitors, in particular, regarded employees and business owners as important for facilitating beneficial host–guest interactions. On Bruny and Magnetic Islands, visitors considered direct interaction with tourism industry employees and business owners, such as accommodation providers and tour guides, as central to increasing awareness of the unique island environments:

> We went out for a day with Andy from reef ecotours ... he told us more about the environment than what type of coral or fish was swimming by ... he explained the delicacy of the ecology surrounding the entire island ... now I understand more about why we have to be so careful.

(Visitor, MI)

Visitors to Bruny Island also emphasized the importance of employees and business owners for building sustainable host–guest relations. On Bruny Island, the owners of other businesses, especially those that sold local products, including strawberries, cherries, wine, oysters and fudge, were considered by many visitors as important ambassadors for the island, leaving lasting impressions. Locals also recognized the importance of employees and owners, even those not perceived to be directly dependent on the tourism industry to survive, such as the general stores and restaurants.

Locals and visitors also acknowledged the work of local councils and parks agencies in ensuring the long-term viability of islands. For example, one visitor to Bruny Island commented on how interacting with a ranger during a previous experience resulted in volunteering during other stays on the island:

> We always put our kids in the summer program with the Tasmanian Parks and Wildlife Service run by a local ranger. We did it at the beginning so we could have some time alone without the kids but soon we found the program added so much to our own experience we have felt compelled to volunteer during previous trips to the island.

(Visitor, BI)

On Magnetic Island, the local council was also a key facilitator of host–guest interaction, with a programme connected to the Townsville Solar Cities project putting an interpretation centre on the island, which was designed to educate locals and visitors to the island about the use of sustainable forms of energy:

> It wasn't until going to the market and talking to the locals that I heard all about this Solar Cities project on the Island. The council had a stall set up this morning at Horseshoe and was telling everyone to visit their information centre down the street. We went there and spent ages learning about the solar technology used on the island ... we have been thinking about getting a solar panel at home and now we really think it's the way to go.

(Visitor, MI)

This programme illustrates an unusual link between structured host–guest interaction and wider sustainability outcomes, with the council potentially shaping the attitudes and modifying the post-visit behaviour of visitors in relation to sustainable energy use.

In addition, a number of visitors and locals alike noted that interaction was facilitated by community-driven signage, interpretation and other tourism literature about the island. Information about the island, compiled by the community, was regarded by locals as important for getting stories and messages through to visitors. A community group, 'Friends of Adventure Bay on Bruny Island', developed a book about the early explorers to Bruny, using the proceeds for maintenance along the island's busiest foreshore, and fostering sustainability.

In summary, this research on Bruny and Magnetic Islands suggests that islands have the potential to facilitate longer, deeper and richer interactions between hosts and guests, more so than tourism in other contexts. To build sustainable host–guest interactions, islands must maximize and mobilize the resources of key events, community group members, agencies and interpretation in order to generate community-driven and desired programmes, with the capacity to build enduring interactions between visitors and locals. The key point of these interactions is the residents' choice to interact, such as by attending events where visitors will be present, and, by choice, they have ownership of the interactions. The corollary is that locals may choose not to attend events, festivals and the like because of the visitors, and thus change the very nature and purposes of these community events, which attract visitors, into visitor events that exclude the local community. The findings point to a number of strategies for enhancing the host–guest interaction that will, among other things, help to keep visitors on islands longer and gain a greater understanding of the islands, promote repeat visitation through positive and endearing experiences, and improve the potential for sustainable island tourism interactions.

The host and guest interviewees reinforce the role of festivals, events and markets in providing positive and voluntary interactions, and the positive longer-term outcomes of relationship building, greater island experience, contribution to the economy and overall enhancement to the quality of island life. Lindroth *et al.* (2007) also note the sustainability role of community-driven festivals, events and markets in generating income, instilling a sense of pride in the local community, preserving local culture and providing visitors with a unique and authentic cultural experience. All the same, there needs to be careful consideration that festivals, events and markets do not transform the host–guest relationship into one of subservience, menial employment and consequent community discontent (Faulkenberry *et al.*, 2000).

Committed island volunteers, business owners and employees are the frontline interaction agents with guests, and are crucially important for any community. From the interviews and observations, the committed individuals are even more important for tourism experiences within these relatively isolated and small island populations. Their role in creating and maintaining the events that facilitate interaction, and in the development of understanding of the important island attributes, including the environment, lifestyle and culture, were identified as leading impacts on the guest experience. Without the commitment and sincerity of islanders in interacting with guests, the experiences of the wider island community and guests would not be sustainable (Greer, 2002).

There were two final points in enhancing the sustainability of island and tourism experiences. First, the crucial role that government played in the provision of services, facilities and infrastructure to support the community and the guests. The roles of government organizations were highlighted (especially as both islands had protected areas) as a positive addition and learning element to the guests' experiences. Secondly, government organizations also facilitated, along with community members and groups, interpretation and communication about the importance of the islands, and about community and sustainable practices on the islands by hosts and guests. Overall, the social interactions between hosts and guests provided positive opportunities for communication, understanding and enhancement of the economic, social and environmental sustainability of the islands, and for tourism on the islands.

Implications, Future Research and Conclusion

This research has implications for island tourism planners and policy makers. First, it demonstrates that managing host–guest interactions can optimize the positive impacts and the longer-term sustainability of island tourism interactions. As such, there are a number of strategies that can be actively pursued to foster positive host–guest interactions and to promote repeat interaction. For example, islands can take a more strategic approach to the use of special events, festivals and markets as a marketing and planning tool. Importantly, the results highlight the fact that community events must be driven by and for the community to engender voluntary interactions (Faulkenberry *et al.*, 2000). In addition, individuals, businesses, community groups, local councils and government authorities can be given incentives, such as funding and resources, to support programmes, communication and infrastructure aimed at enhancing host–guest interactions.

Further research could explore what might be the key inhibitors of sustainable host–guest relations. These inhibitors might include, but are not limited to, perceived negative impacts of tourism and development, negative community attitudes toward tourism and tourists, poor communication and promotion of opportunities for interaction, lack of support for tourism, funding and infrastructure to foster interaction, and lack of coordination, collaboration and planning to sustain interactions. Indeed, it may be that some strategies may either facilitate or inhibit sustainable host–guest relations on islands, depending on the context. As a result, officers need to tailor social interaction programmes to specific island contexts, ensuring that these programmes adhere to the overall strategy for the sustainable tourism on the island.

In conclusion, this chapter has explored the facilitators of sustainable host–guest relations, and discussed implications for the overall sustainability of tourism development on islands. The key facilitators of host–guest relations on Bruny and Magnetic Islands included festivals, events and markets, driven by community groups, clubs, societies and coast-care groups. Tour guides, accommodation providers, other local business owners and employees, parks agencies, community-driven signage and interpretation, and local council programmes, were also facilitators of host–guest relations. Each of these actors has a fundamental role to play in building healthy sustainable host–guest relations on islands. Finally, this research illustrates the usefulness of social exchange theory for understanding not only residents' perceptions of the impacts or consequences of tourism, but also hosts' and guests' perceptions of the facilitating antecedents of host–guest interaction.

References

Andereck, K.L., Valentine, K.M., Knopf, R.C. and Vogt, C.A. (2005) Residents' perceptions of community tourism impacts. *Annals of Tourism Research* 32, 1056–1076.

Ap, J. (1992) Residents' perceptions on tourism impacts. *Annals of Tourism Research* 19, 665–690.

Blau, P. (1964) *Exchange and Power in Social Life*. John Wiley, New York.

Carlsen, J. (1999) Tourism impacts on small islands: a longitudinal study of community attitudes to tourism on the Cocos (Keeling) Islands. *Pacific Tourism Review* 3, 25–35.

CD MOTA (Compact Disk Monitor of Tourism Activity) (2009) Online databases for the International Visitor Survey (IVS) and the National Visitor Survey (NVS). Tourism Research Australia, Canberra, Australian Capital Territory. Available at www.tra. australia.com (accessed 3 June 2010).

Cerulo, K.A. (2009) Nonhumans in social interaction. *Annual Review of Sociology* 35, 531–552.

Chhabra, D. (2007) Exploring social exchange theory dynamics in Native American casino settings. *UNLV Gaming Research and Review Journal* 11, 31–48.

Cropanzano, R., Rupp, D.E., Mohler, C.J. and Schminke, M. (2001) Three roads to organizational justice. In: Ferris, J. (ed.) *Research in Personnel and Human Resources Management, Volume 20*. JAI Press, Greenwich, Connecticut, pp. 1–113.

Davis, B. (2004) Bruny Island ferry – 50th anniversary. *Bruny News* 3, 1–41.

Emerson, R. (1976) Social exchange theory. *Annual Review of Sociology* 2, 335–362.

Faulkenberry, L.V., Coggeshall, J.M., Backman, K.F. and Backman, S.J. (2000) A culture of servitude: the impact of tourism and development on South Carolina's coast. *Human Organization* 59, 86–95.

Greer, J. (2002) Developing trans-jurisdictional tourism partnerships – insights from the island of Ireland. *Tourism Management* 23, 355–366.

Hall, C.M. (1994) Tourism in Pacific Island microstates: a case study of Vanuatu. *Tourism Recreation Research* 19, 59–64.

Jurowski, C., Uysal, M. and Williams, D.R. (1997) A theoretical analysis of host community resident reactions to tourism. *Journal of Travel Research* 36, 3–11.

King, R. and Connell, J. (1999) *Small Worlds, Global Lives: Islands and Migration*. Pinter, London.

Kuo, I. (2007) Where West meets the Middle East – Jumeirah Mosque visit. *Tourism Recreation Research* 32, 31–38.

Layder, D. (1994) *Understanding Social Theory*. Sage, London.

Lindroth, K., Ritalahti, J. and Soisalon-Soininen, T. (2007) Creative tourism in destination development. *Tourism Review* 62, 53–58.

Magnetic Island Holidays (2008) Welcome to Magnetic Island … The Ultimate Destination for Queensland Holidays! Available from: http://www.visitmagneticisland.com. au/ (accessed 20 July 2008).

Markovsky, B., Willer, D. and Patton, T. (1988) Power relations in exchange networks. *American Sociological Review* 53, 220–236.

Mauss, M. (1954) *The Gift*. Free Press, Glencoe, Illinois.

McElroy, J.L., Tarlow, P. and Carlisle, K. (2007) Tourist harassment: review of the literature and destination responses. *International Journal of Culture, Tourism and Hospitality Research* 1, 305–314.

McNaughton, D. (2006) The host as uninvited guest: hospitality, violence and tourism. *Annals of Tourism Research* 33, 645–665.

Moyle, B., Croy, G. and Weiler, B. (2010a) Tourism interaction on islands: the community and visitor social exchange. *International Journal of Culture, Tourism and Hospitality Research* 4, 96–107.

Moyle, B., Croy, W.G. and Weiler, B. (2010b) Community perceptions of tourism: Bruny and Magnetic Islands, Australia. *Asia Pacific Journal of Tourism Research* 15, 353–366.

Scheyvens, R. and Momsen, J.H. (2008) Tourism and poverty reduction: issues for small island states. *Tourism Geographies* 10, 22–41.

Sirakaya, E., Teye, V. and Sönmez, S.F. (2001) Examining the sources of differential support for tourism industry in two Ghanaian cities. *Tourism Analysis* 6, 29–40.

Uriely, N., Maoz, D. and Reichel, A. (2009) Israeli guests and Egyptian hosts in Sinai: a bubble of serenity. *Journal of Travel Research* 47, 508–522.

11 Sustainable Tourism in High-latitude Islands: Shetland Islands

RICHARD BUTLER

University of Strathclyde, Glasgow, Scotland

Introduction

Tourism development in small relatively isolated islands, especially those in cold waters, faces certain advantages in achieving a more sustainable form than does development in islands in warm waters, primarily because of the likelihood that smaller numbers of tourists will be attracted to cold-water destinations than to their tropical or subtropical counterparts (Butler, 2006). Conversely, such islands may face greater difficulty in attracting tourists at all unless they have specific attractions that make them stand out as desirable destinations. The Shetland Islands, the focus of this chapter, are very typical of the first type of islands mentioned above. They are relatively small in area, located at 60° north, not easily or cheaply accessible, have a small population and are on the north-western fringe of Europe, exposed to some of the worst north Atlantic weather and sea conditions. Despite these negative features, the islands have succeeded in attracting numbers of tourists for over 200 years, partly because of some unusual features, and partly because, in recent years, of the improved accessibility, accommodation and visibility that have resulted from the discovery and exploitation of offshore oil resources in the late 20th century (Butler, 1996, 1997). Current tourist numbers are approximately 100,000 annually, of which just over one third are cruise ship passengers (SIC, 2008). The discovery of oil has proved beneficial overall to tourism in Shetland, perhaps somewhat paradoxically considering the generally negative relationship between resource extraction and tourism. One of the reasons for this is because the discovery and exploitation of the oil resources resulted in the Shetland Islands achieving a level of control over their resources and development not shared by many island groups, unless they are sovereign states. This level of control, along with a distinctive attitude towards development, has allowed Shetland to determine its own future to a significant degree, and has ensured that it is able to prevent development, both of tourism and in other areas, from becoming unsustainable. This chapter reviews the characteristics of the Shetland Islands, their tourism development, the achieving of controls and the policies adopted to ensure a high degree of sustainability for tourism and other development.

Setting

The Shetland Islands represent the northernmost extension of the British Isles. They comprise mostly granite rock, which, because of the constant battering of the North Atlantic Ocean, has weathered into impressive sea cliffs dissected by deep and narrow fjords on the western side of the islands. The eastern side is lower, with occasional sandy beaches. The climate is typically maritime temperate, with cool summers (15°C average maximum) and winters (5°C average maximum), constant wind (average 15 knots), and a high proportion of days with rain (around 200 annually), conditions that are not particularly encouraging for tourism. The island population of some 21,950 is located on 15 of the over 100 islands, with the largest centre of population being the capital, Lerwick, which has 6830 inhabitants (SIC, 2008). The population is scattered, with few large settlements, mostly in small groups located around harbours or sheltered fertile pockets of land. The islands were settled several thousand years ago, and successive waves of invaders included Picts, Vikings and Scots. They were one of the first parts of Britain settled by the Vikings in their westward expansion a 1000 years ago and served as a final stop before the exploratory voyages to Iceland, Greenland and North America at that time. Many of the features of the island reveal Scandinavian roots in their names and the Shetland dialect has strong links to the Norwegian language to this day. The islands belonged to Norway until 1469, when they were given to Scotland as part of a wedding dowry and were never redeemed (Irvine, 1985). They are, thus, along with the Orkney Islands to the south, the last parts of the UK to become a part of Great Britain. As such, they have always represented somewhat of an anachronism, with a distinctive outlook from the rest of Scotland, and an outward rather than introverted attitude. Over the centuries, Shetlanders have taken advantage of their maritime location and become seamen of note, many being employed in both the Royal Navy and the Merchant Marine (or Merchant Navy), as well as whaling fleets, serving in foreign parts and maintaining strong links with Europe and North America. The location of the islands is highly strategic, lying astride the northern approaches of the North Sea, and this location was reflected in defence-related developments in both the First and Second World Wars, as well as for centuries before.

The islands are low lying, the highest point is only 450 m above sea level, soil is relatively thin and poor, and arable land is in short supply. Most agriculture is crofting (small-scale subsistence farming based on sheep and limited arable crop production), reflecting the marginal climate and soil conditions. Shetlanders have relied heavily on the sea for their survival, and this reliance has continued to the present, with fishing representing one of the mainstays of the Shetland economy, although in the last few decades fish farming (aquaculture) particularly of salmon, has exceeded the value of wild fishing for the first time. Along with fishing, and farming, tourism has become another crucial element in the Shetland economy. Knitwear, based on wool, was for many years a fourth leg of the economy, but has declined over the last half century in the face of competition from machine-produced products and artificial fibres. Today, the mainstay of the Shetland economy is revenue (past and present) from offshore oil, the discovery of which changed the nature of the Shetland way of life quite dramatically, although at the same time, perhaps, ensuring its survival.

Not surprisingly, the primary way of reaching Shetland has always been by sea, and this remains true today. Roll-on roll-off car ferries provide service between Shetland (Lerwick) and the Scottish mainland at Aberdeen at the present time, both directly and via the Orkney Islands. There is a fleet of inter-island ferries operated by the Shetland Islands Council (SIC), which link the Shetland mainland to the outlying islands of the group. Air services link Shetland with Orkney and the Scottish mainland, and also serve the outlying islands, many of which have airstrips constructed by the armed forces, either during wartime or subsequently. There is a reasonable road network on the islands which has been substantially upgraded in recent decades, funded mostly by oil-related revenue. Communications also underwent a major upgrading in the 1970s and 1980s to serve the oil developments, as did the major airport at Sumburgh. Sumburgh provides the main base for air services to Shetland and to the offshore structures and became one of the most heavily used airports in the UK in terms of total take-offs and landings in the 1980s; air passengers at Sumburgh rose from 47,000 in 1971 to over 1.3 million by 1978, and currently number around 330,000.

Oil-related Developments in Shetland

It is impossible to explain the current nature of life and economic activity on Shetland without reviewing the process and effects of offshore oil discoveries and developments that occurred there in the decades from 1970, because these events have had such major impacts on not only the economy of the islands but also their very fabric and way of life. Oil was discovered beneath the North Sea off the east coast of England and the west coast of the Netherlands in the second half of the 20th century, and exploration continued northwards towards Scotland and Norway through the 1960s and 1970s. Major fields were discovered to the east of Shetland and Orkney in 1971 (Wills, 1991), and the island groups were the obvious and nearest landfall for pipelines and hence for the development of oil terminals for the transshipment of the oil. At the time of the discoveries, the British economy was performing badly and the government of the day was keen to extract and sell oil as rapidly as possible to ease pressure on the economy and the currency. Local authorities, which in the UK exercise control over development, were encouraged and pressured to approve rapid and large-scale proposals for oil-related developments such as terminals, oil rig construction sites and ports for ships servicing the rigs. Shetland received a large number of requests for approval of pipelines and terminals, in general with each oil company involved requesting its own pipeline and terminal. Shetland faced the possibility of up to 16 terminals with associated shipping berths and pipeline connections being constructed at a very rapid rate on a massive scale, which threatened the lifestyle and economy of the islands.

At that time, the Shetland economy was performing well, unemployment was below the national average, income from fishing, agriculture and tourism was increasing and the island authorities argued that the islands did not 'need' the offshore oil developments. The Islands Council accepted the national interest in having Shetland as an onshore base, but stated that it would 'give no encouragement to developments and (would) oppose proposals where these … put Shetland at unnecessary risk … and will at no time put commercial or industrial development before those of the Shetland Community' (SIC, 1978). Led by a highly articulate and committed chief executive, the Council rejected all of the proposals and announced that it would approve only one terminal which all companies would have to share, with one pipeline access (Butler and Nelson, 1994b). In addition, the Council was to have equity in the terminal, to be in charge of marine operations as the harbour authority, to provide the power for the terminal, to impose various conditions of employment on the construction labour force for the terminals and to receive compensation for each barrel of oil brought ashore to be processed at the terminal. Such conditions were previously unheard of, but the Council held firm and ultimately succeeded in having a private bill (*Zetland County Council Act 1974*, UK Parliament, 1974) passed in Parliament which gave the Council those powers and rights to license dredging and construction up to 3 miles offshore, thus effectively controlling all pipelines coming to Shetland. The national government agreed to these conditions to ensure a speedy resolution of the planning issues, and also agreed that an oil compensation fund would not be considered in the calculation of the support grant given by central government to the local council (Nelson and Butler, 1993). While there was still some opposition to the oil developments, subsequent evaluation of the Council's actions has seen Shetland held up as the appropriate way for local authorities to deal with such major developments and Shetland has often been quoted as being one of very few local governments to have been successful in controlling and managing major developments, particularly those controlled by external agencies and corporations working with the at least tacit support of the central government (Butler and Nelson, 1994a).

The Shetlanders' argument, that their way of life was worth preserving in the face of major development and political pressure, set an example which unfortunately few other small island authorities have been inclined or able to follow. Of relevance to tourism, and particularly to sustainable tourism, is the fact that the powers and attitude which the local authority in Shetland gained allow that authority to ensure that any and all development is in line with maintaining the desired 'quality of life' of the community, and that when granting permission for development 'the Council will apply the precautionary principle to limit those risks, even where scientific or technical knowledge is inconclusive' (SIC, 2004). This has translated into development which is appropriate in scale to Shetland, which supports rather than conflicts with existing activities, which helps ensure the long-term future of Shetland, and which is environmentally benign and is, in essence, sustainable in terms of the economy, the community and the environment. The *Shetland Local Plan*, adopted in 2004, is based 'on the principle of sustainable development ... which means that all development proposals should achieve the best possible outcome in environmental, social and economic terms, helping to ensure that new development allows future generations of people at least the same level of opportunities and choices as we enjoy today' (SIC, 2004).

Tourism in Shetland before 1970

Unlike many areas, Shetland has collected reliable and consistent statistics on many aspects of the islands and their population and economic activity. The argument was made immediately following the discovery of oil that, in order to deal with the ensuing requests for development approval, the Islands Council would need good and reliable information of its own and not have to rely on other sources. Thus, in 1972, the Council started collecting data and publishing this in an annual report, *Shetland in Statistics*, a document which has been produced now for over three decades. From the point of view of tourism, basic information is collected on accommodation, visitor arrivals, membership in local associations, levels of use and the overall contribution of tourism to the economy of the islands. Unfortunately, there have not been regular visitor surveys so little can be said about the activities of visitors, their preferences or general behaviour, but surrogate information exists on some aspects of visitation patterns.

For many centuries, visitors to Shetland – other than occupying forces such as the Vikings – were mostly shipborne traders, Shetland having strong connections, for example, with the ports of the Hanseatic League in Europe and with the fishing fleets of countries such as the Netherlands. Tourists, i.e. those coming to Shetland for pleasure or curiosity rather than business, were very few in number through the 19th century. Accounts exist of intrepid travellers visiting the northern isles of the UK in the 18th century, Sir Walter Scott set one of his novels (*The Pirate*) in Shetland, and the lighthouse builders, the Stevenson family, explored the islands as well as constructing lighthouses there; but such visitors were rare. Few facilities existed for tourists, accommodation was extremely basic and limited to a few settlements only, and the general economy was precarious. Life was extremely hard, survival difficult, and landlords absent on the mainland and ruthless in extracting their rents. There was considered little reason to visit Shetland and, more pertinently, the sea voyage has always been hazardous. The tide race to the south of the mainland runs at 7 knots, a speed higher than many sailing ships could manage, and the islands have experienced many shipwrecks, including at least one from the Spanish Armada. It was not until the advent of steam power that a visit to Shetland could be expected to have reliable arrival and departure dates, although even now storms are severe enough to delay sailings for several hours, if not days.

By the late 19th century, small numbers of tourists were arriving on Shetland, and these comprised several distinct groups. One was of fishermen seeking trout in the inland lochs, another was of painters and artists, another of scientists – particularly geologists exploring the geomorphology of the islands; another group consisted of historians and archaeologists, with a final group of curiosity seekers. Virtually all such tourists were male, with only a very small number of women among the curiosity seekers. Such a composition of the tourist market in Shetland was very similar to that of tourists to Scotland as a whole until the mid-19th century. Tourism to mainland Scotland changed significantly from the 1820s onwards, with large numbers of educated affluent tourists visiting scenic parts of Scotland to witness the landscapes described in Sir Walter Scott's novels, and later popularized by poets such as Wordsworth and Southey, and painters such as Turner and Landseer (Butler, 1985). Of equal importance, from the 1850s onwards, was the presence in Scotland each summer of the Royal family, holidaying at Balmoral Castle and setting an example for other visitors (Butler, 2008).

The popularity of Scotland widened in the late 19th century and tourists spread from the mainland to the islands, first to the Hebrides in the west, and then to Orkney and Shetland. Hotels began to appear in Shetland, and the idea of catering for tourists in terms of accommodation, meals, transport and guiding had taken some small hold among the population. Through the 20th century, tourism continued to grow slowly, with numbers increasing as far as can be seen from the limited information available. One particular attraction which became of increasing importance by the middle of the century was wildlife, particularly birds. Shetland has some of the largest seabird colonies in the world, which include gannets, skuas, terns and auks (including puffins). Also, the islands sit astride one of the great migratory bird routes, and in spring and autumn considerable numbers of birds pass through the islands, including an incomparable number of extreme rarities. Shetland quickly became known as a bird-watching centre, and an internationally respected bird observatory was established in the 1960s on Fair Isle, the southernmost island.

It is likely that the slow expansion of tourism would have continued through the 20th century, with visitor numbers being 'controlled' by limited and costly access, the relatively high cost of facilities on the islands, and the sparse and somewhat low-grade accommodation and services. Visitor numbers increased from 17,000 in 1960 to 23,000 by 1963 (Luckhurst, 1964), and to 38,000 in 1990, with an average length of stay of seven nights (System Three, 1991). Few hotels had en-suite rooms, many were open for only short seasons, meals were often available only to residents, car hire was almost absent and other facilities were lacking. A holiday on Shetland was, therefore, an acquired taste, and while repeat visitation rates appear to have been similar to those of the more remote areas of the mainland, there was little to suggest that tourism would become a major factor in the Shetland economy. Its perceived relatively low level of importance can be judged by the fact that when the Islands Council was creating its policy towards oil developments, it did not list tourism as one of the 'traditional' forms of economic activity which it intended to protect (Nelson and Butler, 1993). It is perhaps ironic, therefore, that it was the discovery of offshore oil that brought about a significant positive change to tourism in Shetland, while those developments may well have been anticipated to be something which would impact negatively on tourism and threaten the landscape and wildlife that were the principal attractions for tourists.

Tourism in Shetland Post Oil Development

The impacts of the discovery of oil on tourism have been discussed at more length elsewhere (Butler and Fennell, 1994) and need only be summarized here. One immediate effect was the arrival on the islands of considerable numbers of employees of oil and related companies, tasked with acquiring properties and establishing facilities for the even larger numbers who would follow once the oil was being extracted and brought to Shetland for treatment and onward movement. These individuals needed to be accommodated, fed and provided with services and transport. Money was of little concern, speed was all important, but many of these individuals had travelled widely and had expectations and demands of the accommodation and related services. The upshot was a massive overhaul and improvement in the accommodation and other tourist stock. Hotels were not only redecorated but often completely redeveloped, en-suite rooms became the norm, restaurants were expanded, car-hire firms established, communications greatly improved, and a new airport terminal constructed, roads rebuilt and ferries enlarged and improved. Of equal importance to the tourism industry on Shetland was the fact that these new visitors were not present only for a few weeks in the summer but throughout the year, and they and their replacements would be visiting for several years. Thus hotels and other services had to remain open year-round rather than just maintaining a skeleton staff and service for 8 months of the year and relying on local bar and meal trade from October to May, as had been the pattern. There were major implications. One was that staff could be employed full time on a year-round basis, resulting in the ability of hotels to retain trained staff and also to pay them better, although this did have implications for those who employed the hotel staff during the off-season, and Shetland began to experience a labour shortage in all areas of employment. A second implication was that the oil companies were not prepared to have staff arrive in Shetland and not be able to find accommodation; therefore, they block-booked rooms or even establishments for several weeks or months, paying for the accommodation even if staff did not arrive because of bad weather or other demands on their services. Accommodation establishments were free to make these rooms available after a certain time each day, which allowed some establishments to achieve an occupancy rate in excess of 100% at times, with rooms being paid for and not used, and then re-rented to visitors who did show up needing accommodation. Overall, those in the tourism industry in Shetland experienced almost a decade of guaranteed full take-up of services and rooms, providing them with funds to undertake the massive upgrading required by the new visitors. By 1980, Shetland had a higher proportion of en-suite rooms and upgraded establishments than any other part of Scotland, with services to match. The value of these 'oil tourists' can be seen from the fact that visitor expenditure in Shetland rose from £3.6 million in 1982 to £10 million in 1991; by 2006, the visitor expenditure was estimated at £16.4 million (SIC, 2008).

Not all was beneficial for conventional tourism however, as most 'traditional' tourists could not get to Shetland or be sure of accommodation if they did travel there. Regular flights to Shetland were virtually all fully booked by business 'tourists', as were hotel beds and hired cars. Few tourists were willing to face a 12-hour boat trip with no guarantee of a bed when they arrived, and so 'pleasure' tourism to Shetland declined for over a decade. While full advantage was taken of the high reliable income to improve facilities, little thought was given to what might happen when the 'rush' related to oil ended. Little advertising of Shetland as a tourist destination was undertaken; as one hotel operator commented 'Why would I advertise for more tourists when my hotel was always completely full? I could not have taken any more bookings' (Survey respondent, 1989). Thus, potential tourists were not being 'sold' Shetland, and those in tourism in Shetland were neglecting, for understandable reasons at the time, their traditional conventional tourist market. When the oil boom ended, accommodation occupancy rates in some establishments declined from 100% to 20% in a year. The excellent upgraded accommodation and food establishments, the car-hire stock, the enlarged airport and rebuilt roads and ferry services became heavily underused, and permanent employment in those establishments and agencies declined equally rapidly. Recent (2007) occupancy levels in Shetland are lower than those in equivalent establishments in the Scottish Highlands and Islands, with Shetland figures being almost the same in the first third of the year, 10–20% lower in the peak summer season, and about 10% lower for the last third of the year (SIC, 2008). There is currently considerable oversupply of accommodation in Shetland in all categories, even in the peak summer months, with only self-catering establishments enjoying over 50% occupancy in that period. Table 11.1 shows the bed spaces available in accommodation establishments that are members of VisitShetland; it indicates that there has been relatively little growth in total beds available over the last 20 years, with most of the limited expansion being in Lerwick, the administrative and transport centre.

The sudden and somewhat surprisingly unforeseen downturn in business left the Shetland Islands tourism operators facing severe economic problems. Not only had most of their high-paying guaranteed customers now ceased to arrive, but there was no obvious replacement market. The former conventional tourist visitors had to be attracted back to Shetland and any negative media coverage of oil-related development counteracted with positive marketing. Rather fortunately for Shetland, the development of the concept of sustainable development was taking hold in the 1980s, along with a rise in popularity of ecotourism and nature-related holidays. Shetland was an attractive destination for both market segments. The local government had earned considerable praise for its stand against uncontrolled development by the oil and gas

Table 11.1 Bed spaces listed by VisitShetland. (Source: SIC, 2008.)

Type of accommodation	1976	1981	1986	1991	1996	2005	2006	2007
Hotels Lerwick	149	231	272	294	296	328	336	309
Hotels country[a]	292	342	310	301	295	215	152	175
Guest houses Lerwick	–	–	29	31	75	137	127	140
Guest houses country[a]	–	–	124	97	95	48	47	52
Bed and breakfast Lerwick	206	103	71	93	143	128	102	87
Bed and breakfast country[a]	154	203	107	208	65	40	32	28
Self-catering Lerwick	169[b]	271[b]	285[b]	23	38	101	114	125
Self-catering country[a]				515	383	364	549	496
Hostels Lerwick	76[b]	81[b]	146[b]	48	64	64	64	64
Hostels country[a]				99	61	35	35	35
Campsites Lerwick	0	0	117	28	60	60	50	50
Campsites country[a]	–	–	117	42	39	144	104	104
Böds[c]	0	0	0	0	63	76	76	76
Total	1046	1231	1461	1779	1677	1740	1788	1741

[a]'country', all Shetland Islands locations outside Lerwick.
[b]Includes Lerwick and 'country' numbers.
[c]A böd is an old fisherman's store (a mix of bothy and camping barn).

industries, and thus the islands were seen as 'unspoiled' and protected natural areas, and their populations of seabirds and other forms of wildlife, including marine mammals, made them attractive to nature or ecotourists (Butler and Nelson, 1994a). The abundance of distinctive cultural attributes, including archaeological and historic sites and the long summer days (with over 20 hours of light skies) also added to their appeal. A series of well-designed promotions featuring key lines such as 'Get away to it all', and an image of a Shetland landscape in evening light entitled 'Shetland at 11.00 pm' next to a black blank scene entitled 'London at 11.00 pm' proved very effective, and occupancy levels increased back to pre-oil levels within 2 years in many locations in Shetland.

Despite a potential disaster in January 1993 (Wills and Warner, 1993), when the supertanker 'Braer' was driven ashore on Shetland, losing its cargo of 100,000 tons of crude oil, tourism has continued a slow and steady growth. The severe storm which wrecked the 'Braer' created its own mini-boom for tourism, with over 500 media representatives arriving on the islands within 2 days of the wreck. So severe was the shortage of accommodation that a belated visit from a government minister saw him sleeping on the floor of the local school. The oil was dissipated by the severe wind and seas, and appears to be buried in one or two locations under the seabed south-west of Shetland (Ecological Steering Group on the Oil Spill in Shetland, 1994). The anticipated catastrophe did not occur, and the fact that the wreck took place during the winter spared many millions of seabirds from oiling (MPCU, 1993). A mass of tourist cancellations was avoided, and while numbers declined slightly, the reduction in visitor numbers was minimal and short lived. Despite some of the world's strongest safety and control measures on tankers visiting Shetland, the possibility of another wreck cannot be dismissed (Wills and Warner, 1993). It was the ultimate irony that the 'Braer' was not visiting Shetland at all, but was en route back to North America having taken on board oil from a Norwegian terminal.

While the oil terminal and associated business is still of crucial importance to the Shetland economy, and continued exploration is taking place to the west of Shetland, where new oil fields have been developed (in 2005), it now has little direct effect on tourism. Its legacy is still very much present, however, not only in the improved infrastructure, tourism related and otherwise, but also in the planning and development controls possessed by the islands authority and, perhaps as importantly, the attitude that exists on Shetland that if it has proved capable of dealing with large-scale oil companies, it can certainly deal with and control any other form of development and thus ensure the 'Shetland way of life'. This is an intangible attribute which is one of the tourist attractions of the islands and which enables Shetland to ensure that tourism, as other forms of economic activity, grows at a sustainable rate and remains at a scale that is in keeping with the resources and priorities of the islanders. While Shetland possesses limited tourist attractions, which may have meant that its tourism was likely never to become 'mass', it has the added advantage that its decision makers are able to prevent excessive or inappropriate development that might remove the level of sustainability it now enjoys. The overall development policy is stated in the following extract, which is found in both *The Shetland Structure Plan 2001–2016* (SIC, 2000) and in the *Shetland Local Plan* (SIC, 2004): 'To protect, sustain and enhance Shetland's natural resources and cultural heritage for future generations to enjoy and ensure that new development contributes to environmental quality'. In the context of tourism, the goal of the Islands Council is 'To create a sustainable tourism industry that achieves long-term economic development and avoids damage to the natural and built environment' (SIC, 2000, 2004).

The current tourist attractions or 'lions' (Fennell, 1994) of Shetland fall into two categories, those pertaining to the natural environment and those resulting from human settlement. The 2005/6 Shetland Visitor Survey reported that 77% of visitors to Shetland came 'to experience its natural and cultural heritage, whether that be Shetland's wildlife, history archaeology or landscapes' (SICDC, 2008). The magnificent cliff and coastal scenery, including some of the highest sea cliffs in western Europe, superb beaches and long fjords or voes, combined with the long summer days, attract many tourists. These attributes are combined with the wildlife, mammals such as otters, seals and whales and, in particular the extremely large seabird colonies and migratory rarities. Shetland has three National Nature Reserves and 81 Sites of Special Scientific Interest, and 13.5% of its total area is covered by statutory conservation sites. The cultural attractions include castles, brochs (Pictish towers), Viking structures and prehistoric underground villages, with some 7842 archaeological sites identified (SIC, 2008), as well as more recent constructions from the Middle Ages, up to and including the Second World War and the oil terminal at Sullom Voe. The nature of these attractions, their dispersed locations and, in some cases, difficult access mean that staying visitors tend to stay longer than in many tourist venues. This tendency is encouraged by the cost and time involved in reaching Shetland from most other places. The dispersed locations of many of the attractions have meant that most visitors hire cars on arrival in Shetland, either at Sumburgh Airport or Lerwick, the county town and site of the ferry terminal. The improved road network and the system of drive-on drive-off ferries allow good access to all parts of the Shetland 'mainland' and to many of the closer inhabited islands. The more remote islands, such as Foula and Fair Isle, have non-vehicular ferry services less frequently (once or twice a week) and also an air service from Tingwall Airport near Lerwick.

Tourist accommodation is located primarily within Lerwick, including the largest hotels, most bed and breakfast and some self-catering establishments, with a smaller number of establishments in Scalloway (Table 11.1). Single hotels are found in smaller settlements, such as those at Sumburgh, Brae, Balstasound and Busta, along with bed and breakfast establishments and a range of self-catering and hostel accommodation. There is one youth hostel in Lerwick and a recently rebuilt (2010) bird observatory on Fair Isle. On the outer islands, such as Foula and the Out Skerries, accommodation is nearly all in private homes. Provision of such accommodation provides a fairly direct income source in many communities as these establishments are almost all locally owned and operated, and tourism employment, apart from in the largest hotels, is generally of local people. Outside the established centres, particularly Lerwick, there are few facilities for tourists. Most of the premises licensed for food and beverages are in hotels, and facilities such as film theatres are often mobile and visit different centres on a regular but limited basis. Swimming pools exist only in Lerwick and Brae. Limited sports facilities exist, gymnasia are normally in conjunction with schools except for one that remains from the construction workers' camp in central Shetland near Sullom Voe.

The appeal of Shetland is, therefore, very much its outdoor natural environment, and given its location, its appeal can vary considerably with the weather being experienced. In recent decades, Shetland, like many of the Scottish island groups, has become increasingly popular with cruise lines. The number of cruise liners visiting Shetland has increased significantly, doubling since 1986, and the size of vessels has increased such that passenger numbers over the same period have increased more than fivefold (Table 11.2). Other smaller cruise vessels visit some of the outlying islands, Fair Isle in particular, where pressures on a small island population (there are 60 people on Fair Isle) are somewhat more intense (personal communication, 1999). In the low season, there are few attractions other than the annual music festival and Up Helly Aa, the reconstituted January 'Viking' ceremony, in which a specially constructed galley is set afire in the harbour after a torchlight parade by around 1000 participants through the streets of Lerwick. The limited attractions and facilities undoubtedly determine the fact that Shetland maintains a low rate of growth in tourism, with limited numbers of visitors, thus allowing the industry to remain at what might be felt to be a sustainable level. There is little or no crowding at any tourist site; only for the Up Helly Aa festival and the music festival is there excessive demand for accommodation and, under normal

Table 11.2. Cruise liner arrivals and passengers, Lerwick Harbour, Shetland. (Source: SIC, 2008.)

Year	1981	1986	1991	1996	2001	2005	2006	2007
Cruise liner arrivals	20	21	35	42	48	48	43	42
Cruise liner passengers	3564	6279	5240	12852	11601	17352	25966	18462

conditions, the current level of access by plane and boat is adequate for the numbers wishing to travel.

It is important to note that these transport services are not under the control of the Islands Council, although all services are subsidized by different levels of government, particularly the North Link Ferry Company. They are truly lifelines for the islands, not just for tourism but for the transport of all goods and almost all people. Not having control over these services is a serious issue and concern for the islanders, as they, and their tourist industry, are thus vulnerable to market changes, oil prices and the profitability of these routes and the companies serving them. As with many cold-water remote island communities (Baldacchino, 2006), with respect to access, the concern is its provision and maintenance rather than any potential or existing excessive capacity.

The Future

In many respects, the prognosis for tourism in Shetland is relatively optimistic, and this was recognized in both *The Shetland Structure Plan* (SIC, 2000), and in the *Shetland Local Plan* (SIC, 2004) which noted that 'Shetland's economy is becoming increasingly reliant on its service sector, and tourism has the greatest potential for growth in that sector'. At present, tourism's total economic value is much less than that of the fish or oil sectors, being approximately the same value to the Shetland economy as agriculture (just under 3%). However, tourism employs approximately 1200 people in Shetland out of an employment total of just over 12,000, more than those in all aspects of fishing, the same as all those involved in agriculture, and more than half as many as are employed in the oil terminal operations. If the current apparent increase in demand for nature-related tourism continues, then Shetland is in a good position to benefit from such a trend. In addition, its unique historical cultural attributes offer strong future potential as tourist attractions. From the point of view of sustainability, the political and geographical aspects of Shetland all point to continued sustainable growth and development of tourism. The political viewpoint of placing a high priority on the quality of life in Shetland, and in the maintenance of traditional activities and the distinctive way of life, suggest that Shetland will not rush headlong into mass tourism development, even if such a possibility existed. The geographical reality, the relatively poor climate, the limited access and the above-average cost of holidays in Shetland also mitigate against rapid and unsustainable growth in tourism.

All is not entirely guaranteed however. The initial flush of economic well-being brought about by the discovery and exploitation of oil in the 1970s that has already been discussed saw many Shetland tourism establishments benefit greatly, and most invested their profits in upgrading their establishments, an opportunity that had been beyond their financial ability before the income generated by the oil business. Such income levels are not available in the current economic climate and consequently, while standards in Shetland exceeded those in most of Scotland for at least two decades, this is no longer the case. The rest of Scotland has improved significantly in the quality of its tourism establishments and Shetland has not been able to maintain its lead over its competitors as normality has returned to the islands with respect to occupancy levels and there has been a need to promote the islands to ensure visitation. While the Island Council is more supportive of tourism now than 40 years ago when tourism was not regarded as a 'traditional' economic activity, it only rates two mentions in the islands' *Corporate Plan – Halfway Point Update* (SIC, 2009). The first mention is of four tourism projects to be undertaken, of which one, 'The Promote Shetland' project, had been approved and the second is the establishment of a Tourism Panel, one of four proposed, which 'is now in operation'. So while non-sustainable growth is extremely unlikely, the main problem facing the islands now is to maintain the market that they have gained over the past two decades. Success will depend on a number of factors, the reliability of sufficient and reasonably priced access, continued interest in natural and cultural tourism attributes and the political desire to maintain Shetland's distinctive characteristics. Perhaps, fortunately for Shetland, these three elements appear to be relatively secure for the foreseeable future.

References

Baldacchino, G. (2006) *Advances in Tourism Research, Extreme Tourism: Lessons from the World's Cold Water Islands.* McMillan, London.

Butler, R.W. (1985) The evolution of tourism in the Scottish Highlands in the 18th and 19th centuries. *Annals of Tourism Research* 12, 371–391.

Butler, R.W. (1996) Problems and possibilities of sustainable tourism: the case of the Shetland Islands. In: Briguglio, L., Butler, R., Harrison, D. and Filho, W. (eds) *Sustainable Tourism in Islands and Small States: Case Studies.* Cassell, London, pp. 11–31.

Butler, R.W. (1997) Tourism in the northern isles: Orkney and Shetland. In Lockart, D. and Drakakis-Smith, D. (eds) *Island Tourism: Trends and Prospects.* Cassell, London, pp. 59–80.

Butler R.W. (2006) Contrasting coldwater and warmwater island tourist destinations. In: Baldacchino, G. (ed.) *Advances in Tourism Research, Extreme Tourism: Lessons from the World's Cold Water Islands.* Macmillan, London.

Butler, R.W. (2008) The history and development of royal tourism in Scotland: Balmoral, the ultimate holiday home? In: Long, P. and Palmer, N.J. (eds) *Royal*

Tourism: Excursions Around Monarchy. Channel View Publications: Clevedon, UK, pp. 51–61.

Butler, R.W and Fennell, D.A. (1994) The effects of North Sea oil development on the development of tourism. *Tourism Management* 15, 347–357.

Butler, R.W. and Nelson, J.G. (1994a) Evaluating environmental planning and management: the case of the Shetland Islands. *Geoforum* 25, 57–72.

Butler, R.W. and Nelson, J.G. (1994b) The importance of local controls: the case of oil related development in the Shetland Islands. *People and Physical Environment Research* 45, 9–20.

Ecological Steering Group on the Oil Spill in Shetland (1994) *The Environmental Impact of the Wreck of the Braer.* Scottish Office, Edinburgh.

Fennell, D.A. (1994) An activities based analysis of the space-time characteristics of tourist travel: the lions of Shetland, Scotland. PhD thesis, University of Western Ontario, London, Ontario.

Irvine, J.W. (1985) *Lerwick: the Birth and Growth of an Island Town.* Lerwick Community Council, Lerwick, Scotland.

Luckhurst, C.R.P. (1964) *Tourism in Shetland.* Zetland County Council, Lerwick

MPCU (Marine Pollution Control Unit) (1993) *The Braer Incident, Shetland Islands, January 1993.* Department of Transport, Southampton, UK.

Nelson, J.G. and Butler, R.W. (1993) Assessing, planning, and management of North Sea Oil effects in the Shetland Islands. *Environmental Impact Assessment Review* 13, 201–227.

SIC (Shetland Islands Council) (1978) *Shetland's Oil Era.* Shetland Islands Council, Lerwick.

SIC (2000) *The Shetland Structure Plan 2001–2016.* Shetland Islands Council, Lerwick. Available at: http://www.shetland.gov.uk/splan/splan.pdf (accessed 9 September 2010).

SIC (2004) *Shetland Local Plan.* Shetland Islands Council, Lerwick. Available at: www.shetland.gov.uk/developmentplans/documents/AdoptedLPpolicies.pdf (accessed 21 September 2010).

SIC (2008) *Shetland in Statistics 2008.* Shetland Islands Council, Lerwick. Available at: http://www.shetland.gov.uk/council/shetinstat.asp (accessed 9 September 2010).

SIC (2009) *Corporate Plan – Halfway Point Update.* Report CE-57-F, Shetland Islands Council, Lerwick. Available at: http://www.shetland.gov.uk/coins/viewSelectedDoc.asp?c=e%97%9Db%95l%82%8E (accessed 21 September 2010).

SICDC (2008) *Heritage Tourism Investment Programme.* Report DV048-F, Shetland Islands Council Development Committee, Lerwick.

System Three (1991) 1991 *Shetland Visitor Survey.* Edinburgh

UK Parliament (1974) *Zetland County Council Act 1974.* Her Majesty's Stationery Office, London.

Wills, J. (1991) *A Place in the Sun: Shetland and Oil Myths and Realities.* Institute of Social and Economic Research, St John's, Newfoundland.

Wills, J. and Warner, K. (1993) *Innocent Passage: The Wreck of the Tanker Braer.* Mainstream Publishing: Edinburgh.

Economically Sustainable Perspectives of Island Tourism

Rejuvenating Paradise: Changing Products, Changing Markets and Changing Visitor Behaviour in Mauritius

GIRISH PRAYAG

SKEMA Business School, Sophia-Antipolis, Nice, France

Introduction

According to the United Nations World Tourism Organization (UNWTO) Deputy Secretary General, Dr David de Villiers, at the United Nations Conference on Small Islands in the year 2005, 'tourism has become the leading economic activity in many small islands and a key element of their development strategies and their economic development is positively affected by tourism growth' (Croes, 2006). The island of Mauritius, located off the east coast of Africa, where tourism has been a significant economic activity, has been no different. It has a multi-racial population estimated at 1.2 million in 2007 (CSO, 2008) with a lineage of immigrants from India, Europe, China and Africa. Mauritius has enjoyed unprecedented economic success, driven by industries such as agriculture (sugarcane), manufacturing (textiles) and, more recently, services (tourism, information technology and financial). Tourism contributes approximately 25.4% (US$2.5 million) to the gross domestic product (GDP) and employs 27.2% of the country's formal workforce (WTTC, 2008).

The beginning of a formal tourism industry can be traced back to the 1950s, driven by the recognized potential of the island as an attractive '3S' (sun, sand and sea) destination and the potential contribution of tourism to economic diversification, given that the island was then heavily dependent on primary industries. Tourism was also seen as a major economic alternative for employment creation. By the 1980s, tourism enclaves became the norm, with hotels such as La Pirogue and Le Saint Géran. Tourism development centred on restricting visitor numbers, air accessibility and the types of holiday activities undertaken by visitors, offering the advantage of limiting the negative impacts of tourism to a specific area, while at the same time seriously limiting linkages between the tourism industry and the local community (Kokkranikal *et al.*, 2003). For almost 20 years (1980–2000), this form of tourism development has persisted, with the number of hotels increasing dramatically from 43 in 1980 to 102 in 2008, and with an average occupancy rate of 70% in 2008 (CSO, 2008). The '3S' positioning of the island, tourism growth through controlled visitor numbers and job creation were the main objectives of government's tourism policy. Hence, economic sustainability was, and remains, the priority of tourism development (Ministry for Employment and Tourism, 1988).

While this approach has been successful, the period 2000–2005 saw year-on-year growth in tourist arrivals plummeting to its lowest levels in comparison with the previous decade (Tables 12.1, 12.2). This forced the government to review and redefine its tourism development strategy. Therefore, the purpose of this chapter is to provide a historical overview of tourism development in Mauritius, through an emphasis on economic sustainability driven by market concentration in the early stages of tourism development, and market diversification in the later stages but, also, increasing concern for environmental sustainability.

Data for this case study were collected using a multi-method approach, consisting of primary and secondary sources. Secondary sources included a literature review to identify the pertinent issues informing island tourism development, and selected trade information such as Mauritius Tourism Promotion Authority (MTPA) reports and newsletters, and policy documents such as the National Tourism Development Plan (NTDP). Primary data came from in-depth interviews in 2007 with a sample of 103 visitors on their perceptions of place. Visitors were asked mainly what they liked and disliked about the destination. The primary data were cross-referenced with official statistics and policy documents for improved credibility of findings.

In the next section, the concept of Tourism Area Life Cycle (TALC) is introduced as a basis for understanding tourism development. This includes a description of the evolution of the destination in terms of tourist numbers and tourism receipts by categorizing official statistics into three eras, which incorporate the stages defined by TALC.

Tourism Area Life Cycle for Mauritius

While there are many models for understanding destination development, Butler's (1980) TALC model has received the most attention. This model provides an analytical framework for examining the evolution of tourist destinations within their complex economic, social and cultural environment (Cooper and Jackson, 1989). The model suggests that destinations evolve through seven stages (exploration, involvement, development, consolidation, stagnation, decline and rejuvenation), each with specific characteristics as they pass through time. Many studies have been published on the applicability of the model to different destinations (Cooper and Jackson, 1989; Rodriguez *et al.*, 2008), but the focus seems to have been on mature destinations in the stagnation phase and their corresponding restructuring and rejuvenation strategies (Rodriguez *et al.*, 2008), which is also the case here. As with most models, TALC has been criticised mainly for its static nature. Consequently, Butler (2000) revisited the model and highlighted aspects such as dynamism, carrying capacity of destinations and long-term planning to avoid decline; further changes were brought to the model as well (e.g. Butler, 2006a,b) so that it can have continued relevance.

The first era (1980–1989)

In Mauritius, the exploration stage of destination development started in the early 1950s, with the first hotel opened in 1952 by Beachcomber. This stage was of short duration given that by 1974, the number of hotels had risen to 30, and from 1974 to 1979, tourist arrivals had, on average, risen by 12.3% annually, indicating that the destination had moved into the involvement stage and, subsequently, by the early 1980s, into the development phase. As shown in Table 12.1, the period 1980–1989 was characterized by declining numbers in tourist arrivals, specifically in the early 1980s. From 1984 onwards, double-digit growth numbers were not uncommon. The trend for tourism receipts during that 10 year period showed a consistent year-on-year growth (Table 12.1). This consistency fuelled further development of the hospitality sector with more upmarket resorts. The government provided incentives to hotel developers through the *Hotel Development Incentive Act of 1974*, which included import duty exemptions on capital equipment, favourable corporate taxes, free repatriation of profits and dividends, income tax concessions and loans at reduced interest rates from the Mauritius Development Bank (Brown, 1997). By the mid 1980s, hotel occupancy rates had peaked to 80%, although they had declined to 66% by 1988 (Brown, 1997).

Table 12.1. Tourism statistics for the period 1980–1989. (Source: CSO, 2010.)

Year	Number of hotels	Tourist arrivals (TA)	Year-on-year growth (TA%)	Tourism receipts (TR) (Rs)[a]	Year-on year growth (TR%)
1980	43	115,080	−10.3	325	25.0
1981	51	121,620	5.7	433	33.2
1982	51	118,360	−2.7	450	3.9
1983	55	123,820	4.6	503	11.8
1984	54	139,670	12.8	630	25.3
1985	55	148,860	6.6	845	34.1
1986	56	165,310	11.1	1190	40.8
1987	60	207,570	25.5	1786	50.1
1988	64	239,300	15.3	2381	33.3
1989	67	262,790	9.8	2796	17.4

[a]Rs, Mauritian rupees.

The second era (1990–1999)

The 1990s saw the destination moving into its consolidation phase, with the rate of hotel expansion slowing down. By 1992, an oversupply of hotel rooms existed and the government responded with a freeze on the issue of hotel development certificates (Carlsen and Jaufeerally, 2003). Table 12.2 shows that the number of hotels declined from 95 in 1995 to 92 in 1999. Year-on-year growth in tourist arrival numbers was more erratic, starting at 10.9% in 1990 to reach 3.6% in 1999. This is consistent with Butler's (1980) prescription of the difficulties facing destinations at that stage of their life cycle. As regards tourism receipts, Table 12.2 indicates that despite positive year-on-year growth, incremental growth was declining in comparison with the figures in Table 12.1. Carlsen and Jaufeerally (2003) noted that tourist spending in real terms had declined from 1990 to 1997. This era saw international hotel groups such as French Accor opening hotels, while existing groups, such as Beachcomber, were consolidating their position in Mauritius. There was also growth of four- and five-star hotels in particular.

The third era (2000–2008)

At the start of the new millennium, Mauritius moved into what can be characterized as the stagnation phase of TALC. Stagnation is characterized by a number of features, including economic, social and environmental problems, a bed-capacity surplus, a heavy reliance on repeat visitation and a destination image that is no longer fashionable (Butler, 1980). While most of these indicators were replicated for the Mauritian tourism industry, one aspect that was significantly different was the lack of sufficient bed capacity.

Table 12.2. Tourism statistics for the period 1990–1999. (Source: Ministry of Tourism, Leisure and External Communications, 2008a.)

Year	Number of hotels	Tourist arrivals (TA)	Year-on-year growth (TA%)	Tourism receipts (TR) (Rs)[a]	Year-on-year growth (TR%)
1990	75	291,550	10.9	3,630	29.8
1991	80	300,670	3.1	3,940	8.5
1992	84	335,400	11.6	4,655	18.2
1993	85	374,630	11.7	5,362	15.2
1994	90	400,526	6.9	6,415	19.7
1995	95	422,463	5.5	7,472	16.5
1996	90	486,867	15.3	9,048	21.1
1997	87	536,125	10.1	10,068	11.3
1998	90	558,195	4.1	11,890	18.1
1999	92	578,085	3.6	13,668	15.0

[a]Rs, Mauritian rupees.

For a 6-year period (2001–2006), Mauritius experienced an average year-on-year growth of less than 4% in tourist arrival numbers (Table 12.3). In comparison with the previous two eras, the tourism industry felt a looming decline stage. The current positioning of the island and its tourism product were inadequate at sustaining tourist arrival numbers and receipts. As can be seen in Table 12.3, annual growth in tourism receipts was constant but not consistent.

This lack of consistency in tourist arrival numbers and tourism receipts forced government to review destination development. As a result, in the year 2000 the European Community (EC) funded the consulting firm Deloitte & Touche for the development of a national tourism plan for the island (Deloitte & Touche, 2002). One of the recommendations of the report was to diversify and rejuvenate the traditional '3S' product. Similar to other island destinations, short-term measures for rejuvenation included reorientation of tourist attractions, environmental enhancement and repositioning (Agarwal, 2002). The destination went through an extensive upgrading of existing hotel facilities, especially at the luxury end of the market, and increased its overall tourist capacity by building new hotels (six new hotels for the period 2003–2004) to further position itself in the luxury segment. The destination also increased its visibility and accessibility in traditional and non-traditional markets, which led to a significant increase in tourist numbers in 2007. These measures corresponded to the rejuvenation strategies recommended by TALC (Agarwal, 2002; Butler, 2006b).

Economic Sustainability as a Priority

The NTDP suggested that tourism growth can be sustained by diversification of the tourism product base and generating markets with the intention of further

Table 12.3. Tourism statistics for the period 2000–2008. (Source: Ministry of Tourism, Leisure and External Communications, 2008a.)

Year	Number of hotels	Tourist arrivals (TA)	Year-on-year growth (TA%)	Tourism receipts (TR) (Rs)[a]	Year-on-year growth (TR%)
2000	95	656,453	13.6	14,234	4.1
2001	95	660,318	0.6	18,166	27.6
2002	95	681,648	3.2	18,328	0.9
2003	97	702,018	3.0	19,415	5.9
2004	103	718,861	2.4	23,448	20.8
2005	99	761,063	5.9	25,704	9.6
2006	98	788,276	3.6	31,942	24.3
2007	97	906,971	15.1	40,687	27.4
2008	102	930,456	2.6	41,213	1.3

[a]Rs, Mauritian rupees.

positioning the destination upmarket. In essence, economic sustainability was to be achieved through strategies of market concentration and/or market diversification. Market concentration involves focusing marketing efforts on existing markets with a view of increasing visitors' spending, repeat visitation and length of stay, etc. The diversification route involves developing new tourism products and attracting new markets. An example of market concentration is the launching of the campaign 'Travel without Passport' for the French and Italian markets in an effort to boost tourist numbers in 2008. An increase of 10.5% can be noted in tourist arrivals figures from France for the period January–October 2008, while the Italian market showed no sign of recovery (Ministry of Tourism, Leisure and External Communications, 2008c).

Diversification of the tourism product

The diversification approach adopted was not new. Lockhart (1997a) suggested that island destinations need to diversify away from the '3S', which is typical of mass tourism, into special activity holidays and business travel, with a focus on higher-spending tourists and the creation of niche markets. However, unlike other island destinations, such as Malta (Lockhart, 1997b) and Isle of Man (Cooper and Jackson, 1989), Mauritius had from the outset rejected mass tourism as an appropriate form of tourism development. The government recognized that although growth in tourist numbers was important, a better strategy to control the negative impacts of tourism was to increase tourism receipts from visitors at the higher end of the market (Deloitte & Touche, 2002). This form of economic sustainability was thought to be more beneficial than traditional '3S' tourism. The focus on the luxury segment over the years had created a reputation of quality and excellence for the core product – the resort-based experience, and further opportunities for diversification. In 2008, the Hotel Development Strategy (HDS; Ministry of Tourism, Leisure and External Communications, 2008b) recommended that hotel development should be centred on setting up of only 4- and 5-star rated hotels.

The government also reviewed its tourism policy with regard to foreign ownership of properties on the island. The Integrated Resort Scheme (IRS) was created in 2002 to allow foreign ownership of luxury villas developed as part of 'marinas' and/or 'golf resorts'. Foreigners are permitted to buy property only with a minimum investment value of US$500,000. This scheme will create more tourism receipts and jobs locally, but its focus on increasing tourist numbers can move the destination away from environmental and social sustainability. In other island destinations, such as Hawaii and Majorca, 'second-home' tourism has created negative environmental and social impacts (Essex, 2004; Sheldon, 2005).

In parallel, tourism policy actively promoted the development of other niche markets such as 'cultural tourism', 'golf-tourism', 'adventure-tourism', 'wellness tourism', 'medical tourism' and the Meeting Incentive Conference and Exhibition (MICE) market. These different initiatives show government and private sector commitment for product diversification, moving away from '3S' towards niche market development. This is a more sustainable form of tourism development for small islands only if the concept of carrying capacity is understood (Lockhart, 1997b; Bull and Weed, 1999). Yet some of the initiatives adopted, such as the IRS scheme, may comprise social and environmental sustainability at the expense of economic sustainability.

Diversification of generating markets

Traditionally, Mauritius has relied on European markets for the success of its tourism industry. It has been able to attract affluent European tourists, but attempts at increasing visitor numbers from Asia have been largely ineffective (Brown, 1997). In the involvement and development stages of TALC, Europe was the main generating market for the island, while Asia, Oceania and America were insignificant markets. Double, triple or quadruple increases in tourist arrival numbers from countries such as France, Germany, the UK and Italy were not uncommon. A similar pattern of tourist arrival numbers persisted for the next 10 years (1990–1999) as Mauritius moved into the consolidation stage (Table 12.4). However, non-traditional European markets, such as Austria, Belgium and the Netherlands, and Asia, with countries such as India, were becoming increasingly important generating markets.

In the stagnation stage of TALC, the percentage increase in tourist numbers from traditional European markets was smaller compared with Asia and Oceania (Table 12.5), driven by countries such as India, China and Australia. Over the years, the improved economic trade with countries such as India and China naturally generated an interest in the destination beyond business tourism. A more open-sky policy improved connectivity of the island with other Asian destinations. The increasing budget of the MTPA for advertising and promotion purposes improved visibility of the destination in international markets.

The Way Forward

While the strategies of market concentration, and product and market diversification have ensured a constant increase in tourist arrival numbers from 2005 onwards, the detrimental effects of increasing tourist numbers are often localized. A survey of outgoing tourists (Ministry of Tourism, Leisure and External Communications, 2006) reports that visitors had unsatisfactory experiences with three aspects of the destination, namely, infrastructure (e.g. road conditions, public transport and traffic jams), hotel facilities (e.g. quality of food, price and service levels) and natural environment (cleanliness of beaches and pollution). These issues were also identified in the in-depth interviews that were carried out. For example, a French visitor commented:

> The aggressiveness of hawkers on the beach, they force you to buy things that you don't want to. They rip you off for the prices they charge. They don't have a

Table 12.4. Generating markets and increase in tourist arrivals for the period 1990–1999. (Source: CSO, 2010.)

Generating markets	1990	1991	1992	1993	1994	1995	1996	1997	1998	1999	% Increase (1990–1999)
Europe	126,750	132,170	161,810	190,690	225,001	237,745	273,456	314,380	339,659	364,823	187.8
Africa	130,330	135,110	137,730	145,000	134,113	139,208	157,931	158,493	156,864	150,366	15.4
Asia	17,800	19,050	17,740	20,050	21,142	21,608	24,926	25,679	23,528	24,145	35.6
Oceania	3,520	3,230	5,520	4,950	4,448	5,902	8,144	9,896	9,349	8,503	141.6
America	3,180	2,660	2,650	3,130	3,111	3,250	3,849	4,541	4,742	4,851	52.5
All countries	281,580	292,220	325,450	363,820	387,815	407,713	468,306	512,989	534,142	552,688	49.1

Table 12.5. Generating markets and increase in tourist arrivals for the period 2000–2007. (Source: CSO, 2010.)

Generating markets	2000	2001	2002	2003	2004	2005	2006	2007	% Increase 2000–2007
Europe	425,053	420,829	432,464	444,470	453,889	475,113	477,276	557,694	31.2
Africa	157,150	161,977	166,637	166,201	168,682	178,740	182,466	204,132	29.9
Asia	29,036	31,338	34,555	37,600	38,617	42,142	50,817	58,948	103.0
Oceania	9,460	9,441	9,030	9,754	12,068	14,424	17,704	20,656	118.4
America	5,516	5,768	5,958	6,350	6,646	7,009	7,518	8,041	45.8
All countries	626,215	629,353	648,644	664,375	679,902	717,428	735,781	849,471	26.3

sense of business. You cannot charge more for the same things to tourists compared to locals. It's an indication that these people are looking for an easy deal but it's not the mentality of all Mauritians though. Also, there is pollution here, garbage should be cleaned up, it's too much. They need to treat rubbish properly. Hygiene must be improved outside of hotels.

A British visitor commented:

The guy at the botanical garden was not very nice, at the entrance, he did not treat me well and they need to improve the garden itself, I mean how can they maintain the place, if it's dirty and has bottles and plastic bags in the ponds. The climate was not too good at times, windy and rainy. Very poor signposting, we did not want to do all the touristy things, and we did not get where we wanted at times.

The weaknesses of the current tourism development approach for Mauritius are related to the overemphasis on tourist numbers as opposed to yield from visitors. For example, the carrying capacity was estimated at 400,000 visitors in 2000 and revised to a million per year (Apostolopoulos and Gayle, 2002) and, currently, the Minister of Tourism suggests 2 million visitors by 2020 (Watt, 2007). There is no national framework that supports and embraces the adoption of concepts of sustainable development, despite the existence of the 'Mauritius Strategy', discussed below, as a guideline for sustainable practices. The NTDP is outdated, given that it was formulated 7 years ago and that tourism policy is not necessarily integrated with other aspects of the destination, such as environmental management (Watt, 2007). There are no indicators for the evaluation of community-based tourism impacts in the NTDP. None the less, some initiatives exist for environmental and social sustainability which have been implemented; these are also discussed below.

Environmental Quality

From Barbados '94 to Mauritius '05, the UNESCO recommendations for sustainable development in small island developing states (SIDS), now known as the 'Mauritius Strategy', suggest that 'if tourism is not developed sustainably, it can damage or even destroy the natural environment that attracts tourism in the first place. Small islands should monitor the impacts of tourism development to ensure that tourism development and social and environmental priorities are mutually supportive at all levels' (UNESCO, 2010). In response to these recommendations, 'Ile Maurice Durable', a government initiative, was launched in 2008 to promote sustainable development. Two of the main objectives of the programme are to:

- Finance schemes for the preservation of local natural resources with a view to achieving sustainable development and adapting to climate change; and
- Finance projects and programmes to support efforts to protect the environment through recycling of waste, to encourage more efficient use of energy, and to increase reliance on renewable energy.

It is too early to evaluate the effectiveness of this initiative, but a white paper on the new national environment policy (Ministry of Environment/ National Development Unit, 2007) is being drafted with the aim of reconciling environmental sustainability with economic and social development, in response to the environmental concerns that exist. For example, McElroy (2003) found that Indian Ocean Islands were characterized by small facilities, long stays and a limited infrastructure which still had a negative impact on the environment. Owing to tourism development, unplanned urbanization, sand mining, mangrove destruction and coastal pollution, the native plant species in Mauritius and Seychelles were endangered while some beach resorts were under threat from rise in sea level. The government's concern for the environment can also be seen in the HDS, which suggests that 'to preserve the natural, exquisite and pristine characteristics of our seascapes, the Planning Policy Guidance (PPG) for coastal development should be strictly adhered to'. Private sector initiatives, such as the Green Globe award for the hotel Le Prince Maurice, and ISO 14000 certification for others, indicate that environmental issues are becoming increasingly important for hoteliers as well.

Social Sustainability

Besides environmental sustainability, social sustainability is a critical aspect of tourism development for island destinations. Social sustainability focuses on community participation and sharing of the economic benefits of tourism. This has only recently begun to emerge as an important criterion for resort development in Mauritius. The *Tourism Fund Act* was enacted in 2006 (Parliament of Mauritius, 2006), with the objective that hotel developers will contribute to this fund to enable infrastructural development and other associated works for the benefit of the inhabitants of the areas in which tourism projects are being implemented. This was necessary to reduce inequity between individuals who profit directly from tourism and the local community which do not always see the benefits. In 2002, the government also enacted the *Tourism Employees Welfare Fund Act* to provide for the social and economic welfare of the employees of tourism enterprises and their families (Parliament of Mauritius, 2002). Private-sector practices include hoteliers such as Naiade Resorts promoting corporate social responsibility by setting up, for example, 'Les Pavillons School of Music', for the less privileged youngsters in villages around resorts.

Social sustainability is also an area of concern for SIDS, given that the 'Mauritius Strategy' '05 states: 'there is a particular challenge to make appropriate linkages between tourism and other sectors, including local service providers so as to retain resources within the country, and in particular to create synergistic linkages between tourism and the agricultural sector by promoting island foods and beverages supply chains, rural hospitality and agro-tourism. In addition, they should develop and implement community based initiatives on sustainable tourism' (MIDF, 2010). Therefore, grass-root level initiatives that encourage local community participation in tourism development are seen as necessary for economic sustainability and social sustainability, although such initiatives are more private-sector driven.

Changing Visitors' Behaviour

Certainly, the changing nature of the tourism product and generating markets are indicators of visitors' changing behaviour with respect to destination choice and attractiveness factors. While the traditional sun-lust tourist is perceived as a pleasure seeker engaging in hedonistic activities, the 'new' sun and sand tourist shows an increasing interest in the environment and local people. For example, the survey of outgoing tourists (Ministry of Tourism, Leisure and External Communications, 2006) indicated that the main motives of destination choice were the 'island image' and 'people'. The in-depth interviews undertaken showed the same. For example, a French visitor said:

> I like the welcoming feeling that you have here, the climate, the kindness of people, the scenery, the sea with so many fish, we loved everything about this place. You have mountains, lakes, everything is close to each other, it's very varied, even the colour of the water, it varies from place to place. The fish we saw when we went for diving, coral reefs that are different from other places we have visited.

This quote indicates that visitors are still drawn by the '3S', but that environmental integrity and local people and hospitality are also important. Therefore, if the environment is not protected, the very attributes that create the destination appeal may disappear over time. By the same token, if local communities are not involved to a greater extent in tourism development, and their cultural identity is not preserved, the kindness and hospitality that so far has been an asset for the island, may erode.

Implications and Conclusion

TALC indicates that it took approximately 50 years (1950–2000) for Mauritius to move from the exploration stage to its stagnation phase. The changing products, markets and visitors' behaviour are indicative of attempts to rejuvenate. Yet how long will it take for the destination to find itself in the stagnation stage again? Surely, existing pitfalls with regard to the carrying capacity of the island and management of tourism impacts at local community level will have to be addressed in the overall planning of destination development. Currently, there is no indication of acceptable levels of change for local communities. For island destinations, this should be the starting point for sustainable development. Without such indicators, it becomes difficult to balance economic, social and environmental concerns.

While the government and the private sector are conscious of the importance of environmental and social integrity, economic difficulties often leave limited options for tourism development. Consequently, tourism policy becomes ineffective at measuring and controlling tourism impacts. The IRS scheme is an example of economic sustainability being preferred at the expense of environmental and social sustainability. This will be detrimental for the island in the long term. Tourism development should be integrated into quality-of-life objectives. For local communities, sustainable forms of tourism should be characterized by a small-scale, local, bottom-up and grassroots approach in tourism planning (Sharpley, 2003). Dodds (2007) recommends participatory and open working methods, overall analysis of local and island space, specific lines of action, initiatives and a working programme for islands. Often though, environmental and social sustainability are difficult to implement because of barriers to policy implementation in the form of lack of stakeholder involvement, lack of integration with national frameworks and policies, lack of accountability by politicians and lack of coordination with the private sector. This seems to be the case for Mauritius too, implying that economic sustainability will remain a priority unless the government, through integrated planning, management, legislative and conservation measures, decides that sustainability has three facets (economic, environmental and social).

In conclusion, the island of Mauritius has had unprecedented economic success, but like other islands, in the current economic climate, tourism growth has slowed. The various strategies to rejuvenate island tourism seem to fit with current trends globally. However, the focus on economic sustainability, weak policies to support environmental sustainability and little concern for social sustainability have the potential to damage the tourism product. As a result, there is a need to review destination development plans and tourism policy, and these need to be integrated into quality-of-life objectives for the local population to ensure continued success of the island for tourism purposes.

References

Agarwal, S. (2002) Restructuring seaside tourism: the resort lifecycle. *Annals of Tourism Research* 29, 25–55.

Apostolopoulos, Y. and Gayle, J.D. (eds) (2002) *Island Tourism and Sustainable Development: Caribbean, Pacific, and Mediterranean*. Praeger, Westport, Connecticut/London.

Brown, G.P. (1997) Tourism in the Indian Ocean – a case study of Mauritius. In: Lockhart, D.G. and Smith, D.D. (eds) *Island Tourism: Trends and Prospects*. Pinter, London, pp. 229–248.

Bull, C., and Weed, M. (1999) Niche markets and small island tourism: the development of sports tourism in Malta. *Managing Leisure* 4, 142–155.

Butler, R.W. (1980) The concept of a tourist area cycle of evolution: implications for management of resources. *Canadian Geographer* 24, 5–12.

Butler, R.W. (2000) The resort cycle two decades on. In: Faulkner, B., Laws, E. and Moscardo, G. (eds) *Reflections on Experience*. Cassell, London, pp. 284–298.

Butler, R.W. (2006a) *The Tourism Area Life Cycle Model, Vol. 1: Applications and Modifications*. Channel View Publications, Clevedon, UK.

Butler, R.W. (2006b) *The Tourism Area Life Cycle Model, Vol. 2: Conceptual and Theoretical Issues*. Channel View Publications, Clevedon, UK.

Carlsen, J. and Jaufeerally, K. (2003) An analysis of tourism trends in Mauritius 1979 to 1998. *Current Issues in Tourism* 6, 235–248.

Cooper, C. and Jackson, S. (1989) Destination life cycle: the Isle of Man case study. *Annals of Tourism Research* 16, 377–398.

Croes, R.R. (2006) A paradigm shift to a new strategy for small island economies: embracing demand side economies for value enhancement and long term economic stability. *Tourism Management* 27, 453–465.

CSO (Central Statistics Office) (2008) *Digest of International Travel and Tourism Statistics – 2008*. Ministry of Finance and Economic Development, Port Louis, Mauritius. Available at: http://www.gov.mu/portal/goc/cso/report/natacc/tourism08/toc.htm (accessed 13 September 2010).

CSO (Central Statistics Office) (2010) Historical Series – Tourism. Ministry of Finance and Economic Development, Port Louis, Mauritius. Available at: http://www.gov.mu/portal/site/cso/menuitem.dee225f644ffe2aa338852f8a0208a0c/?content_id=a93de924d448a010VgnVCM1000000a04a8c0RCRD (accessed 13 September 2010).

Deloitte & Touche (2002) *National Tourism Development Plan for Mauritius and Rodrigues*. Report by Deloitte & Touche Consulting.

Dodds, R. (2007) Sustainable tourism and policy implementation: lessons from the case of Calvia, Spain. *Current Issues in Tourism* 10, 296–322.

Essex, S. (2004) Tourism development in Mallorca: is water supply a constraint? *Journal of Sustainable Tourism* 12, 4–28.

Kokkranikal, J., McLellan, R. and Baum, T. (2003) Island tourism and sustainability: a case study of the Lakshadweep Islands. *Journal of Sustainable Tourism* 11, 426–447.

Lockhart, D.G. (1997a) Islands and tourism: an overview. In: Lockhart, D.G. and Drakakis-Smith, D. (eds) *Island Tourism:* *Trends and Prospects*. Pinter, London, pp. 3–20.

Lockhart, D.G. (1997b) Tourism to Malta and Cyprus. In: Lockhart, D.G. and Drakakis-Smith, D. (eds) *Island Tourism: Trends and Prospects*. Pinter, London, pp. 152–178.

McElroy, J.L. (2003) Tourism development in small islands across the world. *Geografiska Annaler* 85B, 231–242.

MIDF (2010) About Us. Maurice Ile Durable Fund, Port Louis, Mauritius. Available at: http://www.gov.mu/portal/sites/midf/aboutus.htm (accessed 13 September 2010).

Ministry for Employment and Tourism (1988) *White Paper on Tourism*. Ministry for Employment and Tourism, Port Louis, Mauritius.

Ministry of Environment/National Development Unit (NDU) (2007) *Draft White Paper on New National Environment Policy*. Port Louis, Mauritius.

Ministry of Tourism, Leisure and External Communications (2006) *Survey of Outgoing Tourists. Report by Ministry of Tourism, Leisure and External Communications*. Port Louis, Mauritius.

Ministry of Tourism, Leisure and External Communications (2008a) *Handbook of Statistical Data on Tourism 2008* (Vol. 28). Available at: www.gov.mu/portal/goc/tourist/file/touristsurv08.pdf (accessed 13 September 2010).

Ministry of Tourism, Leisure and External Communications (2008b) *Hotel Development Strategy*. Port Louis, Mauritius.

Ministry of Tourism, Leisure and External Communications (2008c) *Monthly Bulletin of Tourist Arrivals* (October 2008). Port Louis, Mauritius.

Parliament of Mauritius (2002) *Tourism Welfare Employees Fund Act 2002*, Act No. 15. Port Louis, Mauritius.

Parliament of Mauritius (2006) *Tourism Fund Act 2006*, Government Notice No. 22, Section 24 of the Finance and Audit Act. Port Louis, Mauritius.

Rodriguez, J.R.O., Parra-Lopez, E. and Yanes-Estevez, V. (2008) The sustainability of island destinations: tourism area life cycle and teleological perspectives: the case of Tenerife. *Tourism Management* 29, 53–65.

Sharpley, R. (2003) Tourism, modernization and development on the island of Cyprus: challenges and policy responses. *Journal of Sustainable Tourism* 11, 246–265.

Sheldon, P.J. (2005) *The Challenges to Sustainability in Island Tourism*. Occasional Paper No. 2005-01, School of Travel Industry Management, University of Hawaii, Manoa, Hawaii.

UNESCO (2010) Tourism Resources: Extract from the Mauritius Strategy, Chapter VIII, Paras 50–52. Available at: http://portal.unesco.org/en/ev.php-URL_ID=43070&URL_DO=DO_TOPIC&URL_SECTION=201.html (accessed 13 September 2010).

Watt, I. (2007) Sustaining beauty in Mauritius. BBC News, Tuesday 25 September 2007. Available at: http://news.bbc.co.uk/1/hi/world/africa/7010212.stm (accessed 10 September 2010).

WTTC (World Travel and Tourism Council) (2008) Mauritius Travel and Tourism Report, London.

13 Sustainable Island Tourism: the Case of Okinawa

HIROSHI KAKAZU

Meio University, Okinawa, Japan

The Roles of Tourism for Small Island Economies

Bertram and Watters's (1985) well-cited MIRAB (Migration, Remittance, Aid, Bureaucracy) characterization of small-island economies must be modified to include the fast-growing service industry driven by the tourism industry. For an increasing number of the Pacific and the Caribbean islands, the tourism industry is becoming the most important source of foreign exchange earnings (see Table 13.1). About one half of these island economies depend more on tourism income than on their export earnings. In islands such as Palau, Bahamas, Antigua and Barbuda and St Lucia, tourism accounts for more than 30% of gross domestic product (GDP). Tourism income in Hawaii, the largest economy among the Pacific islands, is nearly three times larger than its export earnings. In the future, Papua New Guinea, the Solomon Islands and Haiti can all be considered to have great potential to develop their tourism industries because of their abundant natural tourism resources and low level of development.

Small island economies tend to specialize in the tourism industry, mainly because they lack the natural resources, domestic market and industrial technology to exploit for export production. Although tourist expenditure is recorded as service receipts in the external balance of payment statistics, it is equivalent to exports not only of services but also of goods which are sold to non-resident tourists. Conceptually, the only difference between export earnings and tourism income is where the goods and services are traded and consumed. Tourist receipts imply precisely the same economic effect as exports of goods and services (Kakazu, 1996). Unlike manufacturing and agricultural products, comparative advantage in 'tourism products' is largely determined by both economic and non-economic factors, such as geographical location, culture, history and even by 'the spirit of hospitality' which is difficult to capture in rational economic terms. The tourism industry, of course, faces more or less

Table 13.1. Tourism in selected island countries, 2003. (Source: revised from Umemura, 2006.)

	GDP[a] (US$ million)	Trade balance (US$ million)	Tourism income (US$ million)	Exports/GDP (%)	Tourism income/ GDP (%)	Tourism income > exports[b]
South Pacific Islands						
Hawaii	46,386	−21643	10,054	8.2	21.7	+
Okinawa	28,222	−8921	3,475	15.0	12.3	
Papua New Guinea	3,182	877	60	59.4	1.9	
Fiji	2,036	−464	431	31.5	20.3	+
Vanuatu	283	−78	71	10.3	26.8	+
Samoa	268	−122	53	6.0	18.1	+
Solomon Islands	253	8	9	24.0	3.6	
Micronesia, Federated States of	243	−65	17	6.6	7.0	+
Tonga	163	−75	15	7.8	6.0	
Palau	126	−129	59	11.7	48.0	+
Marshall Islands	106	−46	4	9.8	3.9	
Kiribati	55	−37	3	11.7	5.8	
Caribbean Islands						
Dominican Republic	16,541	−2,444	3,110	27.2	14.5	
Jamaica	8,147	−2,435	1,621	14.8	18.9	+
Bahamas	5,260	−892	1,795	13.7	35.6	+
Haiti	2,921	−841	93	8.7	3.1	
Barbados	2,627	−923	767	9.2	28.0	+
Belize	989	−347	156	19.7	14.6	
Antigua and Barbuda	757	−275	301	5.1	40.1	+
Guyana	742	−60	39	68.7	7.8	
St Lucia	693	−300	282	6.3	37.8	+
Grenada	439	−198	104	13.0	22.4	+
St Vincent and the Grenadines	371	−162	85	11.6	22.8	+
St Kitts and Nevis	346	−207	61	9.6	17.2	+
Dominica	259	−87	51	16.9	18.3	+

[a]GDP, gross domestic product.
[b]+ indicates economies where tourism income is greater than export income.

the same kind of competition, and displays similar characteristics to the goods-producing industry. Hawaii, Saipan and Guam (both in the Marianas archipelago in the western Pacific) and Okinawa, in particular, have been competing with each other for the growing Japanese tourism market. In the past, Okinawa suffered cost disadvantages in comparison with these other tourist destinations mainly because of the rapid appreciation of the yen. Saipan also has a labour cost advantage over Okinawa because it has been able to import cheap labour, primarily from the Philippines (Kakazu, 1994).

The tourism industry is a composite industry, not merely a service industry. In Okinawa, for example, aside from conventional tourism components such as hotels, travel agents, transportation, souvenirs and travel guides, the industry is deeply and extensively related to local cultures, production sectors, information and communication technology (ICT), various entertainments and sports, marketing and promotional activities, conventions and the conservation of natural and cultural assets. In this sense, the tourism and goods-producing sectors are supposed to be complementary towards each other and not necessarily trading off against each other as many economists have asserted in their development theories (Kakazu, 1998). This suggests that tourism can be considered as a powerful engine for industrial diversification for small island economies in which the domestic market is extremely limited by the small size of the population and by the small, fragmented markets.

Small island economies need to minimize the leakage of tourist spending, which, in the case of Okinawa, has accounted for 40% of the total, in order to improve the economic impact of the tourism industry. Producing more locally made products for tourist consumption, providing local entertainments and attractions, and improving transportation and information systems are all measures to be taken by policy makers, as well as by industry leaders. It should also be noted that successful island tourist destinations in the Pacific are part of or are surrounded by richer countries such as the USA and Japan, and have well-organized transportation networks, political stability and offer warm hospitality to visitors.

Okinawa's Tourism Development

Okinawa, a prefecture of the westernmost part of Japan, is located between the northwestern edge of the Pacific Ocean, just east of China, and the southwestern tip of Japan. It covers a distance of 1000 km (622 miles) from east to west and 400 km (248 miles) from north to south. The archipelago consists of three major island groups: the Okinawa Islands, Miyako Islands and Yaeyama Islands (Fig. 13.1).

Okinawa is the only Japanese prefecture to lie wholly within the subtropical oceanic climatic zone. The average annual temperature is 22.4°C, and average annual precipitation is 2037 mm. Except for occasional typhoons during the summer, no natural disasters have been reported in recent years. The Ryukyu archipelago, the pre-modern Chinese name for Okinawa, with its abundant flora and fauna, including world-renowned species such as the Iriomote wildcat,

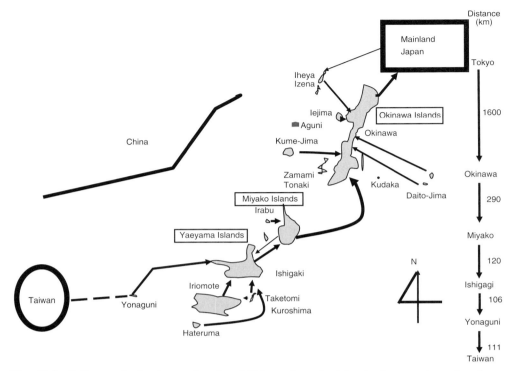

Fig. 13.1. Patterns of migratory networks of Okinawa's major islands. Arrows show direction of net migration among islands. (Constructed by author.)

Pryor's woodpecker, Okinawa rail and others, has sometimes been called the 'Galapagos of the Orient'.

Nearly four decades have elapsed since the administrative reversion of Okinawa from the USA to Japan, in 1972. Despite significant changes in the international politico-economic environment in the Asia-Pacific region since reversion, Okinawa's geo-military position as the 'Keystone of the Pacific' has remained almost unchanged. It is still the case that 75% of all military base facilities for the exclusive use of USA forces in Japan are located in Okinawa Prefecture, which comprises only 1% and 0.6% of Japan's total population and land area, respectively. In positive contrast, the successful hosting of the year 2000 G8 Summit of world leaders publicized Okinawa globally, thereby promoting its image as a culture-rich, healthy, international tourist destination.

Like many other small-island economies, Okinawa's economy possesses general characteristics that have presented challenges for its economic development. These include: (i) specialized rather than diversified economic activities; (ii) a small domestic market; (iii) reliance on a limited number of primary products and tourism for export earnings, while at the same time dependence on imports of consumer and capital goods; (iv) chronic trade-balance deficits;

(v) diseconomies of scale; (vi) high transportation costs; (vii) rising population pressure on a small arable land area; and (viii) a heavy reliance on government expenditure and activities as a major source of income and employment (Kakazu, 2003).

The tourism industry has played an increasingly important role in Okinawa's economic development, particularly since its reversion to Japan in 1972. The number of inbound visitors, mainly from mainland Japan, has increased sharply from a mere 17,000 in 1970 to about 6 million in recent years (Fig. 13.2).

According to a survey of by the Japan Travel Bureau (JTB, 2008), Okinawa is the most popular island tourist destination for Japanese travellers and may surpass Hawaii within a few years in terms of the numbers of visitors. The

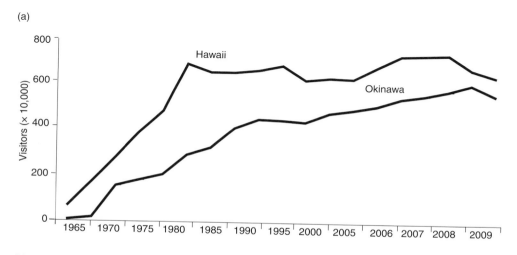

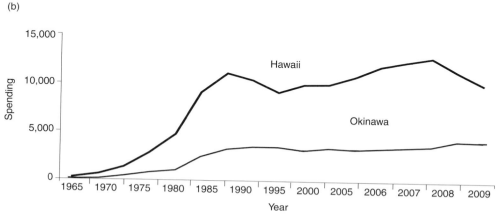

Fig. 13.2. Inbound visitors (a) and visitor spending (b) in Hawaii and Okinawa (1965–2009). (Constructed by author using data from the Okinawa Prefectural Government and Hawaii Department of Business, Economic Development & Tourism. Figures for 2009 estimated based on January–June actual figures.)

survey also indicated that the main attractive features of Okinawa's tourism are its pristine beaches, diversified chain of islands, semi-tropical climate, abundant flora and fauna, rich culture, healthy foods, hospitality-minded people and low crime rate. For mainland visitors in particular, Okinawan islands are cheap, near and safe vacation destinations with exotic Asian taste. Mainly because of a short-stay type of domestic tourism destination, Okinawa's total visitor spending is about one half of that of Hawaii, reflecting lower per capita visitor consumption (Fig. 13.2).

Of the total tourist expenditure in Okinawa, lodging accounted for 34%, followed by souvenirs (26%), meals (18%), transportation (11%), entertainment (8%) and other (3%). The tourism industry generated about 12%, 15% and 12% of Okinawa's gross prefectural income, total external receipts and total employment, respectively, in recent years. One unit of tourist expenditure generated about 1.5 units of gross income. This multiplier effect is higher than that in Aomori and Shizuoka prefectures, which are located in the heartland of Japan. Unlike Japan 'proper', Okinawa has recorded a huge surplus in tourism balance of payments.

Challenges for Okinawa's Sustainable Tourism

As already discussed, tourism has been a main engine for Okinawa's economic growth since the 1970s. The industry continues to be the most powerful engine for future development because it has the archipelago's potential comparative advantage. However, the tourist industry, faces challenging problems that need to be resolved.

First, despite the rapid growth of tourists in the past decade, tourism expenditure has not grown commensurate with the number of visitors. As a matter of fact, tourism incomes have declined in recent years, despite the increased number of visitors. The decline is reflected in a sizeable decrease in per capita tourism spending. Deepening the structure of tourism is the most effective measure that can be taken to address this declining trend of per capita tourism spending. A US$100 decrease in per capita spending means a loss of 450,000 visitors in terms of total tourism income. This clearly suggests that the tourism industry, which consumes local resources, should not be a mere numbers game. Okinawa is facing the problem of how to upgrade its tourism industry. 'Cheap, Near, and Short' has been a recent slogan to attract mainland tourists to Okinawa. As a result, despite high hotel-room occupancy rates, per-room revenue has declined substantially. Such excessive competition by means of price-cutting may eventually damage tourism in Okinawa, which needs to shift its paradigm from a quantity-oriented tourism policy to quality-oriented policy.

Second, tourism is becoming more important in Okinawa's smaller outlying islands, where comparative advantage lies in the location of specific indigenous endowments, including marine resources, local culture and hospitality. We should note, however, that economic benefits such as rising incomes and employment from tourism differ greatly from island to island. The number of visitors to Kumejima Island, for example, has stagnated in recent years compared with the more popular Ishigaki and Miyako Islands. It is a daunting task to spread tourism benefits among islands and regions, as well as to upgrade tourism quality so that per capita tourism spending will increase.

Third, the tourism industry in Okinawa is meticulously tailored towards the mainland Japanese market, which accounts for more than 95% of the total tourists, mainly from the metropolitan areas such as Tokyo, Kansai (Osaka and Kyoto) and Fukuoka. Okinawa should learn a lesson from the bitter experience of Miyazaki Prefecture, where tourism boomed once and bust soon after. Although Okinawa may continue as the most favourite resort in Japan for the foreseeable future, this assessment depends largely on its comparative advantages in the environmental quality, rich cultural heritage and hospitality which support the industry. Although Okinawa has been struggling to diversify its tourism markets in order to reduce instability in the tourism industry, as well as to capture the emerging East Asian market, it is not succeeding. One important bottleneck for the diversification is the lack of networks in terms of transportation, hotels and promotional activities between Okinawa and other Asian countries.

Fourth, despite a welcoming attitude towards tourists, there are always deep-rooted fears among the island people that their fragile environments and rich culture might be eroded or degraded by a massive and continuous intrusion of outsiders. There are also constant complaints on the part of island economies that major tourism businesses, including hotel facilities and airline transportation, are dominated by mainlanders, and that the majority of tourism-generated revenue is reverted back to the mainland. In particular, Yaeyama and Zamami Islands seem to have overexpanded their visitor industry through the use of migrated labour from the mainland, which has created various socio-economic problems and uncertainty for the life of islanders, including water shortages, waste disposal, food insecurity, imported inflation and family problems. It is an urgent task for tourism-dependent island economies to determine the tourism 'absorptive capacity' of the island in relation to its sustainable development.

Fifth, there is a clear pattern of seasonality in the utilization rates of Okinawa's hotel occupancy and other tourism-related facilities, which is directly related to the seasonal variations in visitors. As expected, summer time (July–September) and March are the busiest season in the year, reflecting Japanese holiday-taking patterns, while the rest of the months are slack. Seasonality itself is a big management issue for any small island's tourism. In Okinawa, particularly in Miyako and Yaeyama islands, the tourism season overlaps with occasional typhoons, which totally disrupt travel schedules and purposes and tourists, naturally, are most sensitive to their own inconvenience and security. Terrorism, outbreaks of SARS (severe acute respiratory syndrome) and avian and swine flu, and tsunamis and typhoons have all scared off potential visitors. Therefore, the bottom line for sustainable tourism is to secure peace and stability in tourist destinations. Islands are particularly vulnerable to such unforeseen incidents and, in this context, island tourism policy makers have to learn about how to assess geo-political as well as unexpected risks arising from travel. Although insurance is one of the means of reducing such risks, it usually does not cover unexpected socio-political risks.

Sixth, what is crucial in enhancing tourism activities is the availability of a highly flexible, skilled labour force. Okinawa has been experiencing a growing mismatch in the labour market, which has arisen from a rapid transformation in economic structure and lagging human resource development. Despite the rising unemployment rate – which is an indicator not only of an underutilized labour force, but also of multiple deprivations such as social exclusion, loss of self-reliance, self-confidence and psychological and physical health – many resort hotels are having a difficult time finding qualified workers and managers. This widening mismatch can be addressed by improved human resource development in tourism-centred economic activities.

Finally, the future growth of Okinawa's tourism industry will be constrained by its limited carrying capacity, which will be discussed in more detail in the following section. In particular, the limited supply of quality water and environmental degradation are the most important constraints. Although the Okinawa Prefectural Government (OPG) has planned to achieve 7 million tourists by 2011, and 10 million by 2017, there is no convincing data at all to support any belief that these targets are consistent with Okinawa's limited tourism resources.

The Road Block to Okinawa's Sustainable Tourism Development

According to the United Nations World Tourism Organization (UNWTO, 1998), sustainable tourism development (STD) meets the needs of present tourists and host regions, while protecting and enhancing opportunity for the future. It is envisaged as leading to management of all resources in such a way that economic, social and aesthetic needs can be fulfilled while maintaining cultural integrity, essential ecological processes, biological diversity and life support systems. We must also add that STD should meet the needs and wants of the local host community in terms of improved living standards and quality of life (QOL). The concept should also satisfy the demands of tourists and the tourism industry, and continue to attract them in order to meet the above-mentioned wants and needs and also safeguard the environmental resource base for tourism. Sustainable tourism is synonymous with responsible tourism, which attempts to make a low impact on the environment and local culture, while helping to generate income, employment and the conservation of local ecosystems (Harris *et al.*, 2002).

Amid the growing tourism industry, coupled with a rapid population growth, Okinawa's sustainable tourism indicators and constraints have deteriorated in recent years. Among public utilities, particularly water supply, in terms of quantity and quality, has been a serious issue for Okinawa Island and for small outlying islands. Water supplies have rapidly shifted from river water (from 55% to 21%) and underground water (from 31% to 8%) to dams (15% to 68%) in the past 30 years to meet the increasing demand for water consumption. The site to construct a future dam, however, is extremely limited on all islands. It is reported that a tourist consumes, on average, more than three times the freshwater than does a resident consumer (Kameya, 2007).

Miyako Island has been a location for occasional water shortage and droughts because of its flat topographical conditions (Miwa *et al.*, 1988). The island has no river, so groundwater has been a lifeline for nearly 50,000 islanders. Despite the construction of expensive underground dams, Miyako Island's water balance (supply minus demand) has been deteriorating every year owing largely to the influx of tourists (Fig. 13.3). It is highly questionable whether or not the current water supply capacity can meet future demand.

In addition to the increasing demand for water and energy resources as the population and the number of tourists increase, the economy's carrying capacity and environmental disruption will become serious impediments to future development. There is already sufficient evidence to suggest that Okinawa's world-renowned coral reefs are on the verge of extinction due largely to global warming and high predation of coral by *Acanthaster* (crown-of-thorns starfish) (Tsuchiya, 2004). A recent study suggests that, with intense coral bleaching, close to a third of Okinawa's corals have already gone, with 60% expected to be lost by 2030 (UNEP-WCMC, 2006).

With the increasing number of tourists and rented-car users, air pollution and waste disposal are other serious obstacles for future sustainable tourism in Okinawa. Okinawa's air pollution in terms of CO_2 emission has increased by over 40% since 1990 along with a rapid increase of automobiles. Okinawa's per-capita CO_2 emission is twice as high as that of Japan proper. The increasing air pollution is not only a limiting factor for Okinawa's sustainable tourism, but it also damages the image of its clean air and healthy lifestyle. We need to assess whether or not Okinawa's small, environmentally fragile islands can

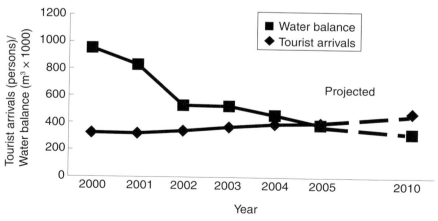

Fig. 13.3. Tourism arrivals and water balance (supply minus demand), Miyako Island 2000–2010. (Constructed by author from Water Resource Statistics, Miyoko Water Enterprise Bureau.)

sustain their ever-increasing de facto population (residents + tourists) with the extremely limited capacity of their renewable as well as non-renewable resources, based on reliable data on per capita demand for islands' infrastructures such as water, sewers, electricity, gas, solid wastes and CO_2 emission.

Evaluation of Tourism Resources and Carrying Capacity of Tourist Sites

The contingency valuation method (CVM) has been used widely in recent years to evaluate the economic value of tourism resources such as landscapes, coral reefs, flora and fauna and amenities, which are not easily valued through market transactions. The CVM method involves asking people directly about how much they would be willing to pay (WTP) for the specific value of environmental services, or how much they would be willing to accept (WTA) in compensation for giving up specific environmental services. Therefore, the method is contingent upon a specific hypothetical scenario and on the questions asked. There are, of course, many limitations and assumptions that need to be recognized when the method is applied.

Figure 13.4 demonstrates the basic concept of the CVM method using a conventional diagram. The vertical axis indicates the cost or income a consumer should pay in order to improve environmental quality (EQ), which is drawn on the horizontal axis. S_1 and S_2 indicate the level of consumer satisfaction or 'utility function', with S_2 giving greater satisfaction than S_1, and any point on

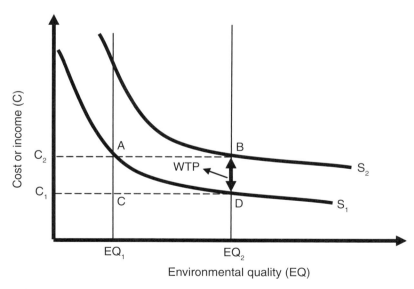

Fig. 13.4. Concept of the contingent valuation method (CVM). C, cost or income (C_1, C_2); EQ, environmental quality (EQ_1, EQ_2); S, level of satisfaction (S_1, S_2); WTP, willingness to pay. (Source: Kakazu, 2009.)

the same curve gives precisely the same level of satisfaction which is called 'indifference satisfaction curve'. The WTP can be defined as the difference between S_2 and S_1 ($S_2 - S_1$) because the level of consumer satisfaction has not changed from A to D despite the consumer having to pay environmental costs ($C_2 - C_1$) in order to improve the environmental quality from EQ_1 to EQ_2. Thus, $C_2 - C_1$, or BD in the figure, can be considered as 'compensating surplus' or the maximum amount of cost or income forgone in order to obtain the EQ_2 level of environmental goods.

Based on a CVM study (Sukpil, 2003), Zamami Island, which has been experiencing severe water shortages and environmental disruption as a result of influx of tourists, has decided to introduce island entry tax for environmental conservation. According to the study, visitors to Zamami Island were willing to pay about US$100 per trip to the island for the conservation of beaches and environments. The Zamami Island Authority imposed a 5% tax on the ferry fare between the island and Naha port in Okinawa Island. The tax rate was much lower than what each visitor was willing to pay for his or her trip to the island according to the CVM study. Theoretically, the optimum amount of tax is represented by BD in Fig. 13.4. As could be expected from the CVM study, the number of visitors to the island has not declined in response to the additional tax cost. The result demonstrates that the fragile tourist resources in these islands are underpriced. This is particularly true for a resort island such as Zamami Island where heavy repeaters are attracted to its pristine beaches and marine leisure. The CVM study also demonstrates that the value of environments will differ greatly by place, incomes, interviewees, age, sex and probably the way a survey is conducted. Therefore, the CVM method needs a lot of refinements and improvements for it to be usefully applied to a particular project and island.

The United Nations Environmental Programme (UNEP) also calculated the value of Okinawa's coral reef based on the CVM method. According to this study, the total economic value of coral reefs is estimated at between US$100,000 and US$900,000 per km^2 a year (UNEP-WCMC, 2006). The value of coral reefs critically depends on the incomes generated through utilizing costal zones.

This author also conducted a preliminary study on Okinawa's tourism social carrying capacity (SCC) (Kakazu, 2009). The SCC of tourist sites can be defined as the socially determined maximum number of tourists that are tolerated by local communities; it is usually analysed from both the standpoints of local residents and tourists. The latest study, by Marzetti and Mosetti (2005), concluded that the residents' SCC is lower than the visitors' SCC, and that the site SCC is the result of a compromise between these two aspects of the SCC. They suggested two approaches to measuring the SCC. One is a conventional cost-benefit analysis (CBA) based on the maximization of individual preferences; the other approach is to let local residents determine the maximum number of acceptable tourists through the majority vote rule.

Figure 13.5 illustrates the tourism SCC applied to Okinawa by this author. In this diagram, the upper vertical axis and the horizontal axis indicate the costs and benefits (or tourist expenditure) and the forecast number of tourists

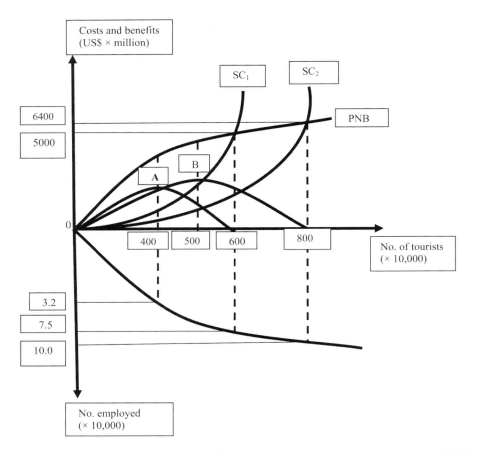

Fig. 13.5. An illustrative representation of Okinawa's tourism social carrying capacity (SCC) in 2008. A, function A; B, function B; PNB, private net benefit; SC, social cost (SC$_1$, SC$_2$) (Source: Kakazu, 2009.)

from 1995 to 2015, respectively. The lower vertical axis indicates the amount of employment generated directly and indirectly by tourist expenditure. These figures exclude the private, as well as the social, costs of accepting tourists. The total net benefit from tourism activity (TNB) is defined as:

TNB (N) = PNB (N) − Cs (N) − Ce (N)

where PNB is private net benefit, N is number of tourists per day, Cs is social costs such as noise, pollution and stress from crowding and Ce is value of environmental losses. The maximum number of tourists tolerated by local communities can be determined by the following utility maximization rule:

net marginal benefit = social and environmental marginal costs

This is where the social cost (SC) curves (SC_1, SC_2) intersect with the PNB curve in Fig. 13.5.

The net marginal benefit is the additional net benefit generated from the additional number of tourists. Social marginal cost is the additional cost per tourist arrival in Okinawa. If we assume that Okinawa's utility (satisfaction) curve from tourism rises as the number of tourists increases, and declines as a result of overcrowding and environmental disruptions, then we can draw the utility functions A and B in Fig. 13.5 depending on the degree of tolerance. Obviously, function B is more hospitable to tourists than function A. If function A is the genuine utility or tolerance curve, then Okinawa's optimum SCC is determined at the intersection of SC_1 and PNB, where 6 million tourists, US$5 billion in tourist expenditure and 75,000 in local employment are the maximum social net benefits that Okinawa can generate from tourism activities. Okinawa will experience net social loss if tourist arrivals exceed 6 million. However, if the tolerance curve is more like function B, the optimum number of tourists will be 8 million where SC_2 intersects with PNB in Fig. 13.5. The optimum SCC depends on a number of geographical, socio-economic, ecological, cultural, administrative and political factors, on which reliable data are not always available; none the less, the CVM method (or voting rule) can be used to determine the optimum SCC. Okinawa's popular outlying islands such as Zamami, Tonaki, Ishigaki, Taketomi and Iriomote, where the number of visitors is more than ten times the resident population, may offer a good comparative case study to determine the optimum number of tourists.

Concluding Remarks: Okinawa's Sustainable Tourism Development

The tourism industry will continue to grow in the Asia-Pacific region at the fastest rate of any region in the world. It is becoming a leading industry in the region, and is expected to contribute to regional sustainable development, stability and peace through the creation of employment, incomes and the exchange of peoples. Tourism is becoming the most competitive industry in the Pacific islands, including Okinawa, on both domestic and international scales.

Okinawa consists of 40 inhabited small islands with limited and fragile human and non-human resources. This requires balanced development that takes into account economic, social and environmental sustainability, with particular emphasis on the conservation and sustainable use of coral reef and marine ecosystems, underground freshwater resources, coastal and inland forests, agricultural lands and infrastructure. We have to recognize that the terrestrial, freshwater and marine ecosystems of these islands are closely interconnected, and attempts must be made to maintain the quantity and quality of groundwater resources to protect these islands from pollution and to use the terrestrial freshwater and marine biodiversity as a foundation for sustainable livelihoods.

Although Okinawa's tourism industry has expanded more than thirteenfold since the early 1980s, the economy could capture only 40% of total tourist spending through the sale of domestic goods and services. The rest leaked out on imports. The first important research question is how to internalize the growing tourist spending through expanding domestic production of goods and services. In particular, the pursuit of high-value tourism, in conjunction with its socio-economic sustainability, will be the most important issue to be resolved.

There are multifaceted ways to fill the gap between tourist spending and the economy's capacity to meet demand. Many surveys indicate that tourist spending on restaurants and souvenirs, which accounts for only 8.1% and 5.9%, respectively, of total spending can be expanded further because Okinawans are well known for their longevity and healthy foods. In fact, health food products have grown so rapidly within Japan's major markets to the point where an 'Okinawa brand' could be established. The second key question is how to diversify Okinawa's tourism in terms of visitors and stakeholders in the tourism-related industry. The excessive competition in the industry has also resulted in a widening income gap among households and islands, as measured by the Gini index (Kakazu, 2009).

Okinawa's tourism industry is facing serious challenges resulting from its high growth rate, which has inevitably been accompanied by increasing demand for water and energy resources, as well as environmental degradation, as the population and the number of tourists increased. There are already supply constraints with public utilities such as water and electricity for which demand has increased more than Okinawa's economic growth rate. Recent severe water shortages in some outlying islands indicate that there is a potential risk to island tourism arising from water supply, which is the most important lifeline for these isolated islands. The economy's carrying capacity and environmental disruptions will become serious constraints on future tourism development. Therefore, the third key question is how to assess Okinawa's tourism social carrying capacity under a de facto ever-increasing population.

References

Bertram, I.G. and Watters. R. (1985) The MIRAB economy in South Pacific micro-states. *Pacific Viewpoint* 26, 497–519.

Harris, R., Griffin, T. and Williams, P. (eds) (2002) *Sustainable Tourism: A Global Perspective.* Butterworth-Heinemann, Oxford.

JTB (2008) *Travel Intention Survey.* Japan Travel Bureau, Tokyo.

Kakazu, H. (1994) *Sustainable Development of Small Island Economies.* Westview Press, Boulder, Colorado.

Kakazu, H. (1996) Effects of tourism growth on development in the Asia-Pacific Region: the case of small islands. Paper presented at: *UNESCO Conference on Culture, Tourism, and Development: Crucial Issues for the XXI Century,* 26–27 June 1996, Paris, France.

Kakazu, H. (1998) Sustainable tourism development: the case of small islands. Paper presented at: *Inter-island Cooperation in Asia: Tourism Policy in Island Area,* 24 July 1998, Busena Resort, Okinawa, Japan.

Kakazu, H. (2003) The challenge for Okinawa: thriving locally in a globalized economy. In: Hsin-Huang M.H., Chao-Han, L. and

Huei-Min, T. (eds) *Sustainable Development for Island Societies: Taiwan and the World*. Asia-Pacific Research Program (APARP), Academia Sinica/Southeast Asia Regional Committee for START (SARCS), National Central University, Taipei, Taiwan, pp. 201–232.

Kakazu, H. (2008) *Island Sustainability: Challenges and Opportunities for Okinawa and Other Pacific Islands in a Globalized World*. Trafford Publishing, Bloomington, Indiana.

Kakazu, H. (2009) *Island Sustainability: Challenges and Opportunities for Okinawa and Other Pacific Islands in a Globalized World*. Trafford Publishing, Victoria, Canada.

Kameya, D. (2007) A study on water shortages in Okinawa's small islands. Paper presented at: *Annual Meeting of the Japan Society of Island Studies*, 16 September 2007, Yonaguni, Okinawa, Japan.

Marzetti, S. and Mosetti R. (2005) *Social Carrying Capacity of Mass Tourist Sites: Theoretical and Practical Issues about its Measurement*. FEEM Working Paper No. 144.05, Fondazione Eni Enrico Mattei, Milan, Venice, Viggiano, Italy/Brussels, Belgium. Available at: http:ssrn.com/abstract=856024 (accessed 12 December 2005).

Miwa, N., Yamauchi, H. and Morita, D. (1988) *Water and Survival in an Island Environment: Challenge of Okinawa*. University of Hawaii, Honolulu, Hawaii.

Sukpil, O. (2003) *A Study on Coastal Conservation and Utilization: Valuations on Coral Reefs and Ecosystem of the Kerama Islands*. Research Institute of Subtropics, Naha, Okinawa, Japan.

Tsuchiya, M. (2004) Ecosystem function and carrying capacity of coral reefs. Paper presented at *Experts Meeting on Projects Designing for Pacific Islands: Environment, Health and Human Resources Development*, 3–5 March 2004, Naha, Okinawa, Japan.

Umemura, T. (2006) An empirical analysis on international tourism and economic growth in small island developing states. *The Journal of Island Sciences* No. 1 (December 2006), p. 51 [in Japanese]. Copy available at: http://www.geocities.jp/umemurat2001/ (accessed 10 September 2010).

UNEP-WCMC (United Nations Environment Programme-World Conservation Monitoring Centre) (2006) *In the Front Line: Shoreline Protection and Other Ecosystem Services from Mangroves and Coral Reefs*. UNEP-WCMC, Cambridge.

UNWTO (1998) *Guide for Local Authorities on Developing Sustainable Tourism*. United Nations World Tourism Organization, Madrid.

14 Tourism in Mediterranean Islands: a Comparative Analysis

GIOVANNI RUGGIERI

The Observatory on Tourism in the EU Islands (OTIE), Palermo University, Italy

Introduction

From ancient times, the Mediterranean basin has connected peoples from different countries, facilitating both commercial and cultural exchanges. Within the Mediterranean basin, both large and small islands have always been transit and temporary stopping places, thereby promoting trade and acting as sorting centres for goods and knowledge. Today, these territories, which differ in size, population and economic and cultural activities, are the core of new exchanges and activities, among which tourism stands out (CPRM, 2002).

The Mediterranean basin has more than 100 islands belonging to six states that are members of the European Union (EU). However, despite the diversity and uniqueness of each island, these territories share the same permanent handicaps as a result of their insularity (Briguglio and Kisanga, 2004). This condition has been recognized by the EU as both a geo-cultural factor and a permanent handicap because of additional constraints on competitiveness in the areas concerned (CESE, 2002, 2005), and is seen as the main reason for the formulation of specific policies addressed to these territories. Awareness of such a condition has developed recently, dating back to the end of the last century, and has led to the insular areas being identified as regions 'which suffer from severe or permanent natural or demographic handicaps' for which it is necessary to adopt specific measures aiming to 'reduce disparities between the levels of development of the various regions and the backwardness of the least favoured regions' (CESE, 2002). The difficulties related to the condition of insularity of Mediterranean islands include the following:

- Structural disadvantages stemming from isolation, limited area, distance from mainland and residential density;

- Limited resources, in particular water and energy resources;
- Presence of fragile ecosystems;
- Developmental backwardness in comparison with the rest of the country;
- Increased investment costs for local enterprises;
- Isolation from large markets;
- Loss of quality human potential; and
- Economic weakening due to the presence of a single sector of activity, such as tourism.

In contrast to these difficulties, Mediterranean islands experience a strong tourist demand that ensures high levels of tourism consumption with positive effects on local employment and production. Not only does tourism in islands tend to be central for the local economy, it is also the principal factor of economic, environmental and social imbalances (Costa and Manente, 2000; Candela and Figini, 2005).

However, the islands cannot all be placed at the same stage of tourism development (Butler 1980), because in the Mediterranean, destinations coexist at various stages of maturity. This makes it impossible to formulate strategic guidelines of sustainable development that are valid and generally applicable in all islands (Baldacchino, 2006; Fairbairn, 2007). It is, therefore, necessary to start from a comparative analysis of tourism in the islands (CESE, 2002; Gomel and Roccas, 2002) to develop the most appropriate tourism policies for the territory concerned.

Tourism in the Mediterranean Islands

The EU recognizes more than 280 insular regions comprising islands that:

- Have an area of over 1 km^2;
- Are located at least 1 km from mainland;
- Have no permanent links with mainland; and
- Boast a stable population of at least 50 inhabitants.

As already mentioned, in the Mediterranean there are more than 100 islands belonging to six EU countries – Cyprus, Greece, Italy, Malta, France and Spain. Furthermore, a comparative analysis of tourism in these European Mediterranean islands identified 18 international insular regions that are officially recognized (OTIE 2008). Depending on their overall areas, these islands could also be classified into four size groups (OTIE, 2008):

- 1 km^2 < micro island <1000 km^2;
- 1001 km^2 < small island <5000 km^2;
- 5,001 km^2 < medium island <10,000 km^2; and
- Large island >10,001 km^2.

Analysed in this way, the EU Mediterranean islands are grouped as follows (see Table 14.1):

- *Micro islands*: Sporades, Malta archipelago, Argosaronicos Islands, Tuscan Islands, Flegree Islands, Pontine Islands and Tremiti Islands;
- *Small islands*: Balearic Islands, north-eastern Aegean Islands, Evia, Ionian Islands, Dodekanisa and Cyclades;
- *Medium islands*: Cyprus, Corsica and Crete; and
- *Large islands*: Sicily and Sardinia.

These islands have an overall population of over 11 million inhabitants on an area of 97,308 km^2 (Table 14.1). The population/area ratio reveals that micro islands have a greater residential density and that the islands with the highest concentration of inhabitants are the Flegree Islands and the archipelago of Malta, both of which belong to the *micro-islands* category.

Like population, tourism is not uniformly distributed over the islands. In 2008, the Mediterranean islands attracted 32,798,552 tourists, generating 222,392,408 overnight stays, with an average length of stay of 6.8 nights. The Balearic Islands are the major archipelago in the Mediterranean in terms of tourist numbers, receiving one third of tourist arrivals and more than half of the tourist overnight stays of all the islands considered (INESTUR, 2007). The

Table 14.1 Geo-demographic indicators of European islands of the Mediterranean, 2008. (Source: OTIE, 2008.)

State	Category	Island/Archipelago	Area (km^2)	Population/area
Italy	Large	Sicily and its small islands	25,703	196
Italy	Large	Sardinia and its small islands	24,090	69
Cyprus	Medium	Cyprus	9,251	86
France	Medium	Corsica	8,680	34
Greece	Medium	Crete	8,261	74
Spain	Small	Balearic Islands	4,968	216
Greece	Small	North-eastern Aegean Islands	4,260	47
Greece	Small	Evia	3,662	56
Greece	Small	Ionian Islands	2,443	95
Greece	Small	Dodekanisa	2,393	49
Greece	Small	Cyclades	2,267	82
Greece	Micro	Sporades	417	37
Malta	Micro	Malta, Gozo and Comino	316	1309
Greece	Micro	Argosaronicos Islands	261	202
Italy	Micro	Tuscan Islands	261	122
Italy	Micro	Flegree Islands	61	1418
Italy	Micro	Pontine Islands	11	356
Italy	Micro	Tremiti Islands	3	159
All European Mediterranean Islands			97,308	113

other islands share the rest of the tourist flows with diverse numbers, but display a mild predominance of medium-sized islands receiving more tourists (Table 14.2). If the geographical position is considered (excluding the Balearic Islands), tourist demand is most substantial in the eastern part of the Mediterranean – involving all the Greek islands and Cyprus.

In terms of changes in the average lengths of stay from island to island, two groups of islands may be identified: those recognizable as holiday destinations, with average stays longer than a week, and those characterized by stays shorter than four nights. This implies that there is no relationship between the island size and the average length of stay. Variations in tourist stays from one island to another mostly depend on the level of attractiveness of the island and the type of tourism offered by the destination.

In a comparison of tourist demand with accommodation supply, it can be noted that most islands show a low occupancy rate and are not able to fill more than half of the beds supplied over a year (overnight stays/beds × 365). The

Table 14.2. Tourist flows in the European islands of the Mediterranean, 2008. (Source: OTIE, 2008.)

State	Category	Island/Archipelago	Tourist arrivals	Overnight stays	Length of stay
Italy	Large	Sicily and its small islands	4,174,276	13,609,672	3.3
Italy	Large	Sardinia and its small islands	2,363,496	12,290,514	5.2
Greece	Medium	Crete	2,287,742	15,729,316	6.9
Cyprus	Medium	Cyprus	2,403,744	14,380,375	6.0
France	Medium	Corsica	1,966,121	6,240,956	3.2
Spain	Small	Balearic Islands	13,103,901	116,436,211	8.9
Greece	Small	Dodekanisa	1,666,972	12,750,703	7.6
Greece	Small	Ionian Islands	1,091,790	7,414,829	6.8
Greece	Small	North-eastern Aegean Islands	423,706	2,314,209	5.5
Greece	Small	Cyclades	502,734	1,795,440	3.6
Greece	Small	Evia	212,018	861,533	4.1
Malta	Micro	Malta, Gozo and Comino	1,290,856	11,262,026	8.7
Italy	Micro	Flegree Islands	648,477	3,551,444	5.5
Italy	Micro	Tuscan Islands	443,541	2,771,310	6.2
Greece	Micro	Sporades	107,748	604,734	5.6
Greece	Micro	Argosaronicos Islands	65,751	193,716	2.9
Italy	Micro	Pontine Islands	27,469	98,820	3.6
Italy	Micro	Tremiti Islands	18,210	86,600	4.8
Mediterranean Islands			32,798,552	222,392,408	6.8

only exceptions are Malta and the Balearic Islands, which record occupancy rates higher than 75% (Table 14.3).

The islands attracting the largest number of tourists are those which make the best use of available bed places, thereby reaching high occupancy rates. This indicator undergoes variations over the year and is tied to seasonal variations in tourism demand, which is heaviest from May to October. Tourist flows are more evenly distributed during the year in those islands with a wider tourism demand (Malta and the Balearic Islands), while the islands with fewer tourist arrivals and stays are characterized by a greater seasonality.

Comparative analysis of tourism in the islands

The Mediterranean islands are at different stages of the tourist product life cycle, and some have reached the maturity stage. Sustainable development

Table 14.3. Bed-place capacity and occupancy rates in the European islands of the Mediterranean, 2008. (Source: OTIE, 2008.)

State	Category	Island/Archipelago	Bed places	Occupancy rate of bed places[a]
Italy	Large	Sardinia and its small islands	198,072	17%
Italy	Large	Sicily and its small islands	190,583	20%
Greece	Medium	Crete	154,492	28%
France	Medium	Corsica	139,000	12%
Cyprus	Medium	Cyprus	90,398	44%
Spain	Small	Balearic Islands	425,097	75%
Greece	Small	Dodekanisa	123,183	28%
Greece	Small	Ionian Islands	92,370	22%
Greece	Small	Cyclades	51,799	9%
Greece	Small	North-eastern Aegean Islands	21,077	30%
Greece	Small	Evia	17,345	14%
Malta	Micro	Malta, Gozo and Comino	39,167	79%
Italy	Micro	Tuscan Islands	37,204	20%
Italy	Micro	Flegree Islands	27,886	35%
Greece	Micro	Sporades	10,742	15%
Greece	Micro	Argosaronicos Islands	8,037	7%
Italy	Micro	Tremiti Islands	1,435	17%
Italy	Micro	Pontine Islands	1,229	22%
Mediterranean Islands			1,629,116	37%

[a]Occupancy rate of bed places = overnight stays/beds × 365.

implies some limitations in the use of resources and this is true, in particular, in places with high levels of tourist pressure, territorial exploitation and environmental impact. On comparing these indicators, it is possible to classify islands and suggest the tourism policies that need to be followed which might improve sustainability.

Use of the territory of Mediterranean islands, which considers both the resident population and tourists, is calculated by an territorial exploitation index, whereby: (arrivals/area + population/area)/100. This indicator allows islands to be classified according to the level of use of their area or territory. Only six islands/island groups out of the 18 under examination record high values of this territorial exploitation index (Table 14.4). Thus, two groups of islands may be contrasted and compared: (i) the Tremiti Islands, Pontine Islands and the Tuscan Archipelago, whose exploitation and development is mostly connected with tourism; and (ii) Sicily and the Argosaronicos Islands, where exploitation by the resident population in the form of traditional economic activities prevails.

The tourist pressure index – (overnight stays + population)/area – reveals that the tourism and population pressure is high in proportion to the island area in five insular regions. These values are noticeably higher than average in the Flegree Islands, the Malta archipelago, Tremiti Islands, Balearic Islands and Tuscan Archipelago.

However, in some islands, the impacts generated by tourism are higher in specific limited areas of the territory, namely, those where the supply of tourist facilities is more concentrated. In these areas, tourist activity is often accompanied by more marked impacts on the environment, corresponding to higher levels of tourist pressure. The impact index – (overnight stays/population × 365) × 1000 – reflects the number of tourists present for every 1000 permanent inhabitants. It shows a higher level in some Grecian archipelagos, where tourist flows are particularly concentrated. It can be seen that the higher the values, the higher the sociocultural impacts triggered by tourism on the traditions and culture of the local population.

Strategies for the Development of Sustainable Tourism

The availability of bed places is widespread and easily accessible in many islands, but only in a few cases is this feature used effectively. In most islands, only partial utilization at best is observed, and sometimes bed-space use is limited to only a few months in the year. In the case of islands in particular, growth and development policies and the resultant strategies that should be followed must be considered in relation to the load capacity that insular territories are able to bear (Bosetti *et al.*, 2004).

In these territories, which are often fragile and highly vulnerable to tourist activities, as well as being characterized by developmental backwardness, the strategies to be defined and approaches to be followed must take into account the peculiarities of each individual island. A correlation between the values of the two indicators already discussed – tourism pressure and occupancy

Table 14.4. Tourism indicators in the European islands of the Mediterranean, 2008. (Source: OTIE, 2008.)

Island/Archipelago	Territorial exploitation index	Island/Archipelago	Tourist pressure index	Island/Archipelago	Impact index
Flegree Islands	120.8	Flegree Islands	59.8	Tremiti Islands	477.4
Tremiti Islands	59.8	Malta, Gozo and Comino	37.0	Balearic Islands	297.3
Malta, Gozo and Comino	54.0	Tremiti Islands	29.0	Tuscan Islands	237.5
Balearic Islands	28.5	Balearic Islands	23.7	Dodekanisa	178.2
Tuscan Islands	27.7	Tuscan Islands	10.7	Flegree Islands	112.8
Pontine Islands	18.2	Pontine Islands	9.0	Sporades	106.0
Dodekanisa	7.8	Dodekanisa	5.4	Ionian Islands	87.7
Ionian Islands	5.4	Ionian Islands	3.1	Malta, Gozo and Comino	74.6
Argosaronicos Islands	4.5	Crete	2.0	Crete	70.8
Sicily and its small islands	3.6	Cyprus	1.6	Pontine Islands	66.8
Crete	3.5	Sporades	1.5	Corsica	58.5
Cyprus	3.5	Argosaronicos Islands	0.9	Cyprus	49.4
Sporades	3.0	Cyclades	0.8	Cyclades	44.2
Cyclades	2.7	Corsica	0.8	North-eastern Aegean Islands	31.7
Corsica	2.6	Sicily and its small islands	0.7	Sardinia and its small islands	20.2
Sardinia and its small islands	1.7	North-eastern Aegean Islands	0.6	Evia	11.4
North-eastern Aegean Islands	1.5	Sardinia and its small islands	0.6	Argosaronicos Islands	10.1
Evia	1.1	Evia	0.3	Sicily and its small islands	7.4

rate – can be used to outline a more clear and definable strategic framework in terms of potential actions and initiatives (Figueroa, 2004). Based on the values obtained from these indicators, four possible development strategies can be outlined; these are indicated and summarized in Table 14.5.

The Balearic Islands and the Malta archipelago (A Strategy in Table 14.5) show considerable tourism pressure with a relatively high occupancy rate. In such cases, it is argued to be inadvisable to increase bed place availability but, rather, that the existing levels of tourism demand should be maintained. If demand was increased by the provision of additional bed places, such a high level of tourism pressure could accelerate the process of decline of these destinations, with resulting negative effects on the environment and the resident communities, thus alternative approaches are needed. In these islands, the possible strategies that emerge are:

- Stabilization and/or maintenance of the balance already achieved;
- Gradual upgrading of supply but without an increase in tourism pressure; and
- A generalized, although gradual, shift towards an upmarket segment of customers, through a coherent readjustment of the quality of supply and prices (Knowles and Curtis 1999; Kotler *et al.*, 2006).

In contrast, some smaller-sized archipelagos (micro islands), such as the Flegree and Tremiti Islands (B Strategy in Table 14.5), have a high tourism pressure index and a low occupancy rate. This indicates that in these islands, the supply of bed spaces is being underutilized but, despite this, the level of impact is high. In this case, tourism policies aimed at moving towards

Table 14.5. Strategic matrix for tourism development in the European islands of the Mediterranean. (Source: OTIE, 2008.)

Occupancy rate	Tourism pressure	
	High	Low
High	*A Strategy (stabilize and maintain flows)* Balearic Islands Malta, Gozo and Comino	*C Strategy (increase accommodation capacity)* No islands
Low	*B Strategy (design growth strategy)* Flegree Islands Tremiti Islands	*D Strategy (develop a targeted positioning strategy)* Argosaronicos Islands North-eastern Aegean Islands Cyprus Pontine Islands Cyclades Sardinia Corsica Sicily Crete Sporades Dodekanisa Tuscan Islands Evia Ionian Islands

sustainability should be focused on seasonality reduction, tourism restraint and the upgrading of, but not increasing supply of, tourism.

At present, no Mediterranean islands show low tourism pressure and a medium-to-high bed occupancy rate (C Strategy in Table 14.5). This suggests, therefore, that there are no islands in the Mediterranean which are currently suitable for the establishment of new facilities without compromising the environment.

Most Mediterranean islands tend to show a low tourism pressure and low bed occupancy rate (D Strategy in Table 14.5). This last group of islands can be argued to possess the highest potential for growth in tourism demand, both in the short and in the long term. They also have greater freedom of choice in terms of possible strategies (e.g. diversification over the full range of possible segments: high – medium – low). In their case, accurate analysis of the restraints to development is of crucial importance in order to prevent any bed place increase from giving rise to lower occupancy rates. This situation applies to Cyprus, all the Greek islands and the two large Italian islands (Sardinia and Sicily), to the Pontine islands and the Tuscan archipelago, all of which share similar characteristics.

This analysis reveals that small and medium-sized islands in general have increased their tourism supply in terms of bed places, such as in new hotels, generating an increase in tourism pressure on the territory. However, although tourism demand has grown in almost all the Mediterranean islands over the past few decades, it has been increasingly concentrated more heavily in some periods of the year. This is a result of both the supply of a single product, generally sea- and sports-related holidays, and also to the presence of a primarily local or domestic tourism market. For those islands where the bed-place occupancy rate is low, it would be desirable to increase tourism demand, for example through policies aimed at integrating coastal holidays with cultural tourism, and targeting international markets rather than the existing domestic market only.

For large-sized islands, e.g. Sardinia and Sicily, tourism has lower importance vis-à-vis other economic activities, and issues of sustainable development, even though significant, seem to be less urgent. For these territories, a growth strategy can be supported by policies that differentiate tourism products, linking them with the cultural activities and natural resources that are often more prevalent in larger islands. The integration of existing tourism products and the creation of a differentiated tourism supply, related to cultural activities, should be the major growth guidelines.

Finally, the Balearic Islands and the Archipelago of Malta have chosen and pursued over time a development policy exclusively based on tourism. As a consequence, these territories need now to constantly monitor tourist demand and promptly detect the beginning of any decline stage, thus allowing them to undertake a 'restyling' of the destination and possibly change the existing types of tourism.

Some Considerations on the Tourism Policies of Mediterranean Islands

All Mediterranean islands, although different in individual characteristics, share not only the same restraints and limitations, but also geomorphology, history, traditions, archaeology and art. Tourism in these territories still has broad potential for development, but in order for economic growth to be sustainable, development must be planned in a systemic rather than an independent perspective, both inside and outside the island context (Figueroa, 2004; Gómez *et al.*, 2004). Therefore, cooperation in two dimensions is necessary: the first involves the local actors involved in tourism development, while the second is to be carried out through partnerships among island groups identified as 'Mediterranean'.

In a situation of continued growing competition within the tourism market, cooperation among islands could be an appropriate instrument of economic and social development, which could offer an integrated product and result in inter-regional tourism among territories. Such partnerships are encouraged by EU cohesion policies aimed at fostering cooperation, thereby increasing competitiveness of weaker regions, which include many of the Mediterranean islands.

In the current situation of growing international competition, which every single island faces, cooperation and partnerships appear to be a particularly logical strategy which could result in the construction of a 'Mediterranean insular region'. Such an aggregation may guarantee a unique positioning of these islands, strengthening the appeal and distinctiveness of Mediterranean insularity (Cook, 2003).

References

Baldacchino, G. (2006) Serving sustainable islands tourism: hot or cold? *Insula* 15 (2), 15–22.

Bosetti, V., Cassinelli, M. and Lanza, A. (2004) Measuring efficiency in sustainable tourism management. In: AA.VV. I Conference on Tourism Economics, University of Balearic Islands, Palma de Mallorca, Spain, 28–29 May 2004. *Economía del Turismo*, AECIT (Asociación Española de Expertos Científicos en Turismo), Castellón, Spain, pp. 399–415.

Briguglio, L. and Kisanga, E.J. (2004) *Economic Vulnerability and Resilience of Small States*. Formatek, Malta.

Butler, R.W. (1980) The concept of a tourist area cycle of evolution: implications for management of resources. *Canadian Geographer* 24, 5–12.

Candela, G. and Figini, P. (2005) *Economia dei Sistemi Turistici*. McGraw-Hill, Milan.

CESE (2002) *Parere del Comitato delle Regioni sul Tema 'La Problematica delle Regioni Insulari dell'Unione Europea e le Prospettive in Vista dell'Allargamento'*, 12 agosto 2002. Comitato Economico e Sociale Europeo/European Economic and Social Committee, Brussels.

CESE (2005) *Parere di Iniziativa sul Tema 'Verso una Maggiore Integrazione delle Regioni Gravate da Svantaggi Naturali e Strutturali Permanenti*, 10 febbraio

2005. Comitato Economico e Sociale Europeo/European Economic and Social Committee, Brussels.

Cook, S. (2003) *Guida Pratica al Benchmark. Come Creare un Vantaggio Competitivo*. FrancoAngeli, Milan.

Costa, P. and Manente, M. (2000) *Economia del Turismo. Modelli di Analisi e Misura delle Dimensioni Economiche del Turismo*. Touring Club Italiano, Milan.

CPRM (Conference of Peripheral Maritime Regions) (2002) *Off the Coast of Europe*. Calligraphy-Print, Chateaubourg, France.

Fairbairn, T.L.J. (2007) Economic vulnerability and resilience of small islands states. *Islands Studies Journal* 2, 133–140.

Figueroa B., E. (2004) The economics of sustainable tourism: making green and cultural viable. In: AA.VV. I Conference on Tourism Economics, University of Balearic Islands, Palma de Mallorca, Spain, 28–29 May 2004. *Economía del Turismo*, AECIT (Asociación Española de Expertos Científicos en Turismo), Castellón, Spain, pp.417–431.

Gomel, G. and Roccas, M. (2002) *Le Economie del Mediterraneo, Relazioni Conclusive del Progetto di Ricerca della Banca d'Italia 'Economie del Mediterraneo'*. Banca d'Italia, Rome.

Gómez G., C.M., Lonzano, J. and Rey-M., J. (2004) A dynamic analysis of environmental and tourism policies. In: AA.VV. I Conference on Tourism Economics, University of Balearic Islands, Palma de Mallorca, Spain, 28–29 May 2004. *Economía del Turismo*, AECIT (Asociación Española de Expertos Científicos en Turismo), Castellón, Spain, pp.435–456.

INESTUR (Instituto de Estrategia Turística de las Islas Baleares) (2007) *Estudio del Impacto Economico del Turismo sobre la Economia y Empleo en las Balears*. Palma, Majorca.

Knowles, T. and Curtis, S. (1999) The market viability of European mass tourism destinations: a post stagnation life cycle analysis. *International Journal of Tourism Research* 1, 87–96.

Kotler, P., Bowen, J. and Makens, J. (2006) *Marketing del Turismo*. McGraw-Hill, Milan.

OTIE (Observatory on Tourism in the European Islands) (2008) *1st Focus on Tourism in the European Islands*. Logos, Palermo, Italy.

15 Sustainable Tourism Transportation in Hawaii: a Holistic Approach

GUI LOHMANN[1] AND DAVID NGOC NGUYEN[2]

[1]Southern Cross University, Gold Coast, Australia; [2]University of Hawaii at Manoa, Hawaii

Introduction

In spite of the differences that exist in regard to size, shape and distance to the continental mainland, islands are heavily dependent on transportation. Nations and sub-national island entities can be remote, relying on air and maritime transportation to connect them to other regions. Small islands in particular are faced with several disadvantages owing to the sizes of their geographical areas and populations, susceptibility to natural disasters, fragile ecosystems and geographical remoteness from major market centres (Abeyratne, 1999). Because of their limited resource base and production capabilities, the ability of islands to export primary products are low, while they rely heavily on the importation of capital and consumer goods (Kakazu, 2007). As a result of these disadvantages that are faced by small islands, tourism development has became an attractive and, sometimes, inevitable industry, as economic diversification remains limited (Rao, 2002).

In Hawaii, tourist arrivals outnumbered the local population by an approximate ratio of 6:1 in 2007, with nearly 7.5 million tourists visiting this Pacific archipelago (DBEDT, 2008). In islands, and particularly in archipelagos like Hawaii, tourism transportation needs to be addressed from different perspectives and scales, such as:

1. Accessibility to/from islands: since the emergence of passenger air transportation, islands, which were previously limited in their interactions in the international arena, have been transformed into destinations as tourists from other parts of the world are interested in travelling to exotic locales. Tourism is inextricably linked with air transportation, as many of these islands could not have been made accessible to foreign tourists without the establishment of transportation links between them and their markets. Any developments in the tourism sector affect air transport by influencing

demand. Conversely, developments in air transportation, such as changes in flight frequency and passenger capacity, have an impact on tourism arrivals (Bieger and Wittmer, 2006). In addition, air transportation is strongly influenced by external factors over which it has limited control, including oil prices, which negatively affect the costs of airline operations.

2. Inter-island accessibility: as many islands are part of an archipelago, air transportation is frequently used to provide inter-island flights. Often, the most populated island in the archipelago serves as a gateway or hub, where international and inter-island flights are accommodated. The peripheral islands are then serviced, usually by local airlines, which connect their airports to the major hub. In 2008, intense competition in the Hawaiian inter-island market resulted in the suspension of all flight operations by Aloha Airlines, the second longest serving inter-island air transport provider in Hawaii. In some cases, peripheral islands may also operate outside this network, establishing direct flights to other regions that bypass the major air transport gateway. This has been experienced in Hawaii; while most international flights are concentrated in Honolulu (Oahu), more and more domestic flights to mainland USA operate directly from other airports, such as Lihue (Kauai Island), Kahului (Maui) and Kona (Hawaii Island) (see Fig. 15.1). Apart from air transportation, a recent initiative in Hawaii was the introduction of a fast ferry catamaran linking Oahu and Maui. This opened up the opportunity for travellers to take their vehicles with them while travelling from one island to the other. However, owing to an ongoing legal battle concerning environmental issues, the operation of the Hawaii Superferry ceased and the company filed for bankruptcy in May 2009 (DePledge, 2009).

3. Accessibility within islands: Oahu's urban area experiences heavy traffic congestion which is a result of high vehicle ownership, insufficient roads and the island's geographical features (the mountains and the sea are separated by only a short land mass). In order to mitigate the severe traffic congestion on Oahu's roads, several attempts have been made to introduce a rail system (Department of Transportation Services, 1991). In 2008, Hawaii residents voted in favour of an amendment to the plans that allowed the Honolulu High-Capacity Transit Corridor Project to be implemented. Although the project targets primarily local commuters, it will also benefit tourists as rail stations will be located near major places of interest, such as the airport, tourist attractions and shopping centres.

This chapter aims to take a holistic approach to the sustainability issues related to the means of transportation used by island tourists. Hawaii provides an interesting case study considering that it is one of the most isolated archipelagos in the world, and has made some interesting attempts to provide different means of tourism transportation, including cruise lines, airlines, fast ferry catamarans and rail.

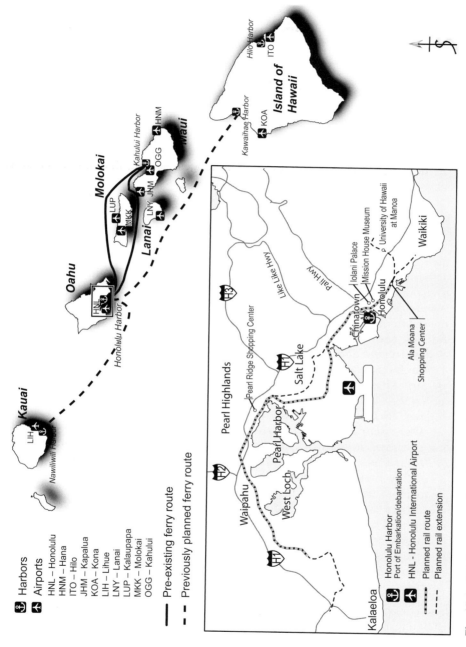

Fig. 15.1. Previous, current and proposed tourism transport initiatives in Hawaii.

Islands and the Sustainability of Tourism Transportation

Archipelagos, defined as a large group of islands or a large number of scattered islands that are either associated with a mainland nation or an island nation state, suffer from problems related to territorial fragmentation. There is often potential for both collaboration and competition between islands in the archipelago. This section provides some examples of sustainable tourism transportation issues on insular destinations.

The Canary Islands are highly dependent on tourism, with over 90% of their tourist access stemming from non-scheduled flights chartered by tour operators. Upon arrival, tourists utilize local airlines for interior travel within the archipelago. With the expansion of their tourism economy, the population of the islands has moved from the primary to tertiary sector, leading to increasing inter-insular mobility. However, there is an imbalance in the demand for transport between each island. Only the larger islands of Tenerife and Gran Canaria offer sufficient administrative, educational, health and transportation services; these are often lacking in the outer islands (Hernandez Luis, 2004).

In the Pacific Islands, distance and isolation are important factors shaping their geographies, economies and societies. Relative differentials in accessibility within the Pacific are greater today than four or more decades ago when air transportation was still in infancy and most inter-island traffic was by sea. Small islands do not generate sufficient traffic to justify ownership or full-time operation of larger aircraft. One example was the overexpansion of Polynesian Airlines, which saw losses of WS$70 million and required 10% budget cuts to all government departments in Samoa to meet government guarantees (Ward, 1998). In October 2005, with the establishment of Polynesian Blue, a joint-venture airline between the Government of Samoa and Australia's low-cost airline Virgin Blue, Polynesian Airlines' operation was downscaled (Polynesian Airlines, 2010).

Diseconomies of scale related to air transportation have also influenced the perceived feelings of time and distance for islanders. For example, Ward (1998) describes the situation of air transportation in Tonga during the mid 1990s, with Auckland and Nadi being relatively closer to Tongatapu, while Pago Pago and destinations within Tonga were pushed further away. The reasons for this include the lack of availability of excursion fares for these routes owing to the use of slower and smaller aircraft and to flight infrequency as a consequence of a lower demand. The government of Tonga considers air transportation vital for Tonga's economic development, but costs of infrastructure maintenance are high, with much capital development funded by overseas aid sources.

Air transportation is often supplemented by other modes of transportation within the islands of an archipelago. Rigas (2009) examined air- and sea-based transportation modes within the Greek Islands. His research found that these modes can complement each other rather than act as substitutes because of different market concentrations. For example, sea travel is preferred by leisure and cost-conscious passengers, while those who are sensitive to time, especially on long-distance routes, prefer air travel. In addition, sea transportation is also preferred by tourists who wish to bring their personal automobiles. Rigas also states that the process of travelling on the sea constitutes part of the travel experience and is preferred by group tours and younger travellers interested in lower fares.

The heavy burden of transportation cost is the single most important barrier to socio-economic development for small islands. This is due not only to the high costs of shipping (because of the distance and small-scale operations), but also to irregularity of supplies, which lead to periodic shortages and erratic price movements (Kakazu, 2007). In Fiji and Papua New Guinea, for example, transport costs to the main distribution centres add 5–10% to the cost of fossil fuels (Weisser, 2004).

Today the proliferation of automobiles is considered to be the main cause of global warming. Air transport, however, is catching up and, if current trends continue, air transportation may have an impact of similar magnitude by the middle of the 21st century. In 1992, aviation was estimated to account for 3.5% of total global warming, measured as radiative forcing and caused by anthropogenic sources (Akerman, 2005). Unlike ground and sea transport, climate change caused by air transport is attributable not only to emissions of carbon dioxide but also to emissions of methane, nitrous oxide and other nitrogen oxides (NO_x), either directly or via chemical processes in the atmosphere (Lee, 2009). As many islands rely on their natural beauty to attract tourists, it is vital to address issues relating to the sustainability of the environment. Owing to a ban on automobile use, the Greek island of Hydra has complete freedom from motorized vehicles; there is an awareness that the island's basic qualities as an attraction will disappear if there are motorized vehicles (Hoyer, 2000).

Challenges to Sustainable Tourism Transportation in Hawaii

In the years 2008 and 2009, the State of Hawaii was the site of a number of failures related to various modes of tourism transportation – from the removal of two permanently based NCL (Norwegian Cruise Line) cruise ships to the bankruptcies of the Hawaii Superferry and Aloha Airlines. In contrast, after a very long and polarizing debate about the proposal to introduce a rail line in Oahu, the project was finally approved. This section depicts these events in more detail. The map in Fig. 15.1 illustrates some of the routes and places of interest for the various modes of transportation described here.

The dismissal of Aloha Airlines

As of October 2009, there are four airlines operating Hawaii's inter-island routes: Hawaiian Airlines; Island Air; go! Airlines; and Mokulele Airlines, the last two of which have recently announced a joint venture. In the past, a number of other airlines have attempted to establish a presence in Hawaii's inter-island market, but were unsuccessful; these included Mid Pacific Air,

Discovery Airways and Mahalo Airlines. Among all these unsuccessful ventures, the failure of Aloha Airlines is worth describing in more detail. Aloha Airlines was one of Hawaii's pioneers in inter-island travel; its operations began in 1946. The pioneer was Hawaiian Airlines, which had operated since November 1929. Aloha Airlines went into bankruptcy on 31 March 2008, 3 days before ATA Airlines, a charter airline providing flights between Hawaii and mainland USA, also ceased operations and declared bankruptcy.

Aloha Airlines experienced serious financial difficulties after the 9/11 attack on the World Trade Center in 2001, which sent the entire airline industry into a giant financial downturn in 2001/2. In addition, energy prices continued to rise, affecting the costs of airline operations. These factors contributed to a decline of visitor arrivals to Hawaii, particularly of Japanese visitors; the Japanese visitor market had already been declining from a peak in 1997 as flights become fewer and fuel surcharges rose (Schaefers, 2008).

In addition to external factors over which Aloha Airlines had limited control, there were concerns that internal factors also contributed to the demise of the company. Within the last 5 years of its operations, Aloha Airlines had declared bankruptcy twice, the first time in December 2004, and the second in March 2008. In a survey conducted by Pacific Business News, 38% of respondents cited poor management as the primary reason for Aloha Airlines' demise, while another 38% said the problem was the airfare wars started by go! Airlines. Third on the list was high fuel prices, cited by 9% of the respondents (Pacific Business News, 2008). With regard to Aloha Airlines' management failures, respondents listed several factors that they believed contributed to the airline's demise: (i) the decision to remove the airline's business class on inter-island flights forced business passengers on to other airlines (Brancatelli, 2008); (ii) mismanagement by the supermarket magnate, Ron Burkle, who became majority shareholder of Aloha Airlines despite having no prior experience in the airline industry (Mayes, 2008); (iii) the airline's continued use of inefficient aircraft; (iv) unreasonable demands by labour unions; and (v) the airline's inability to respond quickly to competitive pressures (Petrello, 2008).

In June 2006, some 3 months after Aloha Airlines emerged from its first bankruptcy, go! Airlines, a subsidiary of Arizona-based Mesa Airlines, established its presence in Hawaii's inter-island market and began lowering prices on its routes. With one-way fares as low as US$9 on select routes, go! Airlines initiated a price war with Aloha Airlines and Hawaiian Airlines, who responded by matching prices and offering other incentives (Charlton, 2007). This intense competition, in conjunction with the existing problems plaguing Aloha Airlines, exacerbated its financial woes and eventually led to its downfall (Blair, 2009b).

The failure of the Hawaii Superferry

The Hawaii Superferry was the first Hawaii-based inter-island ferry system that allowed for the transportation of both passengers and vehicles. The Superferry was founded in 2001 and began its inaugural voyage in August 2007 from

Honolulu to Kahului Harbor on Maui Island. Based in Honolulu Harbor, the Superferry was planned also to include routes to Kahului Harbor, Nawiliwili Harbor on Kauai Island, and Kawaihae Harbor on Hawaii Island. However, the only effective route to exist was the one between Honolulu and Kahului Harbors (see Fig. 15.1).

To operate these routes, the Superferry contracted Austal USA, which built the Alakai and later, the Huakai, at US$80 million per vessel. These ships are aluminium-hulled catamarans capable of transporting up to 866 passengers and 282 cars. The Superferry's final advertised one-way fare was US$39 per passenger and US$57 per vehicle (Pacific Business News, 2009a). To accommodate the Superferry operations, the state paid US$46 million for harbour improvements. On its first voyage to Kauai, the Alakai was met with large protests at Nawiliwili harbour where protestors expressed a number of concerns which can be divided into social, environmental, traffic and legal issues.

The social impact issues revolved around the potential of drugs from Oahu entering the outer islands via the ferry and the migration of the homeless between islands. Outer island communities also expressed anxiety that this new mode of transportation would increase the number of tourists to the outer island, and that this may strain its carrying capacity, thus affecting the local ecosystem. The inclusion of vehicles on the ferry generated alarm on whether or not they would negatively affect traffic on the neighbouring islands. In August 2007, a Maui judge ordered Hawaii's Department of Transportation to implement traffic mitigation measures at Kahului Harbor to accommodate expected traffic from ferry arrivals. However, after conducting a traffic impact study, the department maintained that the ferry would only add a marginal traffic increase on nearby streets (Wilson, 2007).

The list of environmental issues was plentiful. By allowing the inclusion of vehicles on the ferry, there were concerns over the potential of transporting invasive species such as coqui frogs and fire ants to the outer islands. Although vehicles were inspected and washed before boarding the ferry, residents questioned the effectiveness of these preventive methods. The process of travelling between the islands also posed environmental risks as the ferry could discharge ballast water into the ocean, potentially releasing many kinds of bacterial, plant and other life that could be harmful to the local ecosystem. In addition, many of the proposed routes would traverse through areas containing humpback whale habitats, 90% of which inhabit Hawaii's shallow waters (NOAA, 2009), hence the use of two different routes as shown in Fig. 15.1. There was concern that fast-moving ferries with sharp hulls could threaten the whales in a manner similar to an incident in the Canary Islands, where a fast-moving ferry killed a sperm whale (Johnson, 2005).

These environmental concerns led towards a number of legal issues that plagued the operations of the Superferry. In August 2007, the Hawaii Supreme Court stated that an environmental impact assessment would be required on state-funded harbour improvements, overturning the Maui Circuit Court's decision in 2005. Despite this, the ferry went ahead and travelled to Nawiliwili ahead of schedule. Continuing protests in Kauai led towards the suspension of service to Nawiliwili Harbor. In October 2007, the Maui Circuit Court demanded that the Superferry must wait for an environmental impact assessment to be completed before resuming service. However, after a meeting between the Governor and the Hawaii State Senate, the Superferry was later allowed to resume service until the completion of the assessment (Pacific Business News, 2007). By March 2009, the Hawaii State Supreme court found the Superferry operations before the completion of the environmental impact assessment to be unconstitutional (Blair, 2009a). Following this announcement, the Superferry disbanded its workforce, and by May had declared bankruptcy.

Cruise tourism in Hawaii

Cruise-ship lines have also faced difficulties operating in Hawaii's inter-island market. In early 2008, NCL withdrew two of their three ships, leaving a single ship, the Pride of America, to voyage exclusively between islands. Reasons for the downsizing of operations in Hawaii were downward pricing pressure in the Hawaii market and increasing competition from low-cost carriers operating foreign flagged ships based on mainland USA (Wu, 2008). By sailing a foreign flag, cruise line companies escape USA cabotage laws and can stop in or operate from a foreign port while utilizing ships that are built in foreign shipyards and manned by foreign staff; they are also able to escape the strict environmental and labour laws required by USA-flagged ships, thus reducing overall costs. While NCL offers a 7-day itinerary visiting Oahu, Maui, the Island of Hawaii (Big Island) and Kauai, cruise lines such as the Princess and Holland America, which operate foreign flagged ships, offer a 2-week itinerary between the USA mainland and Hawaii. The latter have to provide a stopover in a foreign port such as Ensenada, in Mexico, to comply with the cabotage laws.

Both the state and federal governments have been involved in NCL's operations in Hawaii. The USA Congress allowed NCL's three German-built ships to be registered as American (Pride of America, Pride of Aloha and Pride of Hawaii), thereby bypassing the requirements for ships to be built in American shipyards; this then allows NCL to bypass the need to stop at a foreign port, eliminating previous stopovers at Kiribati, an island nation in the South Pacific (Camire, 2008).

The cruise-ship industry's operations have also been under fire over concerns regarding their environmental impact on Hawaii's ecosystem. The environmental issues expressed were similar to those over the Superferry's operations, and included the discharge of ballast water, which may contain invasive species, threats to the endangered humpback whales that inhabit Hawaii's shallow waters and coral reef damage. In addition, past instances of garbage and solid wastes, contaminated bilge water and other hazardous wastes cast a cloud over the ability of cruise ships to maintain a low ecological footprint in Hawaii's waters. Unlike the catamaran ships used by the Superferry, cruise ships are often powered by diesel electric engines which release a plethora of pollutants such as sulfur dioxide, carbon dioxide, carbon monoxide and nitrogen oxide into the air. The exhausts from these ships produce the equivalent of the exhausts from 12,000 cars daily, which leads to concern over the impact of cruise ships on air quality (Gloor, 2006). Currently, the Memorandum of Understanding (MoU) with the State of Hawaii provides a set of environmental standards and policies that allow the cruise-ship industry to self-report violations and accidents. However, this voluntary reporting is also a sign of inherent weakness, as cruise-ship companies can choose not to be held accountable by their actions simply by not reporting them (Yamanouchi, 2003).

The long battle of the Honolulu transit system

Oahu is currently scheduled to begin construction of the Honolulu High-Capacity Transit Corridor Project in December 2009, as part of the Oahu Regional Transportation Plan 2030. The project consists of an elevated rail-based rapid transit system that will be part of a multi-modal transportation service that utilizes existing bus services, and is intended to reduce the heavy traffic congestion currently experienced on Oahu's roads. Although the project is primarily intended to serve the island's local residents, it has the potential to provide a better experience to tourists wanting to access the airport, hotels and tourist attractions.

The first phase of the proposed rail line will consist of 21 stations, beginning from Ala Moana in Honolulu and going to Kapolei in western Oahu, a 20-mile journey which will take approximately 42 minutes (City and County of Honolulu, 2008). Key stations along the route include major shopping centres (Pearl Ridge and Ala Moana), Pearl Harbor, the Downtown business district in Honolulu, Chinatown and Honolulu International Airport. The complete rail line is to be built in five segments, the first to be in operation by 2013, connecting Kapolei to the Pearl Highlands in Pearl City. All five segments from Kapolei to Ala Moana are expected to be finished by 2019.

There are also plans for possible extensions of the proposed rail route, which might include: a westward expansion from Kapolei to Kalaeloa where Campbell Industrial Park is located; an extension into Salt Lake in western Honolulu which would bypass Honolulu International Airport; a route to the University of Hawaii at Manoa; and a route to Waikiki, the island's most popular tourist area. However, any extension plans will depend on the availability of future funding and the extensions are unlikely to be built before 2019.

According to the Honolulu Transit Authority, construction of the rail line is projected to cost an inflation-adjusted US$5.4 billion (City and County of Honolulu, 2009). Funding for the project will be generated by a 0.5% increase of the general excise tax and also from the Federal Transit Administration. The estimated costs will place the rail project as the most expensive rail line built in the USA within the past decade (Hao, 2009b).

Although the city charter amendment approving the construction of the rail line passed by 53% during the 2008 Honolulu elections, the project remains a highly debated issue, as with past attempts to introduce rail-based transit in Honolulu, which were mired in concerns over costs. In 1981, the then Honolulu mayor terminated a proposal for the construction of a Honolulu Area Rapid Transit system, opting for incremental improvements on the existing bus system. The following mayor revived the rail project in 1986, but was unsuccessful after the city council narrowly voted against the tax increases needed to fund the project in 1992 (Pang, 1998).

Issues over funding continue to plague the current rail line proposal, particularly the burden placed upon taxpayers, as the project relies less on federal funding than other recent rail projects in the USA. In addition, residents living in communities outside the area of the proposed rail lines, such as Kailua and Kaneohe in windward Oahu, have expressed opposition to tax increases on a project that they feel will not benefit their communities (Hao, 2009b).

The nature of an elevated rail line has also led towards aesthetic and noise concerns as the site of the rail line may have a negative impact on Oahu's scenery. Another aspect is that the construction of the pillars to support the elevated rail line may require the reduction of existing road space, which would ultimately lead to slower vehicle speeds and increased traffic congestion. As the proposed rail line will traverse through some of Oahu's most densely populated areas, there is also apprehension about the rail line's effects on land value (Hao, 2009a).

Numerous concerns related to tourism have also been noted. The current rail line proposal does not include a route to Waikiki, Oahu's most popular tourist area, where a large number of hotels are located. Although there are proposals that consider extending the rail towards Waikiki, most likely a Waikiki route will not be a reality before 2019. In other words, an extension to Waikiki will not exist for at least 10 years, at best. However, by integrating the rail route with popular attractions located near the stations, the rail route can benefit from increased tourist ridership. For example, the Chinatown and Downtown stations are located in close proximity to Aloha Tower, Iolani Palace and Mission Houses Museum. The Pearl Harbor station, which will supply riders who are connected with the naval base, can also attract tourists who are interested in visiting the USS Arizona Memorial.

Possible Ways of Addressing Sustainable Tourism Transportation Issues

Modal shifts

As there are few alternatives to air transportation, with its reliance on kerosene, as well as a lack of other transportation modes that can compete in terms of speed of transport, island economies can address energy consumption concerns by promoting shifts in other modes of transportation. Past transport solutions emphasized investments in physical structures, for example travel interchanges, but since the mid 1990s there has been more emphasis on soft modal-shift measures, such as the transition from private cars to sustainable forms of public transportation (Lumsdon *et al.*, 2006).

At Toyama, Japan's least densely populated prefectural city, private car ownership was higher than the national average, and Toyama suffered an immense financial burden resulting from the road maintenance and infrastructural development that was necessary to provide public services for the movement of personnel and goods. Toyama sought to mitigate automobile emissions through the construction and promotion of public transport via light-rail transit and bus rapid transit. Since the introduction of these schemes, there has been a decrease in air pollution which, in turn, has relieved traffic congestion and preserved historical sites by reducing the environmental burdens upon them (Fujimoto, 2008).

Another example of modal shift in islands can be found in Okinawa, also in Japan. Okinawa Island has a higher percentage of private car ownership and lower public transportation ridership than the national average, partially because of its administration by the USA until 1972. Because of the immense traffic congestions, a monorail line was planned in 1981 and began operations in 2003. Within a year, the monorail project led towards a modal switch of 49% from buses, 17% from cars and 16% from taxis. Approximately 38% of passengers used the monorail for commuting to offices/schools, 10% for shopping and 5% for tourism purposes (Toma, 2004).

In Hawaii, the proposal to build a rail transit system in Oahu has been discussed for many decades. The debate about the rail line has been very passionate and almost everyone has had an opinion about it. The referendum became almost a political dispute between the supporting mayor who was running for re-election, and the other two major candidates who were against the project. In a remote and small island like Oahu, where cars and fuel have to be transported from at least 2500 miles from mainland USA, rail public transportation is one of the best alternatives to induce a shift towards the use of public transportation. Tourists will benefit even if the first phase of the project does not reach Waikiki. As parking spaces are becoming more and more expensive in Waikiki, with tourists renting cars just for the day in order to avoid paying prohibitive parking fees, they could still take a bus from Waikiki to the Ala Moana rail station and from there reach the airport, and many tourist attractions and shopping centres, without necessarily having to rent a car or use a taxi.

Although sea-based transportation is often a complement rather than a substitute for air transportation, on some routes, such as in the Canary Islands, new fast ferries are competing with jet aircraft. Nevertheless, fast ferries consume more fuel per seat than do aircraft. In the case of the Tenerife–Gran Canaria route, a jet foil consumes 8.4 litres of fuel per seat, while the ATR-72 aircraft only requires 5.25 litres per seat (Hernandez Luis, 2004). Air transport also has the advantage of offering a higher frequency of travel, which is more tailored to the demand for the area. In addition, the amount of raw materials and energy needed to build a ship is higher than those needed for an aircraft.

In the case of the Superferry, although the environmental impact study (EIS) was never done, the mere fact that another mode of transportation became available for passengers to travel between islands was an important opportunity to increase competition and improve the tourism experience in

Hawaii. Local travellers had the possibility of bringing their own cars in their inter-island displacements, and many business also benefited from the high speed of transporting goods between Oahu and Maui. In this case, there was not only a huge political dispute, as the executive state government was clearly in favour of the Superferry, but a judicial battle was initiated in order to guarantee its operation while the EIS was being prepared. The failure of the Superferry experience in Hawaii is a consequence of the lack of a legal environment to support large investments in transportation. What happened to the Superferry will certainly discourage future initiatives to promote a swift change in the use of other forms of passenger and freight sea transportation between islands.

Regional planning

In a comparison of tourism development in the Balearics and Hawaii, Bardolet and Sheldon (2008) emphasized the role of regional planning, rather than specific island planning, in order to address sustainable tourism development. In Hawaii, one of the main tourist complaints is related to traffic congestion and overdevelopment. The natural landscapes of the Balearics and Hawaii are strong attractors, but these are gradually diminishing as a result of excessive building, especially on the coastline. In addition, signs of tourism stress can be seen in these islands as residents have to compete with tourists, owing to a higher usage of automobiles by tourists, particularly rental cars, which leads to traffic congestion; competition also results from increasing ownership of private dwellings, overcrowding and greater use of public resources. The sustainability paradigm is complex and imprecise at both the destination and the local scale, but it is urgent for islands/destinations that have reached life-cycle maturity. Over-reliance on inbound tourism could lead to symptoms such as slowdown in traditional economic sectors due to lack of diversification, and increased vulnerabilities to changes in current situations, such as economic downturns, increased oil prices and loss of tourist markets.

Regional planning tends to be more effective than destination planning. Both the Balearic and the Hawaiian archipelagos need to decide whether further growth is appropriate and how to achieve balance for all stakeholders now and into the future. Both archipelagos also face redefining their products and consulting with and giving power to their local communities. The suggestions made by Bardolet and Sheldon (2008) include: (i) planning for the archipelago as a whole rather than island by island; (ii) simplifying the layers of policy making; (iii) engaging in land use policies and zoning early before development occurs; (iv) including complexities of transportation between islands in tourism development plans; (v) ensuring that stakeholders on each island have input to the tourism development plans of the archipelago; and (vi) standardizing statistical and economic data collection between the component islands. From the previous discussion about the Superferry, it is clear that a lack of regional planning contributed to its failure in Hawaii. The role of politicians and business leaders was considered as 'pathetic' by the Governor, because although many supported the existence of the Superferry, they did not do much compared with those who were trying to interrupt its operations (Pacific Business News, 2009b).

Air transportation technological improvement

The coming decades promise a wide range of alternatives to the current modes of air transportation. Currently, newer aircraft such as the Boeing 787 and the Airbus A380 utilize lighter materials, achieve increased engine efficiency through ultrahigh bypass engines and offer larger seating capacity. However, continued refinement of conventional turbofan aircraft is not sufficient to reach even the less demanding target levels in reducing the intensity of fuel use. Alternatives include the introduction of radical aircraft configurations, such as an airliner utilizing a flying wing or a blended wing body; these configurations have great potential for reducing aerodynamic drag and fuel consumption, which in turn can reduce intensity of fuel use by 65% compared with current production aircraft. A less risky alternative is to develop airliners that are powered by high-speed propellers, such as a prop-fan; these can attain cruise speeds that are 20–25% lower than those of conventional jet aircraft but produce far fewer emissions (Akerman, 2005). Other strategies include emissions trading to address environmental impacts; according to Becken (2006), this is preferable to a tax regime, which is very inefficient in delivering environmental benefits. In the meantime, trips to isolated islands like Hawaii will continue to be an unsustainable choice of destination from the environmental point of view.

The Need for a Holistic Approach to Sustainable Tourism Transportation in Hawaii

In the years 2008–2009, Hawaii was in the central stage of several initiatives related to different means of tourism transportation. Regardless of the success or failure of the four case studies presented in this chapter, what becomes clear is that some key aspects of these were related to tourism transportation ventures. While, clearly, environmental and economic forces were the major drivers involved, political and legal aspects did play an important role in terms of what happened to these initiatives. In the case of the Superferry, it is possible to argue that two other forms of impacts were also related: social, such as concerns over increases in drug circulation and the homeless population; and traffic increases, from vehicles driving out of the ferries. To a certain degree, the traffic issue can be included as part of environmental impacts; social impacts were not really considered to be a key aspect in the dismissal of the Superferry. Hence, this last section concentrates on the environmental, economic, political and legal aspects of the sustainability of tourism transportation initiatives in Hawaii. The argument here is that in the case of Hawaii, sustainable tourism transportation relies on a holistic approach which gathers these four aspects together, as shown in Fig. 15.2. While it is possible to suggest that these forces would be behind other insular tourism transportation projects, further studies are still required.

Environmental aspects

There were legitimate arguments regarding some of the aspects pertaining to the operation of the Superferry, particularly possible accidents with whales, considering the faster speed that the ferries operate at compared with other ships. However, other complaints, such as problems with invasive species carried by ballast water were not exclusive to the Superferry. The major discussion around the need for an EIS became more a political and legal battle than anything else. The reality is that new modes of operation are subject to an EIS, while most of the modes of transportation that have been in operation for decades have never been the subject of an EIS. From a different viewpoint, the current MoU under which cruise lines operate in Hawaii is very lenient. Why are there two different ways of dealing with environmental issues for maritime passenger transportation? What were the economic powers that were financially supporting the activity of pro-environment supporters against the Superferry? Was the environment used as an excuse to shut down the freight competition that the Superferry introduced against traditional freight-shipping companies that operate in Hawaii?

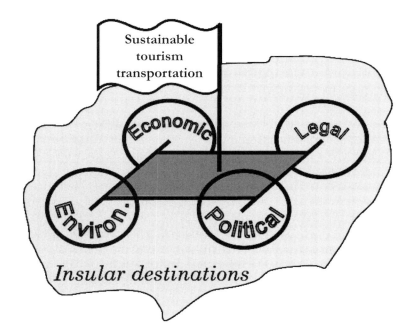

Fig. 15.2. A holistic approach to insular sustainable tourism transportation.

Economic aspects

Two major economic aspects influenced the dismissal of Aloha Airlines and the withdrawal of two of NCL's ships in Hawaii: the rising price of oil – from approximately US$50 in late 2006 to over US$140 by the middle of 2008; and the economic recession in the USA. Islands are heavily dependent on energy for transportation, and the overhead costs of this energy are more expensive in Hawaii as it needs to be transported from faraway places. The funding of large infrastructure projects has always been an issue for islands, as shown by the case of the rail system in Honolulu. Because of the economic situation in the USA in 2008–2009, the project will not rely on a high participation of federal funds, in contrast to similar recent rail projects in continental USA. The Honolulu rail line will only become a reality if higher taxes are charged from the local population.

The withdrawal of the two NCL cruise ships is a sign that in isolated destinations, the right of cabotage needs to be re-discussed. While the Jones Act (*Merchant Marine Act of 1920*) aims to protect and incentivize sea-shipping companies to flag their ships in the USA, giving them the privilege to cabotage rights, there was not enough demand to support the inter-island itineraries with three ships in Hawaii. However, other cruise lines, such as the Princess and Holland America, made use of a flag of convenience to operate return trips between Hawaii and California with a stopover in Ensenada, Mexico, to comply with the cabotage rights. The proximity to Mexico does not much affect these itineraries. Currently, NCL's 7-day itinerary represents half of the Hawaii cruise tourism market, with return trips from mainland USA accounting for a third of the market. Open-jaw trips, including trips made by ships relocating from one region to another or making round-the-world journeys, account for approximately 15% of the Hawaii cruise market.

Political aspects

From a political point of view, Bardolet and Sheldon (2008) have already discussed the challenges faced by archipelagos. These include multiple levels of governance on islands in which policies must be negotiated through complex hierarchal structures, and differing community interests on each island which may make stakeholder involvement in any centralized tourism planning very challenging. The most problematic aspect facing archipelagos is maintaining transportation networks that are vital to tourism development; this can be problematic, especially during multi-island travel. Two examples from Hawaii are the Superferry project, which had the explicit support of the Governor, and the debate around the rail transit, which was the major topic of the 2008 mayor election.

Legal aspects

The lack of a judicial framework to support the planning and trialling of large transport projects created a huge dispute about the need for an EIS for the operation of the Superferry. Why does the EIS need to be done before a new mode of transportation is introduced? How about changing the legislation to allow the EIS to be done while a new transportation such as the ferry is tried out? Would the EIS be much more accurate in this case? While this approach would not be viable for every single type of transportation project, it could have been a possibility. In New Zealand, the Lynx Cook Strait fast-ferry catamaran withdrew from operation because the maritime authorities made the ferries travel at a lower speed so their wash would not damage the environment. The Lynx simply was not economically viable under such restrictive conditions and it was removed from operation. From a wider viewpoint, why does the legislation not require an EIS for those modes of transport that have been in operation for a long time, such as aeroplanes and sea cargo ships?

In Hawaii, lessons from recent examples show that it is not possible to achieve sustainable forms of tourism transportation when environmental, economic, legal and political aspects are not taken into consideration. For example, environmental issues can generate a political debate that will end up being decided in the judicial arena. Conversely, legal and economic aspects can both be tied up, as in the case of cabotage. Many other interrelationships could have been used to illustrate this. So what can be concluded from the examples provided here is that these four forces – environmental, economic, legal and political – are related and that a holistic approach needs to be taken for insular tourism transportation projects to be sustainable.

References

Abeyratne, R.I.R. (1999) Management of the environmental impact of tourism and air transport on small island developing states. *Journal of Air Transport Management* 5, 31–37.

Akerman, J. (2005) Sustainable air transport – on track in 2050. *Transportation Research Part D* 10, 111–126.

Bardolet, E. and Sheldon, P.J. (2008) Tourism in archipelagos: Hawai'i and the Balearics. *Annals of Tourism Research* 35, 900–923.

Becken, S. (2006) Editorial. Tourism and transport: the sustainability dilemma. *Journal of Sustainable Tourism* 14, 2.

Bieger, T. and Wittmer, A. (2006) Air transport and tourism: perspectives and challenges for destinations, airlines and governments. *Journal of Air Transport Management* 12, 40–46.

Blair, C. (2009a) Hawaii Supreme Court rules Superferry law unconstitutional. *Pacific Business News* (Honolulu), 16 March 2009.

Blair, C. (2009b) The sky's the limit for Aloha Air Cargo. *Pacific Business News* (Honolulu), 26 August 2009.

Brancatelli, J. (2008) Seat 2B: The big airlines smell blood ... yours. *News from Yellow Business Pages. Wired: Top Stories*, 8 April 2008.

Camire, D. (2008) Outlook optimistic for Pride of America. *Honolulu Advertiser*, 25 February 2008.

Charlton, B. (2007) Airlines in Hawaii price war offer $9 inter-island flights. *The Seattle Times*, 30 May 2007.

City and County of Honolulu (2008) *Honolulu High-Capacity Transit Corridor Project*. Department of Transportation Services, Honolulu.

City and County of Honolulu (2009) *Honolulu Rail Transit*. Department of Transportation Services, Honolulu.

DBEDT (2008) *2007 Annual Visitor Research Report*. Department of Business, Economic Development and Tourism, Honolulu.

Department of Transportation Services (1991) *Honolulu Rapid Transit Development Project*. Honolulu.

DePledge, D. (2009) Hawaii Superferry files for bankruptcy. *Honolulu Advertiser*, 31 May 2009.

Fujimoto, H. (2008) The modal shift to environmentally sustainable transport: prospects of urban transport systems: LRT, BRT and buses. *Science and Technology Trends* 29, 46–61.

Gloor, L.B. (2006) Riding tourism's new wave: evaluating the cruise industry's. *Hohonu* 4(1).

Hao, S. (2009a) Move sought for rail station: city's plan affects Kamehameha Schools' development project. *Honolulu Advertiser*, 3 May 2009.

Hao, S. (2009b) Honolulu's per-capita cost for rail: $4,000. *Honolulu Advertiser*, 1 August 2009.

Hernandez Luis, J.A. (2004) The role of inter-island air transport in the Canary Islands. *Journal of Transport Geography* 12, 235–244.

Hoyer, K.G. (2000) Sustainable tourism or sustainable mobility? The Norwegian case. *Journal of Sustainable Tourism* 8, 147–160.

Johnson, G. (2005) Collision course – sperm whales and fast ferries in the Canary Islands. In: *Voyage of the Odyssey*, 12 March 2005. PBS (Public Broadcasting Service), Arlington, Virginia.

Kakazu, H. (2007) *Island Sustainability: Challenges and Opportunities for Okinawa and Other Pacific Islands in a Globalized World*. Trafford Publishing, Bloomington, Indiana.

Lee, D.S. (2009) Aviation and climate change: the science. In: Gössling, S. and Upham, P. (eds) *Climate Change and Aviation: Issues, Challenges and Solutions*. Earthscan, London, pp. 27–68.

Lumsdon, L., Downward, P. and Rhoden, S. (2006) Transport for tourism: can public transport encourage a modal shift in the day visitor market? *Journal of Sustainable Tourism* 14, 139–156.

Mayes, B. (2008) Many share blame for Aloha Airlines' death. *Pacific Business News* (Honolulu), 20 March 2008.

NOAA (National Oceanic and Atmospheric Administration) (2009) *Humpback Whale National Marine Sanctuary*. Honolulu.

Pacific Business News (2007) Lingle signs Superferry bill. *Pacific Business News* (Honolulu), 5 November 2007.

Pacific Business News (2008) Aloha couldn't be saved; go! has some explaining to do. *Pacific Business News* (Honolulu), 7 April 2008.

Pacific Business News (2009a) Hawaii Superferry cuts fares. *Pacific Business News* (Honolulu), 27 February 2009.

Pacific Business News (2009b) Lingle: politicians' role in Superferry 'pathetic'. *Pacific Business News* (Honolulu), 16 March 2009.

Pang, G.Y.K. (1998) Will rail fly this time? City revisits the concept of an Oahu-wide light-rail mass transit system – this time with the public's input. *Honolulu Star-Bulletin*.

Petrello, R. (2008) PBN survey: Aloha bosses mostly to blame. *Pacific Business News* (Honolulu), 4 April 2008.

Polynesian Airlines (2010) Welcome to Polynesian Airlines. Available at: http://www.polynesianairlines.com/ (accessed 14 September 2010).

Rao, M.A. (2002) Challenges and issues for tourism in the South Pacific island states: the case of the Fiji Islands. *Tourism Economics* 8, 401–429.

Rigas, K. (2009) Boat or airplane? Passengers' perceptions of transport services to islands. The example of the Greek domestic leisure market. *Journal of Transport Geography* 17, 396–401.

Schaefers, A. (2008) 20-Year low in Japanese visitors seen. *Honolulu Star-Bulletin*, 1 April 2008.

Toma, K. (2004) The opening of Okinawa urban monorail and its expected developments. In: DOCEA (ed.) *Construction,* Naha, Okinawa. Available at: www3.pref. okinawa.jp/site/contents/attach/7864/ The Opening of Okinawa Urban Monorail and its Expected.pdf (accessed 21 September 2010).

Ward, R.G. (1998) Remote runways: air transport and distance in Tonga. *Australian Geographical Studies* 36, 177–186.

Weisser, D. (2004) On the economics of electricity consumption in small island developing states: a role for renewable energy technologies? *Energy Policy* 32, 127–140.

Wilson, C. (2007) Superferry still under Maui traffic order. *Honolulu Advertiser Neighbor Island Edition* (Wailuku), 20 September 2007.

Wu, N. (2008) Another cruise ship to leave: mainland competition drives Pride of Aloha off the islands. *Honolulu Star-Bulletin*, 12 February 2008.

Yamanouchi, K. (2003) Cruise lines admit pollution violations. *Honolulu Advertiser*, 12 December 2003.

16 Planning for Sustainable Island Tourism Development in the Maldives

MARIYAM ZULFA AND JACK CARLSEN

Curtin University, Western Australia

Introduction

McKercher (1993) notes that the debate surrounding sustainable tourism is often polarized by two different perspectives: on the one hand, the perspective subscribed to by the environmentalist and conservationist groups, which calls for a cautious approach to sustainable development and greater ecological preservation and, on the other hand, the perspective of the 'for-profit' industry advocates who envision a more development-oriented approach to sustainability. Is there a middle ground that promotes the principles and practices of sustainable tourism and at the same time enables the use of natural resources for economic development? In exploring answers to this question, this chapter traces the history and development of tourism in the Maldives, a small-island tourism destination where the protection of the natural environment and the economic prosperity of the country are inextricably linked. Tourists visit the Maldives to enjoy white sandy beaches and the pristine marine environment (Ghina, 2003), so any threat to the natural environment represents an obstacle on the journey towards economic as well as ecological sustainability. While these threats can take many forms, not the least of which are those related to climate change, sea level and temperature rise (Ghina, 2003), this chapter will focus on the specific impacts associated with tourism development on the ecologically fragile islands of the Maldives.

Several planning and policy mechanisms are in place in the Maldives to ensure that the impact on the environment from tourism-related activities is avoided (Maldivian Democratic Party, 2008). Successive tourism master plans for the Maldives since 1983 have embraced principles of sustainable development, and environmental plans have stipulated the protection measures that developers must follow strictly. Furthermore, the country's National Development Planning process, which is formulated in cycles of 5-year periods, emphasizes the importance of sustainable development and provides the aegis under which policies for development must proceed. In this chapter, these planning and policy mechanisms are reviewed in relation to the sustainable development of the tourism industry. The account also describes the relevant laws and regulations that are in place and the respective administering authorities that play various roles in enhancing the promotion of sustainable development. The chapter concludes with insights as to how well sustainable development principles have served the Maldives tourism industry. It begins with a brief overview of the Maldives and the development of its tourism industry.

A Brief Overview of Maldives Tourism

The Maldives is an archipelago of 1192 coralline islands occurring in rings of 26 natural atolls situated in the Central Indian Ocean off the south-western tip of India (Fig. 16.1). Most of the islands are quite small (approximately 0.7 km^2 in area on average) with only nine islands larger than 2 km^2 (Ghina, 2003). Over 80% are low lying, with an average elevation above sea level of 1.5 m. The climate is tropical with annual mean temperatures ranging from 28°C to 32°C.

The total population of the country is 298,968, of which 34.7% of the people live in the capital island of Malé. The rest are scattered over 192 inhabited islands which are situated across 19 administrative atolls. The policy to spread tourism across all atolls has the objective of spreading the economic benefits of tourism directly to the people living on all the atolls through the creation of tourism employment opportunities.

In many small-island countries, receipts from tourism account for a large proportion (20–60% or above) of their gross domestic product (GDP) (UNWTO, 1999). The Maldives is no exception, with tourism contributing 30% to GDP (Ministry of Tourism, 2004). In addition, past estimates that include the multiplier effects from tourism-related economic activities (such as construction and the distribution of consumer goods) in the Maldives take the total contribution of tourism to GDP to 80% (MATI, 1998). The annual report of the Maldives Monetary Authority (MMA), the country's Central Bank, confirms that foreign exchange earnings from tourism receipts accounted for about 90% of the service receipts of the balance of payments (MMA, 1999).

Tourism was introduced to the Maldives by an Italian tourist operator, George Corbin, who encouraged three enterprising Maldivians, Mohamed Umar Maniku, Ahmed Naseem and Hussain Afeef, to develop resort facilities for European tourists. Today Mr Maniku and Mr Afeef head two of the largest tourism organizations in the Maldives: Universal Enterprises and Crown Company, respectively. They also founded and have continued to serve on the Executive of the Maldives Association of Tourism Industry (MATI) since its inception in 1982. Under these two pioneers, the tourism industry in the Maldives has transformed itself to an exemplary status, demonstrating the innovative ability of Maldivians and the spirit of Maldivian enterprise (Reimer, 2007).

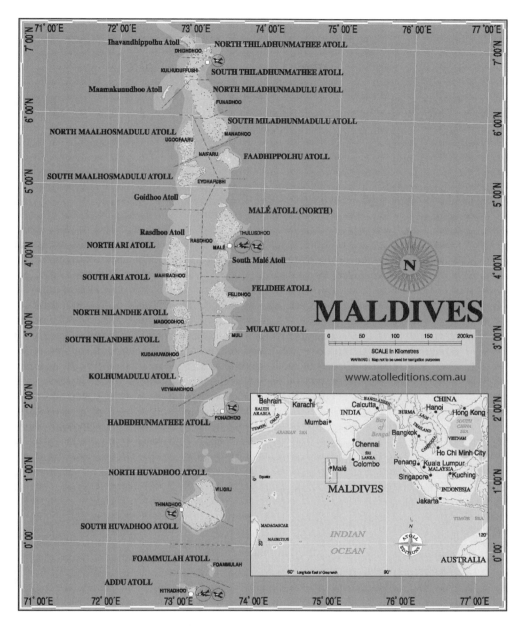

Fig. 16.1. Map of the Maldives. (Source: Atoll Editions, 2004.)

The rate of growth of tourism infrastructure has been controlled and the associated development carried out on a sustainable basis (Nethconsult/ Transtec and Bord Failte, 1996). In North Malé Atoll, the international airport on Hulhulé Island is located next to the capital island of Malé and, logically, most of the uninhabited islands near to Malé International Airport and in the adjacent Ari Atoll (North and South Ari Atolls), are leased as tourist resorts. That is because the distances to these islands are short, and tourists arriving on international flights will only have to have a short journey by sea to get to the resort island of their choice. In the past, the government has, as a policy measure, denied permission to private parties to construct landing strips for the operation of fixed winged or other aircraft (Ibrahim Gasim, personal communication to authors, 14 February 2008) on any island of the Maldives. Hence, the expansion of air services has been restricted. However, as an alternative to fixed-wing aircraft, increasing visitation has supported the introduction of seaplanes and helicopters, operating as add-on services out of Malé International Airport, which has greatly assisted the expansion of tourism to islands further away from the international airport. Hence some islands that were previously seen as located too far away to travel to by boat have become accessible. Tourists getting off an international flight and then travelling to these islands have a short helicopter or seaplane journey. In line with this development, more remote islands that are accessible by seaplane have been progressively released for tourism.

The relevance of tourism to overall regional development within the country, and the necessity to allocate resorts in all atolls of the archipelago, have been recognized since 2003, with the government announcing a policy to create more tourist resorts on every atoll. The new islands coming under this policy have been announced and were leased in 2006, although only a couple had been fully developed by the end of 2009. The policy to introduce tourism to atolls further away from the airports of the country was not, however, complemented by a government policy or investment plan to develop the necessary infrastructure for the development of these distant atolls. Notwithstanding this, the current government has sanctioned the private development of airports, and it remains to be seen how the market responds to the new developments and whether such investments will be sustained in the future.

The volume of international visitors or tourist arrivals has risen from 42,000 in 1980 to half a million in 2003; more than a tenfold increase over the 23-year period. By the end of 2007, a total of 8,382,928 tourists had visited the Maldives from the inception of tourism in 1972. The recorded annual arrival figure for 2007 was 655,852 (Ministry of Tourism, Arts and Culture, 2009). The supply of tourist bed capacity increased from 2400 beds to 19,600 from 1980 to 2004 representing an annual growth rate of 9% compared with the global average of 5% (Ministry of Tourism and Civil Aviation, 2007). According to the Ministry of Tourism figures, tourism bed capacity had an annualized average compound growth rate of 11.65% from 1972 to 2005. By the end of 2007, 92 resort islands had opened for business. A further 53 islands are allocated for tourism development, with a majority of them now leased (Ministry of Tourism and Civil Aviation, 2008).

Each tourist island is an investment worth approximately US$18–20 million as the entire infrastructure and associated facilities are provided individually for each island. The Maldives has followed a one-island one-resort policy, with every resort hosting on average approximately 100 bungalows or less. The *Second Tourism Master Plan 1996–2005* forecast that visitor arrivals would reach a total of 650,000 by 2005 and that provision would be made for 20,500 beds available to visitors by the end of the Master Plan period (Nethconsult/Transtec and Bord Failte, 1996). Those targets were achieved. The United Nations World Tourism Organization (UNWTO) in its report *Tourism Vision 2020* estimated that the Maldives will receive 1,414,000 visitors in 2020 (UNWTO, 2001). With the rate of current expansion now going ahead, it is likely that this target will also be achieved.

It has been the case that given the small volume of supply, there is no other place for the Maldives' tourism product to be placed other than at the top end of the market – thus its often undeserved tag as an expensive destination. It has, up to now, been the basis of an economically sustainable model of development which has served the destination well. However, as tourism expands across all of its atolls, strategies to diversify the Maldives tourism product to cater for market segments other than luxury seekers are necessary in order to maintain financial viability.

National Development Planning Processes

The National Development Planning (NDP) process involves a series of 5-year plans that provide guidance on the economic, social and environmental development of the Maldives. Currently the Maldives is into its Seventh National Development Plan, a plan that covers the years 2006–2010 (Ministry of National Development, 2007). Its key guiding principles are:

> Consistent with the principles of Agenda 21, the development policies to be pursued in 7th NDP should not compromise the ability of future generations to achieve non-declining per capita well being. Thus the Plan shall ensure the optimal use of the available natural resources and pave the way for the protection of critical natural capital such as coral reefs and fish breeding grounds. The new development programs shall consider the carrying capacity of the environment; assess the significant environmental impacts and identify impact mitigation measures where appropriate.
>
> (Ministry of National Development, 2007)

Brown *et al.* (1997) describe the various measures of carrying capacity in the Maldives as related to waste production and management, tourists' perceptions of environmental quality, water (presumably freshwater) availability, and beach and coastal water quality. Solid-waste generation from tourism resorts was found to be well above average household waste generation at about 16.5 kg per visitor per week. Furthermore, the dumping of solid waste at sea was found, anecdotally at least, to be responsible for beach pollution and the necessity for cleaning resort beaches each morning. Consequently, tourists' perceptions of water and beach cleanliness were that both were good to very good, although some problems were perceived with drinking water quality. It must be noted that all islands have drawn on groundwater and rainwater in the past, but now increasingly rely on bottled water and desalination plants as the water lens (water table) declines in level and quality.

However, the main mechanism for the assessment and regulation of the environmental carrying capacity of the islands developed for tourism is through control of the built environment. Regulations stipulate that the total area of the built environment should not exceed 20% of the resort island land area and that every room should be facing the equivalent of 5 m of beach. A total of 68% of beach space must be allocated to guest rooms, 20% to guest facilities (jetty, reception and restaurant), with the remaining 12% as open space between guest rooms. Overwater bungalows can be built to enhance the appeal of the resort but have increasingly been used to overcome a shortage of guest-room space, thereby artificially increasing the physical carrying capacity of resort islands. Thus, carrying capacity may be a useful concept for delimiting the environmental impacts of tourism development, but it has proven to be less effective when the economic imperatives of increasing demand and the need to expand capacity take precedence in planning processes.

National Environmental Planning Processes

The Maldives developed its first National Environment Action Plan (NEAP) in 1989 with the assistance of the United Nations Development Programme (UNDP) and the United Nations Environment Programme (UNEP). This provided for the first time in the country a policy framework for the overseeing of development tasks in all spheres related to environmental management and planning under a national umbrella (Ministry of Housing, Transport and Environment, 2009a). This plan was intended to be used by the government for a term of 7 years. Further subsequent Environment Action Plans were formulated after a review process of each plan. The country is now in its third NEAP cycle (NEAP3). It has been recognized in NEAP3 that all government agents that concern themselves with environmental management must come to agreement with the key objectives and results to be achieved within the currency of the plan. To that effect, NEAP3 formulated 30 results-orientated goals, including the following sustainability-related goals (Ministry of Housing, Transport and Environment, 2009b):

1. Protect critical infrastructure.
2. Protect human settlements.
3. Increase the resilience of coral reef systems to climate change.
4. Reduce climate-related risks to tourism sector.
5. Protect human health from climate change-related vector-borne diseases.
6. Build resilience of fisheries and food production to climate change.
7. Natural disaster preparedness and mitigation.

Targets, to be achieved under each goal were specified in NEAP3, with proposed start dates from 2010 on to 2012, and the list is impressive and comprehensive. Some pilot projects are ongoing, for example, the Atoll

Ecosystem Conservation Project, a project implemented on Baa Atoll in 2009 by UNDP and the Maldives government, assisted by the Global Economic Facility (GEF), which has the purpose of designing and demonstrating an effective management system for atoll ecosystem conservation and sustainable development (AEC, 2009). This key project extends to 2011, at the end of which results will be evaluated with a view to extending main principles across other atolls of the country. Baa Atoll has been strategically chosen for this key pilot project because of its richness in biodiversity; many species of turtles and other marine life forms as well as flora and fauna have been traditionally abundant at Baa Atoll.

Tourism Master Planning Processes in the Maldives

The *First Tourism Master Plan* was made in 1983; Denmark's DANGROUP was commissioned to carry out this task by the Maldives government. This first exercise at formalized planning was effective in the sense that the Maldivian government recognized that any construction of facilities or infrastructure for tourism purposes must be conducted in accordance with guidelines made for the purpose of preserving the environment. Furthermore, the government recognized that any change to the natural vegetation and landscape of the islands must only be made with regard to the physical carrying capacities on each island. No building was to be allowed to be more than two storeys high, and the extraction of material such as coral and sand from any part of the archipelago came to be banned forever, for construction or any other purpose. These principles are in force today, assisting the preservation of the environment as tourism expands.

The *First Tourism Master Plan*, being the first of its kind, made recommendations of an ultra-conservative nature and the legacy of this exercise has been that the passion for environmental preservation among developers in the Maldives became ignited. Despite differences on other issues, public and private sector bodies cooperate fully in enforcing measures to protect the marine resources and natural environment of the country. The *First Tourism Master Plan* had its focus on achieving efficacy from the infrastructure to be provided for tourism; it called for the introduction of what it termed zonal development, with three to four of the larger islands of the country selected and recommended as the central servicing zone islands for tourism. The plan recommended that tourism development be allowed strictly in and around these nodes, to make the service or the recommended nodal islands more efficient. In hindsight, this concept appears unworkable because, given the geography of the islands, the physical provision of infrastructure such as electricity, sewerage and communications from a nodal point to islands in the vicinity is practically impossible. Regardless of whether nodal islands could be established or not, having islands separated by sea means that such provision will, of necessity, have to be provided on an island-by-island basis. Costs will be incurred both literally and environmentally in replicating services on each island. There is no other choice, given the physical separation of the islands by the ocean. Having underwater cables provided from nodal islands to resort islands did not prove to be a feasible or environmentally friendly alternative.

It seemed plausible that every island be made self-sufficient, with its own service infrastructure. In any event, the zonal concept prescribed in the *First Tourism Master Plan* did not materialize, and even during the currency of the plan, islands were sanctioned to developers in all atolls in and around Malé International Airport that were serviceable by seaplane and helicopter. What the *First Tourism Master Plan* did not anticipate was that the operation of services such as seaplanes was environmentally friendly, with landings and take-offs made on floating facilities that were collapsible so that disruption to the land or marine environment was negligible. The seaplane service was, therefore, revolutionary in extending the scope of the islands that may be developed for tourism.

The *Second Tourism Master Plan* was developed in 1996, formulated with grant assistance from the European Union (EU). The nodal development theme of the *First Tourism Master Plan* was re-conceptualized to encompass what was termed regional development, and the need for developing regional airports for tourism-specific purposes was recognized. While the first plan served as a platform for the creation of legislation to protect the environment, the second plan called for greater integration of the NEAP and policies created to promote tourism development. Pursuant to this vision, the selection of Marine Protected Areas (MPAs) in 25 different locations of the country to be frequented by divers visiting the Maldives was made, and the introduction of a Green Resort Award ensured that the spirit of environment preservation instituted during the *First Tourism Master Plan* period was sustained. It must be noted though that the majority of the currently declared MPAs are located in and around Malé Atoll and Ari Atoll (next to Malé Atoll). The sites to be protected have not yet been determined on a nationwide basis. Despite this, the *Second Tourism Master Plan* is also noteworthy for the recommendation that it makes to reposition the Maldives as a premium ecotourism destination, a theme which was to be expanded upon in the *Third Tourism Master Plan*.

The *Third Tourism Master Plan* notes that the Maldives tourism industry has remained mindful of the fragility of the environment. It recognizes that the practice of allowing only 20% of the land surface of each island to be built up has necessarily been maintained to the present day, and that various other planning regulations, such as the protection of the shoreline and setback limits, have been adhered to. However, despite such apparent adherence, in practice, ways to circumvent building restrictions have become evident, with almost all resort islands venturing into the construction of overwater bungalows, thereby avoiding some land-based planning principles stipulated in regulations. Importantly, the *Third Tourism Master Plan* alerts stakeholders to the challenges of these practices and others, which have arisen as a result of the rapid physical expansion of tourism development. For the first time, the *Third Tourism Master Plan* outlined the need to be cognizant of the resource needs of the other major industry of the Maldives – fishery – and the requirement for joint management of resources was outlined. These strategies need follow-through action plans although, to date, a mid-term evaluation has not been conducted nor have strategic assessments been made.

The *Third Tourism Master Plan* was sophisticated in its recommendations, calling for a nationwide environment management system, and detailed the significant areas in this regard – such as solid-waste treatment, engineering solutions and sewage treatment – that must be taken into account in pursuing responsible development. These recommendations sit very well with the provisions of the current draft Environment Law and it remains to be seen in the future as to how such a system will materialize. The *Third Tourism Master Plan* is distinguishable from the other two because, for the first time in the Maldives, it called for development based on renewable energy sources. These recommendations of the *Third Tourism Master Plan* serve, without a doubt, as a foundation on which an integrated environmental management plan for the whole country could be based, given the importance of tourism to the economy.

Tourism Laws and Regulations

All applications related to tourism development have to be tendered to the Ministry of Tourism, Arts and Culture which will, in turn, seek the expertise of the Ministry of Housing, Transport and Environment (MHTE, now the Ministry of Housing and Environment). The law currently in operation is the *Maldives Tourism Act 1999* (Law No. 2/99). Article 15 makes specific reference to the 'felling of coconut palms and trees on an island or land leased for development as a tourist resort, dredging of the lagoon of such an island, reclamation of land, or any other activity … as may be likely to cause a permanent change to the [natural] environment of such places'. Actions such as these may only be carried out after obtaining written permission from the Ministry and in accordance with the relevant regulations. The regulations set out under the *Regulation on the Protection and Conservation of Environment in the Tourism Industry* (Ministry of Tourism, Arts and Culture, 2010) are formulated pursuant to the *Maldives Tourism Act 1999* and they spell out in detail what developers can and cannot do with regard to any developmental activity carried out on an island.

The key Ministry involved in overseeing environmental protection in the Maldives is the MHTE. The law entitled *Environment Protection and Preservation Act 1993* (Law No 4/1993) is the key current legislation governing environmental management in the Maldives. It empowers the Maldivian government to formulate policies, rules and regulations. Additional powers include the mandate to identify areas for protection and preservation (Section 4). Section 6 empowers the government to halt, without compensation, any project that has 'undesirable' environmental impacts, and Section 7 prohibits the disposal of waste, oil and poisonous gases. The government has the powers to impose fines of up to Maldivian Rufiyaas 1 million (US$100,000) for breach of the provisions of this Law.

The *Environment Protection and Preservation Act 1993*, and regulations under this law, formulated in 2007 and entitled *Environmental Impact Assessment Regulations*, are the key legal instruments regulating the protection of the environment. These are currently monitored by the MHTE. Additionally, the Ministry of Tourism, Arts and Culture enforces the separate set of regulations mentioned above entitled *Regulation on the Protection and Conservation of Environment in the Tourism Industry*.

The *Environment Protection and Preservation Act 1993* is currently being overhauled with a draft new legislation compiled with the assistance of UNEP. The proposed legislation is expected to provide even wider environment policing powers to the government and also the ability to introduce a more diverse range of fines for infringements. The draft tabled as a Bill on Maldives' Environment Protection is expected to go before parliament in late 2010 or early 2011. The Bill proposes to bring under the Environment Ministry's umbrella a wider range of functions, such as the introduction of the principles of renewable energy sources (as suggested in the *Third Tourism Master Plan*), delineate coastal protection zones and, for the first time, the protection of genetic resources in the country. Waste management has also been given a wider focus and it is now written into the proposed legislation that importation of plastic bags into the country must be controlled. The Waste Management Corporation is another government agency seeking international assistance in introducing modern methods of waste management in the country. Outside the government structure, organizations such as MATI, the Maldives Association of Travel Agents and Maldives Live-Aboard Association act as key stakeholders who are consulted by the government in formulating policies and legislation in relation to tourism planning, development and the environment.

Key Challenges for the Future

The vulnerabilities facing tourism development in the Maldives will remain because tourism is so central to the country's economic prosperity and it has very few alternatives to pursue other than tourism for increasing its economic wealth. The need for exploitation of its natural environment cannot and will not be halted, as market trends continue to provide evidence that the Maldives tourism product will remain popular for the long-term future. What needs to be ensured is that the management of environmental resources is conducted responsibly.

As has been reviewed above, there are adequate mechanisms and policy instruments in the Maldives that indicate the willpower to achieve responsible methods of environmental management while simultaneously developing island tourism. However, the mechanisms are applied in a piecemeal way and traverse a number of government agencies. The NEAP plan is still not completed, despite the fact that programme dates were expected to commence from 2010. Action plans to prevent environmental damage and address potential impacts to the environment remain to be implemented. A country-wide environmental audit has not yet been conducted and it remains to be seen whether mechanisms for environmental protection will extend to identifying existing environmental damage, as well as to safeguarding proposed future developments.

The *Third Tourism Master Plan* also called for the integration of tourism with environment protection management activities. Pilot projects such as the Atoll Ecosystem Conservation Project have proved promising but remain only that – as pilots. As with the case of determining marine protected areas, which began ambitiously at the time of the *Second Tourism Master Plan* process, only marine-protected areas in Malé and nearby atolls have so far been declared. The expansion of tourism must recognize that important conservation measures such as this need to be extended countrywide before tourist facilities are developed.

Tourism in all atolls will no doubt bring economic benefits, but unless a nationwide system is in place, the policing of environmental protection laws and regulations may not be effectively implemented. For example, the regulations prohibiting waste dumping into the sea are still not enforced effectively. Also, expansion of the land area of the existing resort islands has continued for the purposes of creating overwater bungalows. Although all land reclamation is supposed to be subject to an environmental impact assessment (EIA), anecdotal evidence suggests that some developments may have proceeded without the potential impacts being identified and documented. The construction of overwater bungalows appears to have been a way of circumventing built-environment regulations and the consequent damage to the lagoons, reefs and surrounding marine resources may be substantial.

Conclusion

It is apparent that the Maldives has in place the appropriate plans, laws and regulations for effectively managing environmental impacts while ensuring that the economic benefits of tourism are sustained in the future. Since the 1970s, the Maldives has engaged in a systematic and well-planned programme of tourism development involving gradual expansion of transport and resort infrastructure in accordance with market demand and the environmental carrying capacity. Substantial growth in arrivals and resort capacity has been moderated by the controlled release of islands for resort development. This control mechanism is exercised through the various planning processes in place, including the successive National Development Plans (NDPs), Tourism Master Plans (TMPs) and National Environment Action Plans (NEAPs).

These planning processes and programmes suggest that the government of the Maldives would conduct an audit of the carrying capacity of the environment, as well as an assessment of significant impacts, and provide mitigation measures if there are problems identified. However, the current NDP planning period is now virtually at an end and there is little evidence of any centralized audit or nationwide impact assessment being made by the government. NEAP3 has outlined some targets to be achieved, but there is work to be done if environmental programmes are to be implemented and, more importantly, monitored in the future. There is a need to replicate lessons learnt from pilot projects such as the Atoll Ecosystem Conservation Project in applying conservation principles uniformly across all atolls as tourism expands – for example, the delineation of marine protected areas in and around islands released for tourism. Establishing country-specific data against which EIAs related to tourism development could be assessed is crucial. Furthermore, the limitations associated with the application of carrying-capacity regulations in relation to the built environment have become increasingly apparent, as when the economic imperative to expand accommodation capacity in the form of overwater bungalows in response to increased demand takes precedence over environmental management processes.

However, in the face of the competing demands on tourism to deliver economic benefits to current and future generations of Maldivians, while simultaneously limiting the impacts on the natural environment that is the core of the tourism attraction, the Maldives has made admirable progress over the past four decades. In part, this transformation to more sustainable forms of island tourism resort can be attributed to the foresight of the founders and pioneers of Maldives tourism, who recognized that the pristine marine environment remains the basis for continued prosperity, not only for their businesses, but for the entire country. It is also the result of the various planning processes and programmes described above, which have attempted to embrace the principles and practices of sustainable development that provide a sound basis for responding to the multiple problems and opportunities that will confront the Maldives in the future, on their continued journey towards sustainability.

References

AEC (2009) AEC: Atoll Ecosystem Conservation Project. Our Vision and Implementation Strategy (2009) Available at: http://www.biodiversity.mv/aec/index.php?option=com_content&view=article&id=44 (accessed 15 September 2010).

Atoll Editions (2004) Atlas of the Maldives, Reference for Travellers, Divers and Sailors, 4th edn. Apollo Bay, Victoria, Australia.

Brown, K., Turner, R.K., Hameed, H. and Bateman, I. (1997) Environmental carrying capacity and tourism development in the Maldives and Nepal. *Environmental Conservation* 24, 316–325.

Ghina, F. (2003) Sustainable development in small island developing states: the case of the Maldives. *Environment, Development and Sustainability* 5, 139–165.

Maldivian Democratic Party (2008) *Aneh Dhivehi Raajje: The Strategic Action Plan. National Framework for Development 2009-2013*. Malé, Maldives.

MATI (1998) *Issues of concern to the Maldives tourism industry*, Maldives Association of Tourism Industry, Malé, Maldives.

McKercher, B. (1993) The unrecognised threat to tourism: can tourism survive sustainability. *Tourism Management* 14, 131–136.

Ministry of Housing, Transport and Environment (2009a) *Our Vision and Implementation Strategy: Atoll Eco-System Conservation Project*. Malé, Maldives. Available at: http://www.biodiversity.mv/aec/index.php?option=com_docman&task=doc_download&gid=99&Itemid= (accessed 22 September 2010).

Ministry of Housing, Transport and Environment (2009b) Third National Environment Action Plan. Malé, Maldives. Available at: http://cde.com.mv/wp-content/uploads/2010/05/NEAP_3.pdf (accessed 15 September 2010).

Ministry of National Development (2007) *Seventh National Development Plan 2006–2010: Creating New Opportunities.* Malé, Maldives. Available at: http://www.planning.gov.mv/en/images/stories/ndp/seventh_ndp.pdf (accessed 15 September 2010).

Ministry of Tourism (2004) *Tourism Statistics 2004.* Malé, Maldives. Available at: http://tourism.gov.mv/pubs/stat2004/index.htm (accessed 22 September 2010).

Ministry of Tourism and Civil Aviation (2007) *Maldives Third Tourism Master Plan 2007–2011.* Malé, Maldives. Available at: http://www.tourism.gov.mv/downloads/ttmp.pdf (accessed 15 September 2010).

Ministry of Tourism and Civil Aviation (2008) Fathuruveri kamuge tharaqqee ge 35 aharu (Development of tourism in the last 35 years). *Tharaqqee ge dhuveli* (Speed of Development) No. 23. Malé, Maldives.

Ministry of Tourism, Arts and Culture (2009) *Tourism Yearbook 2009.* Malé, Maldives. Available from: http://www.tourism.gov.mv/downloads/stat_yearbook_2009.pdf (accessed 15 September 2010).

Ministry of Tourism, Arts and Culture (2010) *Regulation on the Protection and Conservation of Environment in the Tourism Industry.* Malé, Maldives. Available at: http://www.tourism.gov.mv/downloads/unofficial-translation.pdf (accessed 15 September 2010).

MMA (1999) *Annual Report of the Maldives Monetary Authority, 1998.* Maldives Monetary Authority, Malé, Maldives.

Nethconsult/Transtec and Bord Failte (1996) *Maldives Tourism Master Plan 1996–2005, Volume 1, Main Report.* Prepared by Nethconsult/Transtec in association with Bord Failte. Ministry of Tourism, Malé, Maldives.

Reimer, K (2007) Paradise in the making: tourism, development, and the Maldive Islands. PhD thesis, York University, Toronto, Ontario.

UNWTO (1999) *Compendium of Tourism Statistics, 17th edn.* United Nations World Tourism Organization, Madrid.

UNWTO (2001) *Tourism 2020 Vision – South Asia.* United Nations World Tourism Organization, Madrid.

17 Conclusions and Implications for Sustainable Island Tourism

RICHARD BUTLER[1] AND JACK CARLSEN[2]

[1]*University of Strathclyde, Glasgow, Scotland;* [2]*Curtin University, Western Australia*

Introduction

In this final chapter we endeavour to draw some conclusions and implications from the preceding chapters about the issues and problems involved, if the island communities that were studied seriously desire to move towards a more sustainable future. As might be expected, the situation is confusing and complicated, not least because there are no simple solutions where sustainability is concerned and there is little homogeneity among the locations that have been analysed. The islands described represent a wide variety of categories, those that are from high and low latitudes, in warm and cold waters, with large and small populations, independent states and subunits of other states, and large and small in area. They all, however, share the common feature of being islands, and thus the issues discussed by the various contributors to this volume: accessibility, small internal markets, vulnerability to exogenous forces, difficulties in relationships between tourism and other activities and between tourists and local residents.

For some of the islands that have been included in the book, tourism is the mainstay of their economies, and it is difficult to imagine life or economic existence without tourism. For others, tourism is a secondary or minor aspect of their economies, subservient to other factors, such as mineral wealth, remittances and income from other sources. Irrespective of the level of importance of tourism to their economies, however, the relationship between tourism and the quality of life of the communities on these islands is of critical importance. Tourism is involved in much more than simply the economies of islands because it is a phenomenon that affects the environment and the social and cultural life of the residents and, through these, the political reality of the islands and their governance. Despite this complex situation, there are some elements of commonality that can be identified that make it possible to sketch out a pathway or programme that might be followed in the pursuit of a more sustainable future, not only for tourism, but for the island communities, their economies and their environments.

To identify key issues, we have focused particularly on the conclusions and implications drawn from each chapter. The authors of the 15 chapters reviewed present close to 50 sometimes specific, and sometimes more generalized, issues in their discussions and conclusions. We have endeavoured to integrate and summarize the issues under the four headings of Economic Priority; Restrictions on Growth; Response to Environmental Change and Extent of Local Input and Direction. One overarching issue that determines economic priorities, the imposition of restrictions, the reception of local input and the response to environmental change is covered under the next heading: Political Commitment to Sustainable Tourism Principles. Insights from each chapter in relation to the issues summarized under the first four headings and the overarching issue of political commitment are also provided under the heading of Research Issues and Implications. We have also included here three key questions arising from each chapter, which may serve to stimulate discussion and thinking, not only about the case in point, but about sustainable island tourism development in general.

Economic Priority

Many authors have commented on the propensity of governments of all political persuasions to place a higher priority on economic policies than on those relating to environmental or sociocultural matters, even when they may be espousing sustainability as a development goal (Dodds and Butler, 2009). The reason for such prioritization is as understandable as it is regrettable; it relates to governments throughout the world at all levels having the desire to retain power and win re-election, and assuming (probably generally correctly), that the best way to do this is to maintain economic growth, even at the expense of other aspects of life. Employment and income generation are at the heart of most public-sector policies, and all too often environmental protection and cultural preservation are seen as being at the expense of economic growth. As Dodds (2007) pointed out in the case of the Balearic Islands, even when a regional level government passed legislation which placed an economic charge on tourists to fund sustainable goals, such measures did not survive the subsequent election and the government was changed to one that repealed the measures.

This issue of economics being given priority over other concerns has been raised in a variety of ways in the context of Macquarie Island, Fraser Island (consumption having priority over protection), St Croix and Christmas Islands (casino profits over community well-being), Mauritius (development beyond capacity limits on economic grounds) and Okinawa (pursuit of high-value tourists despite environmental limitations). If sustainable tourism, and sustainable development in general, do depend on the acceptance of the 'triple bottom line' approach, then clearly, any government that is placing a higher priority on economic development – rather than giving equal importance in planning and development to economic, environmental and social issues – is not serious or honest about moving towards sustainability. This is not to argue that development should cease or that economic growth is not important, for political reality has to recognize as well the fact that local populations generally are growing and need additional jobs and income; rather, it is to recognize that there does have to be a fundamental change in attitude if successful reorientation is to be achieved.

Restrictions on Growth

As with economic prioritization, the imposition of restrictions on growth has political overtones that most governments would wish to avoid. It is clear from the cases discussed, however, that many of these island destinations are concerned about the existing level of development, let alone what might occur in the future. Restrictions, often in the form of regulations, are noted in a number of cases, Macquarie Island has tight regulations (including the removal of alien species), Fraser Island is cited as an area that may lose its World Heritage Status because of ineffectively managed restrictions on use, Green Island has changed the nature of use to a more sustainable form through the imposition of regulations, and on the islands of Lakshadweep tourism has been segregated and restricted spatially. There is discussion of the need for more regulation in Malaysia, and in Mauritius the concept of carrying capacity (with its implied limits) is discussed, as is also the case for Okinawa and the Maldives. In all discussions of carrying capacity, regulation and the imposition of limits or restrictions are integral to the adoption of such a strategy. Restrictions need not imply a reduction in absolute numbers of tourists to a destination, nor a reduction in employment or in the importance of tourism to the economy. It might well be that a restriction on specific forms of tourism development could result in an expansion of other types of tourism, in some cases yielding higher economic returns per capita visitor; limiting the number of cruise-ship visitors while increasing the number of staying visitors would be an example of this, a situation long acknowledged as a possible strategy for islands taking a long-term view of tourism (Wilkinson, 1987).

Response to Environmental Change

An issue raised in several contexts is that of changes in the natural environment, which is a particular problem for islands, owing to their often small land area, limited biodiversity and thus increased vulnerability to impacts. Macquarie Island has experienced considerable impact from the introduction of alien species and, ironically, the presence of tourists has highlighted the effects of this problem, resulting in the elimination of aliens and protection measures to reduce tourism-induced impacts. This is somewhat of an exception however. In the discussion of Fraser Island, for example, the physical effects of tourism are likened to the results of a traditional 'mining and logging' economy, and have been experienced to such a degree that environmental degradation is considered to threaten the World Heritage Status of the island. Much of the new strategy for Green Island is focused on reducing or eliminating environmental impacts such as fishing, feeding marine species and erosion. The Maldives is shown to be particularly vulnerable (along with other ocean island groups) to potential sea level rise driven by climate change, and while tourism on the islands may not be the cause of this problem, adaptive strategies to environmental change, whether locally or externally driven, are clearly necessary. Similar points are made in the context of Malaysian islands, such actions being dependent in part on perceptions and acknowledgement of the problem by both tourists and locals. In Shetland, progressive planning was driven by fear of massive change in both environmental and social spheres as the result of oil development, which has had beneficial results on tourism development. The demands being placed on the natural environment, particularly on water and energy resources, with the resulting impacts and changes, is a key issue in the case of Okinawa, and environmental change is also seen as of potential concern to politics and legal affairs in Hawaii. Finally, the Maldives shows concern over the lack of clarity on carrying-capacity issues, particularly with respect to the ability of the environment to withstand further development. All of these examples emphasize the overwhelming importance to most islands of the need to protect and conserve their physical environment, both marine and terrestrial, as these are the primary drawing cards for tourism, as well as being at the heart of most island cultures. To suffer severe impacts and changes in the physical environment threatens the long-term sustainability of island culture and life, as well as of tourism.

Extent of Local Input and Direction

Community involvement in planning and development, i.e. the local view, is an essential ingredient of sustainable development. The absence of local inputs and perceptions is an issue that has been raised in many of the cases discussed in this volume. This is particularly important in the context of island planning for tourism, for virtually all tourism to islands comes from overseas, if not from foreign parts, and the infrastructure involved – such as transport and accommodation – is often owned and controlled by external interests. While this is not inherently a problem, in reality it often is, as when decisions are made away from the island without local input and in the primary interests of the facility owners. Green Island does not have a local community, but the decisions made about the island, although external, are concerned with ensuring the environmental well-being of the island. In Lakshadweep, the separation of tourism from local communities has both slowed the rate of development of tourism and avoided some of the problems that can result from inappropriate interaction between tourists and locals. One view of the Maldives (Chapter 6) is that local residents have not yet appreciated the potential seriousness of climate change on the island nation, a not uncommon problem in such communities, who are inevitably, by being insular, somewhat divorced from certain aspects of global economies and politics. The comment by Belle and Bramwell (2005) that is cited in Chapter 6 is very apt: 'the failure of SIDS (small island developing states) to invest in policies to respond to climate change may leave them poorly prepared to cope with adverse changes and also increases the probability of severe consequences'. Local input and opinion is not always correct or appropriate when viewed at the global scale, but there is little doubt that at the local scale, island residents generally have a more accurate view of issues than those off-island.

The point made in the context of the Malaysian islands about the need for informing local residents as well as tourists about the effects of tourism is highly relevant. Local input needs additional information, particularly in situations where tourism is not an experience that most island residents are familiar with. In the case of St Croix and Christmas Islands, differences of opinion about casino-based tourism between residents and politicians are important considerations in the achievement of sustainable tourism goals from a sociocultural perspective; similar concerns about public attitudes are expressed in the case of Trinidad and Tobago. In the context of successfully managing resident–tourist interactions on Bruny and Magnetic Islands, the importance is emphasized of having local perspectives that drive events and participation in local politics, and it is noted that without recognizing the role of local input, resident–tourist relations are unlikely to improve. Local feelings and support for local political actions were key to Shetland's success in gaining greater control over planning and development, while the relative lack of integration of local quality of life concerns into policies is seen as a problem in Mauritius. In the Mediterranean context, local agreement over cooperation in dealing with tourism is argued as important, and the audit of impacts and mitigation measures in the Maldives is clearly dependent on local support for successful adoption.

Political Commitment to Sustainable Tourism Principles

All of the preceding issues are important to varying degrees for most of the island communities engaged in tourism. The one factor that overrides all of these, however, is political commitment. Politics is the unstated fourth leg in the sustainable development equation. The 'triple bottom-line' is nothing unless it has political support. Political rhetoric is not sufficient, there are already far too many examples of elected representatives stating their support for sustainable concepts but failing to implement the policies they enact (Dodds and Butler, 2009). Politicians at all levels in democracies have to answer periodically to the electorate, and thus their viewpoint is almost inevitably influenced by the 4- or 5-year time frame between elections. This, in turn, means that short-term 'fixes' or solutions are often seen as preferable to the longer time frame that sustainability requires.

On Macquarie Island, one issue is whether the federal government will continue to financially support the management of tourism and other concerns on the island, particularly in a time of global economic uncertainty. Fraser

Island is seen as a location which has suffered from insufficient political commitment to protection of a special habitat from and for tourism. Politics is of less importance on Green Island, where private control operating in conjunction with state agencies has meant that a more sustainable approach has been possible, and cooperation has been possible in the absence of local residents and politicians. The local policies on Lakshadweep have so far proven effective in separating and minimizing the impact of tourism on local residents and their way of life, possibly at the expense of economic return, an illustration that local management can be effective. This situation is mirrored in Shetland, where strong local politicians putting forward locally supported policies overcame large-scale industrial and higher-level government intentions. While local politicians in Maldives cannot hope to halt climate change and rises in sea level alone, they do need to consider what adaptive actions they may be able to take, given the unlikely situation that others will assist them in any significant way.

The Malaysian approach to information dissemination to local residents as well as tourists is likely to result in more effective local political decision making with respect to including sustainable concepts in planning. In the case of St Croix and Christmas Islands, there appear to be conflicts between policies being enacted and local opinion with respect to casino tourism, at least as far as sociocultural issues are concerned. In Trinidad and Tobago, local differences between different cultural/ethnic groups (distorted by economic inequality) over appropriate actions with respect to the Trinidad Carnival suggest that strong political leadership and action is required. Similar issues arise in the case of Bruny and Magnetic Islands, where policies towards shaping visitor–resident interaction need to involve perceptions of both groups over the conditions of interaction, which are a direct result of development policies. In Mauritius, it seems likely that not having clear indications of acceptable levels of change from the viewpoint of residents is likely to create political issues in the future, and perceptions need to be integrated into local decision making. In Okinawa, more attention needs to be paid by politicians to resource demands resulting from tourism and a growing indigenous population, particularly in terms of water and energy resources, and these concerns need to be recognized in policy formulation.

Such problems also manifest themselves in the Mediterranean islands, where a lack of political cooperation between islands results in less sustainable operations and perhaps threatens the level of sociocultural impacts on local residents. The issue of the need for political commitment is also seen in Hawaii, where it is argued that a much more holistic approach is needed to overcome issues in environmental, economic, legal and political areas. The alternative, it is suggested, is a judicial decision, which may be far removed from local concerns or sustainable goals. Finally, in the Maldives, it is clear that political decisions on determining the appropriate levels of tourism, placing an emphasis on multiple rather than only economic considerations, and giving a high priority to preserving the marine environment, are of crucial importance in any move towards sustainability.

Research Issues and Implications

As comprehensive as the coverage of this book has been, it still raises many questions as to the transition of islands towards ecological, social and economic sustainability. Questions arising from each chapter are outlined below, with the intention of stimulating further research in these and comparable island settings from a sustainable perspective.

Key questions arising from Chapter 2 relate to the way in which the harsh yet vulnerable environment of Macquarie Island in the Southern Ocean should be managed. These questions include:

- How can tourism's ecological impacts be managed in the absence of any empirical data and scientific evidence?
- How will a warming climate affect the island's ecological values and thus the island tourism experience?
- In the current global financial crisis, what will happen to the cost of doing business and other idiosyncrasies of the Antarctic tourism market? Should the federal government continue to underwrite Tasmanian National Parks and limited tourism on the island?

Key issues from Chapter 3, which traces the pathways of Fraser Island towards sustainability, generate further research propositions and imperatives, as follows:

- An island is by definition constrained by its size in its ability to maintain a stable and sustainable environment under pressure from tourist activity, and conservation methods and policies must be tailored to this fact. Systematic comparative research into how this balance is or might be achieved is critically important.
- Organizations with revenue constraints should not manage environments such as Fraser Island, further research is required into the effect of various funding models on responsible management in national parks (this is not just an island environment problem).
- Research is urgently needed into the impact of government environmental conservation actions being considerably at variance with community views and wishes, as is shown with the dingoes in this case study.

The role of national parks organizations in managing for sustainable tourism, supported by appropriate legislation and in consultation with indigenous communities, is clearly evident on Green Island (Chapter 4), but various questions arise, including:

- Are national parks agencies endowed with sufficient resources to manage the multiple impacts of tourism on fragile islands?
- How is it possible to phase out traditional hunting as well as illegal fishing activities through negotiation and enforcement of regulations?
- Would tour operators be willing to end fish-feeding activities and instead educate tourists as to the benefits of conservation of marine life in their natural state?

Segregation of tourists was proposed as a means of managing the environmental and social impacts of tourism on the Lakshadweep Islands in Chapter 5, but a variety of questions arise. These include:

- Is segregation the most effective means of insulating culturally sensitive communities from the undesirable social effects of tourism?
- To what extent does local population pressure compromise the social sustainability of island tourism?
- Do restrictions on tourists arrivals enable a 'high value–low volume' tourism strategy while simultaneously affording protection of the way of life of islanders?

Questions abound over the impacts of climate change on islands such as the Maldives (Chapter 6) including:

- Which components of the Maldivian tourism system are most vulnerable to climate change?
- How do external campaigns on climate change run by the President of the Maldives help the tourism sector in their efforts to adapt to climate change, and how can this be reinforced by appropriate domestic campaigns and policies?
- Who should take the leadership in terms of climate-change adaptation and what partnerships would be most effective to reduce vulnerability as part of the wider goal of sustainable tourism development?

The perceptions of hosts and guests as to what constitutes sustainability in the islands of Malaysia are analysed in Chapter 7, but further questions for analysis could include:

- What is the most effective means of communicating cultural and environmental values to hosts and guests in an island tourism setting?
- To what extent can differences in attitudes towards island tourism be explained by the demographic (age, employment, ethnicity) characteristics of hosts and guests?
- To what extent can differences in attitudes towards island tourism be explained by the physical size of islands and their capacity to accommodate tourism growth?

Sustainable island tourism may preclude certain forms of tourism development, such as the casino development in the cases of St Croix and Christmas Islands described in Chapter 8, but the following questions emerge:

- Why do governments continue to support casino development in socially susceptible island communities?
- Do the economic returns from casino development justify the social costs?
- Is island casino development compatible with socially sustainable island tourism development?

Chapter 9 describes the social tensions that arise on islands when the moral standards of hosts and guests are significantly different, such as in

Trinidad and Tobago. This gives rise to critical questions regarding island tourism events and social sustainability, including:

- How can sustainable island tourism replace other non-sustainable economic activities (such as oil production)?
- Should basic value systems such as the carnival mentality be sanitized and presented as a socially sustainable form of island tourism?
- How can socially sustainable island tourism be compatible with the acute social problems of homelessness, crime and inequity that exist on islands such as Trinidad and Tobago?

Chapter 10 raises three key research questions in relation to the study of social sustainability on Bruny and Magnetic Islands. Addressing these three key questions – which concern the building of healthy and sustainable host–guest relations through social interaction in a tourism context – could evoke positive behavioural outcomes and contribute to sustainability:

- What are the key inhibitors of sustainable host–guest relations and how can these be addressed in order to foster sustainable island tourism?
- How do the facilitators and inhibitors of sustainable host–guest relations differ across different types of islands?
- How can island settings be harnessed to promote sustainable attitudes and behaviours of visitors after their visits?

Three key aspects of tourism on the Shetland Islands (Chapter 11) raise questions regarding sustainability in the future, namely:

- To what extent does geographical isolation, limited transport and seasonal access afford islands some level of protection from unsustainable rates of growth in tourism arrivals?
- How important for sustainable island tourism is the political imperative to maintain quality of life and unique characteristics on islands such as the Shetlands?
- In the future, will the growing trend in cultural and nature tourism support sustainable island tourism in islands such as the Shetlands?

In Chapter 12, the focus was on economic sustainability, coupled with weak policies on environmental sustainability and social sustainability, which generated various questions about the future of tourism on Mauritius, including:

- How can islands diversify their visitor markets and move towards economically sustainable tourism development?
- Does foreign ownership of hotels, private villas and homes compromise the economic sustainability of island tourism?
- At what stage(s) of the Tourism Area Life Cycle (TALC) does economic sustainability take priority over social and environmental sustainability? A corollary question could be at what stage(s) of the TALC do social and environmental sustainability take priority?

Chapter 13 traces the development of tourism on Okinawa, but questions remain regarding the economic sustainability of these islands. These include:

- How to internalize the growing tourist spending through expanding domestic production of goods and services and how to reduce economic leakage?
- How to diversify Okinawa's tourism in terms of visitors and stakeholders in tourism-related industries in order to pursue economic sustainability?
- How to estimate Okinawa's social and environmental carrying capacity under the scenario of a de facto increasing population attributable to tourism growth?

Similarly, economic sustainability is a priority for islands of the Mediterranean, but there is some degree of difficulty experienced by islands in the European Union (EU) in developing tourism (Chapter 14). This raises questions of:

- How can increased cooperation between islands facilitate economically sustainable island tourism?
- Can a grouping of islands be considered as a single insular region for the purposes of sustainable island tourism development?
- How can pressure on islands with high territorial exploitation and high tourist impact indices be reduced?

A holistic approach to tourism transportation systems (and indeed all forms of tourism development) is essential if islands are to move towards sustainability. Yet this type of approach is seldom evident in island tourism development, even on islands such as Hawaii (Chapter 15), where tourism has been long established, leading to questions such as:

- How can island tourism transport sustainability be approached from a holistic perspective?
- Why is a holistic perspective particularly important to understanding tourism transport in islands?
- What are the challenges that islands face in providing sustainable means of tourism transportation?

Finally, the following questions remain regarding the planning and policy processes that facilitate sustainable island tourism development on the Maldives (Chapter 16):

- How can policy and planning processes incorporate sustainable tourism initiatives?
- What are the barriers to the implementation of regulations and restrictions on tourism development that are designed to encourage sustainable island tourism resort operations?
- How can political and legal systems inculcate a sustainable perspective into the development of island tourism?

Conclusion

All islands, regardless of location, political ideology, size or environment, face common problems with respect to moving towards sustainability, whether these are in the context of tourism or other economic activities. In focusing on tourism, this volume has, to some extent, gone against the concept of sustainable development, which is clearly a holistic rather than a thematic goal. This is a point made in Chapter 15, which concluded that 'a holistic approach needs to be taken'; although that specific comment was made in the context of transportation projects, it remains true for all aspects of development. Such an approach demands that decision makers at all levels incorporate not only consideration of all economic activities, but also environmental and socio-cultural issues when they formulate policy. More importantly perhaps, is the commitment of politicians to implement the policies they may select, rather than, as has been the case in many locations, producing an admirable statement of intentions but failing to follow this up with the necessary actions. In the case of islands, such inconsistency is perhaps more serious and problematic than for many large mainland nations or regions. Island locations, which are vulnerable, as has been noted, in many ways (costs of access and operations; small internal markets; lack of power when faced by large-scale multi-national interests; priorities based on mainland, perhaps urban-population dominated, demands; and intense global competition for tourism) are ill served if their own political representatives bow to short-term economic priorities, i.e. 'talking the talk', rather than accepting and accommodating the need to take a long-term view and 'walk the walk' of the difficult path to a more sustainable future.

References

Belle, N. and Bramwell, B. (2005) Climate change and small island tourism: policy maker and industry perspectives in Barbados. *Journal of Travel Research* 44, 32–41.

Dodds, R. (2007) Sustainable tourism and policy implementation: lessons from the case of Calvia, Spain. *Current Issues in Tourism* 10, 296–322.

Dodds, R. and Butler, R.W. (2009) Inaction more than action: barriers to the implementation of sustainable tourism policies. In: Gossling, S., Hall, C.M. and Weaver, D.B. (eds) *Sustainable Tourism Futures*. Routledge, London, pp. 43–57.

Wilkinson, P.F. (1987) Tourism in small island nations: a fragile independence. Leisure Studies 6(2), 127–146.

Index